B&H

EXEGETICAL
GUIDE TO THE
GREEK
NEW
TESTAMENT

1-3 John

"When I was transitioning from classical Greek to the New Testament the summer before seminary studies, I worked through Paul's epistles with the guidance of some nineteenth-century commentaries. The aid was good enough but somewhat hit-and-miss. I wish I'd had the EGGNT series back then, especially this volume on 1–3 John. And I can think of no better guides to the young student of the Greek New Testament than Plummer and Elledge, who have produced a stellar example of careful analysis of Greek and sensitivity to the theology of John. This is an indispensable tool for all emerging Greek students."

—S. M. Baugh, professor emeritus of New Testament, Westminster Seminary California

"Robert Plummer and E. Roderick Elledge provide a methodical and detailed exegesis of the Johannine letters. They expound the various options, views, and interpretations generated by the Greek text, but without forfeiting a sense of wonder and joy at the overarching beauty and sublimity of John's testimony about Jesus, the gospel, and divine love. A terrific resource for students and pastors!"

—Michael F. Bird, deputy principal, Ridley College

"Rob Plummer's decades of helping others understand the intricacies of the Greek New Testament shines through in this exegetical guide to 1–3 John. Greek scholars will appreciate the detailed guidance that Plummer and Elledge provide. Newer students of Greek will find this volume extremely user-friendly, readable, and thorough, and preachers will not only be able to quickly identify exegetical issues and assess competing interpretations but also will find the homiletical suggestions insightful and thought-provoking. Plummer and Elledge's exegetical guide is for everyone who seeks to rightly handle the Word of truth by wrestling with the actual God-breathed words and grammar of 1–3 John."

—Martin Culy, director, Cypress Hills Ministries

"Theologically rich, this commentary expounds the grammar of the Greek text in detail, line by line. On the larger scale, the authors label the parts of the letters to show how they are eminently practical for preaching and teaching about the One whom we worship and about how we should live. This will be a valuable tool for those exegeting these letters, the vocabulary of which seems simple but the message of which is truly profound."

—Craig S. Keener, F. M. and Ada Thompson Professor of Biblical Studies, Asbury Theological Seminary

"The first New Testament book that many beginning Greek students translate is 1 John. The reason is that its Greek grammar and syntax is relatively simple and straightforward. But it still has some challenges. This exegetical guide is ideal for beginning Greek students (and those needing a refresher) to work through line by line, and it is a handy reference for other Greek readers."

—Andy Naselli, professor of systematic theology and New Testament for Bethlehem College and Seminary

"This analysis of the Greek text of John's letters is concise, well-informed, and theologically insightful. It is also much more than a linguistic manual. Those who use it will find practical, down-to-earth help for applying the message of John's letters to their own lives and the lives of those they teach and disciple."

—Frank Thielman, Presbyterian professor of divinity, Beeson Divinity School

"This work is simply the best overall commentary on the Johannine Letters that I have ever encountered. It is most helpful as both an analysis of the Greek text and as a guide to sermon preparation of the passage. It is all here: (1) an overall view of the following pericope; (2) a sentence flow analysis of the passage's structure; (3) a clause-by-clause analysis that includes grammatical and textual features; (4) a semantic analysis of individual words, but never in isolation from their larger context; (5) suggested homiletical outlines for preaching the passage; and (6) further reading on specific features of the passage."

—William Varner, professor of biblical languages and Bible exposition, The Master's University

"I have been greatly helped by the current EGGNT volumes. One of our premier Greek scholars, Dr. Plummer has greatly assisted me in my understanding of the Greek New Testament. To hear about this EGGNT volume is very exciting to me."

—Jerry Vines, pastor emeritus, First Baptist Church, Jacksonville, Florida

Robert L. Plummer &
E. Roderick Elledge

EXEGETICAL
GUIDE TO THE
GREEK
NEW
TESTAMENT

1-3 JOHN

Andreas J. Köstenberger
Robert W. Yarbrough
GENERAL EDITORS

Nashville, Tennessee

Exegetical Guide to the Greek New Testament: *1–3 John*

Published by B&H Academic

Brentwood, Tennessee

ISBN: 978–0-8054–4851–1

Dewey Decimal Classification: 227.9

Subject Heading: BIBLE. N.T. JOHN (EPISTLES)--STUDY \ BIBLE. N.T. JOHN (EPISTLES)--CRITICISM

Printed in the United States of America

29 28 27 26 25 24 VP 1 2 3 4 5 6 7 8 9 10

To our wives, Chandi and Christa

Contents

1 JOHN

2 JOHN

3 JOHN

Acknowledgments

We want to thank the staff at B&H Academic for their consistent support and helpful guidance. Contributing to this significant and impactful series has been a privilege. We also want to express our deep thanks to our students who have challenged and motivated us in our work and to our former professors who led us and inspired us in the learning of the biblical languages. Thank you to Christian Hedland for his time in proofreading the text and for his helpful feedback. Lastly, we want to thank our families for their love and encouragement through this project. We've both been blessed by our investment of time with John's Letters. Our hope is that our efforts in this volume will aid pastors, students, and all readers of the Greek New Testament to understand, embody, and share John's message for the church today.

Publisher's Preface

It is with great excitement that we publish this volume of the Exegetical Guide to the Greek New Testament series. When the founding editor, Dr. Murray J. Harris, came to us seeking a new publishing partner, we gratefully accepted the offer. With the help of the coeditor, Andreas J. Köstenberger, we spent several years working together to acquire all of the authors we needed to complete the series. By God's grace we succeeded and contracted the last author in 2011. Originally working with another publishing house, Murray's efforts spanned more than twenty years. As God would have it, shortly after the final author was contracted, Murray decided God wanted him to withdraw as coeditor of the series. God made clear to him that he must devote his full attention to taking care of his wife, who faces the daily challenges caused by multiple sclerosis.

Over the course of many years, God has used Murray to teach his students how to properly exegete the Scriptures. He is an exceptional scholar and professor. But even more importantly, Murray is a man dedicated to serving Christ. His greatest joy is to respond in faithful obedience when his Master calls. "There can be no higher and more ennobling privilege than to have the Lord of the universe as one's Owner and Master and to be his accredited representative on earth."[1] Murray has once again heeded the call of his Master.

It is our privilege to dedicate the Exegetical Guide to the Greek New Testament series to Dr. Murray J. Harris. We pray that our readers will continue the work he started.

1. Murray J. Harris, *Slave of Christ: A New Testament Metaphor for Total Devotion to Christ* (Downers Grove, IL: InterVarsity Press, 1999), 155.

General Introduction to the EGGNT Series

Studying the New Testament in the original Greek has become easier in recent years. Beginning students will work their way through an introductory grammar or other text, but then what? Grappling with difficult verb forms, rare vocabulary, and grammatical irregularities remains a formidable task for those who would advance beyond the initial stages of learning Greek to master the interpretive process. Intermediate grammars and grammatical analyses can help, but such tools, for all their value, still often operate at a distance from the Greek text itself, and analyses are often too brief to be genuinely helpful.

The Exegetical Guide to the Greek New Testament (EGGNT) aims to close the gap between the Greek text and the available tools. Each EGGNT volume aims to provide all the necessary information for understanding the Greek text and, in addition, includes homiletical helps and suggestions for further study. The EGGNT is not a full-scale commentary. Nevertheless, these guides will make interpreting a given New Testament book easier, in particular for those who are hard-pressed for time and yet want to preach or teach with accuracy and authority.

In terms of layout, each volume begins with a brief introduction to the particular book (including such matters as authorship, date, etc.), a basic outline, and a list of recommended commentaries. At the end of each volume, you will find a comprehensive exegetical outline of the book. The body of each volume is devoted to paragraph-by-paragraph exegesis of the text. The treatment of each paragraph includes:

1. The Greek text of the passage, phrase by phrase, from the fifth edition of the United Bible Societies' *Greek New Testament* (UBS^5).

2. A structural analysis of the passage. Typically, verbal discussion of the structure of a given unit is followed by a diagram, whereby the verbal discussion serves to explain the diagram and the diagram serves to provide a visual aid illumining the structural discussion. While there is no one correct or standard way to diagram Greek sentences, the following format is typically followed in EGGNT volumes:

a. The original Greek word order is maintained.
b. When Greek words are omitted, this is indicated by ellipses (. . .).
c. The diagramming method, moving from left to right, is predicated on the following. In clauses with a finite verb, the default order is typically verb-subject-object. In verbless clauses or clauses with nonfinite verb forms, the default order is typically subject-(verb)-object. Departures from these default orders are understood to be pragmatically motivated (e.g., contrast, emphasis, etc.).
d. Indents are used to indicate subordination (e.g., in the case of dependent clauses).
e. Retaining original word order, modifiers are centered above or below the word they modify (e.g., a prepositional phrase in relation to the verb).
f. Where a given sentence or clause spans multiple lines of text, drawn lines are used, such as where a relative pronoun introduces a relative clause (often shifting emphasis).
g. Underline is used to indicate imperatives; dotted underline is used to indicate repetition (the same word or cognate used multiple times in a given unit); the symbol ⁝ may be used where an article is separated from a noun or participle by interjected material (such as a prepositional phrase).
h. In shorter letters diagrams are normally provided for every unit; in longer letters and Revelation, ellipses may be used to show less detail in diagramming (keeping larger blocks together on the same line) in order to focus primarily on the larger structure of a given unit; in the Gospels and Acts, detailed diagrams will usually not be provided, though less detailed diagrams may be used to illustrate important or more complex structural aspects of a given passage.

3. A discussion of each phrase of the passage with discussion of relevant vocabulary, significant textual variants, and detailed grammatical analysis, including parsing. When more than one solution is given for a particular exegetical issue, the author's own preference is indicated by an asterisk (*). When no preference is expressed, the options are judged to be evenly balanced, or it is assumed that the text is intentionally ambiguous. When a particular verb form may be parsed in more than one way, only the parsing appropriate in the specific context is supplied; but where there is difference of opinion among grammarians or commentators, both possibilities are given and the matter is discussed.
4. Various translations of significant words or phrases.
5. A list of suggested topics for further study with bibliography for each topic. An asterisk (*) in one of the "For Further Study" bibliographies draws attention to a discussion of the particular topic that is recommended as a useful introduction to the issues involved.
6. Homiletical suggestions designed to help the preacher or teacher move from the Greek text to a sermon outline that reflects careful exegesis. The first

suggestion for a particular paragraph of the text is always more exegetical than homiletical and consists of an outline of the entire paragraph. These detailed outlines of each paragraph build on the general outline proposed for the whole book and, if placed side by side, form a comprehensive exegetical outline of the book. All outlines are intended to serve as a basis for sermon preparation and should be adapted to the needs of a particular audience.[1]

The EGGNT volumes will serve a variety of readers. Those reading the Greek text for the first time may be content with the assistance with vocabulary, parsing, and translation. Readers with some experience in Greek may want to skip or skim these sections and focus attention on the discussions of grammar. More advanced students may choose to pursue the topics and references to technical works under "For Further Study," while pastors may be more interested in the movement from grammatical analysis to sermon outline. Teachers may appreciate having a resource that frees them to focus on exegetical details and theological matters.

The editors are pleased to present you with the individual installments of the EGGNT. We are grateful for each of the contributors who has labored long and hard over each phrase in the Greek New Testament. Together we share the conviction that "all Scripture is inspired by God and is profitable for teaching, for rebuking, for correcting, for training in righteousness" (2 Tim 3:16 CSB) and echo Paul's words to Timothy: "Be diligent to present yourself to God as one approved, a worker who doesn't need to be ashamed, correctly teaching the word of truth" (2 Tim 2:15 CSB).

Andreas J. Köstenberger
Robert W. Yarbrough

1. As a Bible publisher, B&H Publishing follows the "Colorado Springs Guidelines for Translation of Gender-Related Language in Scripture." As an academic book publisher, B&H Academic asks that authors conform their manuscripts (including EGGNT exegetical outlines in English) to the B&H Academic style guide, which affirms the use of singular "he/his/him" as generic examples encompassing both genders. However, in their discussion of the Greek text, EGGNT authors have the freedom to analyze the text and reach their own conclusions regarding whether specific Greek words are gender specific or gender inclusive.

Abbreviations

For abbreviations used in discussion of text-critical matters, the reader should refer to the abbreviations listed in the introduction to the United Bible Societies' *Greek New Testament.*

*	indicates the reading of the original hand of the manuscript as opposed to subsequent correctors of the manuscript, *or*
	indicates the writer's own preference when more than one solution is given for a particular exegetical problem, *or*
	in the "For Further Study" bibliographies, indicates a discussion of the particular topic that is recommended as a useful introduction to the issues involved,
§, §§	paragraph, paragraphs

Books of the Old Testament

Gen	Genesis	Song	Song of Songs (Canticles)
Exod	Exodus	Isa	Isaiah
Lev	Leviticus	Jer	Jeremiah
Num	Numbers	Lam	Lamentations
Deut	Deuteronomy	Ezek	Ezekiel
Josh	Joshua	Dan	Daniel
Judg	Judges	Hos	Hosea
Ruth	Ruth	Joel	Joel
1–2 Sam	1–2 Samuel	Amos	Amos
1–2 Kgs	1–2 Kings	Obad	Obadiah
1–2 Chr	1–2 Chronicles	Jonah	Jonah
Ezra	Ezra	Mic	Micah
Neh	Nehemiah	Nah	Nahum
Esth	Esther	Hab	Habakkuk
Job	Job	Zeph	Zephaniah

Ps(s)	Psalm(s)	Hag	Haggai
Prov	Proverbs	Zech	Zechariah
Eccl	Ecclesiastes	Mal	Malachi

Books of the New Testament

Matt	Matthew	1–2 Thess	1–2 Thessalonians
Mark	Mark	1–2 Tim	1–2 Timothy
Luke	Luke	Titus	Titus
John	John	Phlm	Philemon
Acts	Acts	Heb	Hebrews
Rom	Romans	Jas	James
1–2 Cor	1–2 Corinthians	1–2 Pet	1–2 Peter
Gal	Galatians	1–3 John	1–3 John
Eph	Ephesians	Jude	Jude
Phil	Philippians	Rev	Revelation
Col	Colossians		

Other Ancient Jewish and Christian Texts

Haer.	Irenaeus, *Against Heresies*
Hist. eccl.	Eusebius, *Ecclesiastical History*
1 Macc	1 Maccabees
2 Macc	2 Maccabees
1QS	Community Rule (Qumran)
Strom.	Clement of Alexanderia, *Miscellanies*
T. Benj.	Testament of Benjamin
T. Reu.	Testament of Reuben

General Abbreviations

ABD	*The Anchor Bible Dictionary*, 6 vols., ed. D. N. Freedman (New York: Doubleday, 1992)
abs.	absolute(ly)
acc.	accusative
act.	active (voice)
adj.	adjective, adjectival(ly)
adv.	adverb, adverbial(ly)
Akin	Daniel L. Akin, *1, 2, 3 John*, New American Commentary (Nashville: B&H, 2001)
anar.	anarthrous

aor.	aorist
advers.	adversative
apod.	apodosis
appos.	apposition, appositional
art.	(definite) article, articular
attrib.	attibutive(ly)
Bateman and Peer	H. W. Bateman IV and Aaron C. Peer, *John's Letters: An Exegetical Guide for Preaching and Teaching* (Grand Rapids; Kregel Academic, 2018)
Baugh	S. M. Baugh, *A First John Reader: Intermediate Greek Reading Notes and Grammar* (Phillipsburg, NJ: P&R, 1999)
Baugh, *Tense Form Choice*	S. M. Baugh, *Introduction to Greek Tense Form Choice in the Non-Indicative Moods*, PDF ed. (Escondido, CA, 2009), https://dailydoseofgreek.com/new-testament-greek-resources/
Bavinck	Herman Bavinck, *Reformed Dogmatics*, ed. John Bolt, trans. John Vriend, 4 vols. (Grand Rapids: Baker Academic, 2008)
BDAG	*A Greek-English Lexicon of the New Testament and Other Early Christian Literature*, rev. and ed. F. W. Danker (Chicago: University of Chicago, 2000), based on W. Bauer's *Griechisch-deutsches Wörterbuch* (6th ed.) and on previous English ed. by W. F. Arndt, F. W. Gingrich, and F. W. Danker. References to BDAG are by page number and quadrant on the page, *a* indicating the upper half and *b* the lower half of the left-hand column, and *c* and *d* the upper and lower halves of the right-hand column. With the use of dark type, biblical references are now clearly visible within each section.
BDF	F. Blass and A. Debrunner, *A Greek Grammar of the New Testament and Other Early Christian Literature*, trans. and rev. R. W. Funk (Chicago: University of Chicago Press, 1961)
BHGNT	Baylor Handbook on the Greek New Testament
Brooke	A. E. Brooke, *A Critical and Exegetical Commentary on the Johannine Epistles*, International Critical Commentary (London: T&T Clark, 1912)
Brown	Raymond E. Brown, *The Epistles of John*, Anchor Bible (New York: Doubleday, 1982)
BSac	*Bibliotheca Sacra*
Burton	E. de W. Burton, *Syntax of the Moods and Tenses in New Testament Greek*, 4th ed. (Eugene, OR: Wipf & Stock Publishers, 2003)
BW	James A. Brooks and Carlton L. Winbery, *Syntax of New Testament Greek* (Lanham, MD: University Press of America, 1979)
Campbell	C. R. Campbell, *Verbal Aspect and Non-Indicative Verbs: Further Soundings in the Greek of the New Testament* (New York: Lang, 2008)

Carson, *Greek Accents*	D. A. Carson, *Greek Accents: A Student's Manual* (Grand Rapids: Baker, 1985)
Carson and Moo	D. A. Carson and Douglas Moo, *An Introduction to the New Testament*, 2nd ed. (Grand Rapids: Zondervan, 2005)
CBQ	*Catholic Biblical Quarterly*
cf.	*confer* (Lat.), compare
ch(s).	chapter(s)
CJ	*Classical Journal*
comp.	comparative, comparison
cond.	condition(al)
conj.	conjunctive, conjunction
contemp.	contemporaneous
Cox	Leo G. Cox, *I, II, and III John*, vol. 6 of *The Wesleyan Bible Commentary*, ed. Charles W. Carter (Grand Rapids: Eerdmans, 1996)
cstr.	construction, construe(d)
CTJ	*Calvin Theological Journal*
CTQ	*Concordia Theological Quarterly*
Culy	Martin N. Culy, *I, II, III John: A Handbook on the Greek Text*, 2nd ed., BHGNT (Waco: Baylor University Press, 2011)
dat.	dative
DBI	*Dictionary of Biblical Imagery*, ed. L. Ryken, J. C. Wilhoit, and T. Longman III (Downers Grove, IL: InterVarsity, 1998)
dbl.	double
Decker	Rodney J. Decker, *Reading Koine Greek: An Introduction and Integrated Workbook* (Grand Rapids: Baker Academic, 2014)
def.	definite
delib.	deliberative
dem.	demonstrative
dep.	deponent
DJG	*Dictionary of Jesus and the Gospels*, ed. Joel B. Green, Jeannine K. Brown, and Nicholas Perrin, 2nd ed. (Downers Grove, IL: InterVarsity, 2013)
DLNT	*Dictionary of the Later New Testament and Its Developments*, ed. R. P. Martin and P. H. Davids (Downers Grove, IL: InterVarsity, 1997)
DM	H. E. Dana and J. R. Mantey, *A Manual Grammar of the Greek New Testament* (New York: Macmillan, 1927)
DNTB	*Dictionary of New Testament Backgrounds*, ed. Craig A. Evans and Stanley E. Porter (Downers Grove, IL: InterVarsity, 2000)

Dodd	C. H. Dodd, *The Johannine Epistles*, The Moffatt New Testament Commentary (New York: Harper & Row, 1946)
DPL	*Dictionary of Paul and His Letters*, ed. G. F. Hawthorne, R. P. Martin, and D. G. Reid (Downers Grove, IL: InterVarsity, 1993)
dimin.	diminutive
dir.	direct
EDNT	*Exegetical Dictionary of the New Testament*, ed. H. Balz and G. Schneider, 3 vols. (Grand Rapids: Eerdmans, 1990–93)
ed(s).	edited by, edition(s), editor(s)
e.g.	*exempli gratia* (Lat.), for example
Eng.	English
epex.	epexegetic, epexegetical(ly)
esp.	especially
ESV	English Standard Version (2011)
et al.	*et alia* (Lat.), and others
etym.	etymology (etymological)
EvQ	*Evangelical Quarterly*
EVV	English versions of the Bible
ExpTim	*Expository Times*
f(f).	and the following (verse[s] or page[s])
fem.	feminine
fig.	figurative(ly)
FS	Festschrift
Frame	John M. Frame, *Systematic Theology: An Introduction to Christian Belief* (Phillipsburg, NJ: P&R, 2013)
fut.	future
gen.	genitive
Gk.	Greek
GNT	Greek New Testament
Goodell	Thomas D. Goodell, *A School Grammar of Attic Greek* (New York: Appleton, 1903)
Goodwin	William W. Goodwin, *A Greek Grammar* (Boston: Ginn, 1892)
Grudem	Wayne Grudem, *Systematic Theology: An Introduction to Biblical Doctrine* (Grand Rapids: Zondervan, 1994).
Haas	C. Haas, M. de Jonge, and J. L. Swellengrebel, *A Handbook on The Letters of John* (New York: United Bible Societies, 1972)
Harris	M. J. Harris, *Prepositions and Theology in the Greek New Testament* (Grand Rapids: Zondervan, 2012)

Heb.	Hebrew, Hebraism
Hiebert	D. Edmond Hiebert, *The Epistles of John: An Expositional Commentary* (Greenville, SC: Bob Jones University Press, 1991)
Hong	Yohan Hong, "'From the Beginning': Christology and Ethics in 1 John" (PhD diss., The Southern Baptist Theological Seminary, 2023).
i.e.	*id est* (Lat.), that is
impers.	impersonal
impf.	imperfect (tense)
impv.	imperative (mood), imperative(ly)
incl.	including
indecl.	indeclinable
indef.	indefinite
indic.	indicative (mood)
indir.	indirect
inf.	infinitive
ingr.	ingressive
instr.	instrument, instrumental(ly)
intrans.	intransitive(ly)
Int	*Interpretation*
interr.	interrogative
ISBE	G. W. Bromiley, et al., eds., *The International Standard Bible Encyclopedia*, 4 vols. (Grand Rapids: Eerdmans, 1979–88)
iter.	iterative
JBL	*Journal of Biblical Literature*
JBT	*Journal of Biblical Theology*
Jobes	Karen H. Jobes, *1, 2, & 3 John*, ZECNT (Grand Rapids: Zondervan, 2014)
JETS	*Journal of the Evangelical Theological Society*
JSNT	*Journal for the Study of the New Testament*
JSNTSup	Journal for the Study of the New Testament Supplement Series
JTS	*Journal of Theological Studies*
KJV	King James Version
KMP	Andreas J. Köstenberger, Benjamin L. Merkle, and Robert L. Plummer, *Going Deeper with New Testament Greek: An Intermediate Study of the Grammar and Syntax of the New Testament*, rev. ed. (Nashville: B&H Academic, 2020)
Köstenberger, *Theology*	Andreas Köstenberger, *A Theology of John's Gospel and Letters* (Grand Rapids: Zondervan, 2005)

Kruse	Colin G. Kruse, The *Letters of John*, PNTC (Grand Rapids: Eerdmans, 2000)
Law	Robert Law, *The Tests of Life: A Study of the First Epistle of St. John* (Edinburgh: T&T Clark, 1909)
Lenski	R. C. H. Lenksi, *The Interpretation of the Epistles of St. Peter, St. John and St. Jude* (Columbus, OH: Waterburg, 1945)
lit.	literal(ly)
Lloyd-Jones	Martyn Lloyd-Jones, *Life in Christ: Studies in 1 John* (Wheaton, IL: Crossway, 2002)
LN	J. P. Louw and E. A. Nida, eds., *Introduction and Domains*, vol. 1 of *Greek-English Lexicon of the New Testament Based on Semantic Domains* (New York: United Bible Societies, 1988)
LNTS	Library of New Testament Studies
loc.	locative
LXX	Septuagint (= Greek Old Testament)
Marshall	I. Howard Marshall, *The Epistles of John*, NICNT (Grand Rapids: Eerdmans, 1978)
MBG	William D. Mounce, *The Morphology of Biblical Greek* (Grand Rapids: Zondervan, 1994)
McGaughy	Lane C. McGaughy, *Toward a Descriptive Analysis of* Εἶναι *as a Linking Verb in New Testament Greek*, Dissertation Series (Missoula, MT: Society of Biblical Literature, 1972)
Metzger	B. M. Metzger, *A Textual Commentary on the Greek New Testament*, 2nd ed. (London: United Bible Society, 1971)
MH	J. H. Moulton and W. F. Howard, *Accidence and Word-Formation*, vol. 2 of *A Grammar of New Testament Greek*, ed. J. H. Moulton (Edinburgh: T&T Clark, 1939)
mid.	middle
MM	J. H. Moulton and G. Milligan, *The Vocabulary of the Greek New Testament Illustrated from the Papyri and Other Non-Literary Sources* (London: Hodder and Stoughton, 1929)
mng.	meaning
MNTG	Ted Hildebrandt, *Mastering New Testament Greek* (Grand Rapids: Baker Academic, 2003)
Morris	Leon Morris, *The Apostolic Preaching of the Cross*, 3rd ed. (Cambridge: Cambridge University Press, 1967)
Moule	C. F. D. Moule, *An Idiom Book of New Testament Greek*, 2nd ed. (Cambridge: Cambridge University Press, 1959)
Moulton	J. H. Moulton, *Prolegomena*, vol. 1 of *A Grammar of New Testament Greek*, 3rd ed. (Edinburgh: T&T Clark, 1908)
ms(s).	manuscript(s)

n.	note
NA[27]	*Novum Testamentum Graece*, Nestle-Aland, 27th ed.
NA[28]	*Novum Testamentum Graece*, Nestle-Aland, 28th ed.
NASB	New American Standard Bible (1995)
NDBT	*New Dictionary of Biblical Theology*, ed. T. Desmond Alexander and Brian S. Rosner (Downers Grove, IL: InterVarsity, 2000)
neg.	negative, negation
Neot	*Neotestamentica*
NET	New English Translation Bible (2005)
neut.	neuter
NICNT	New International Commentary on the New Testament
NIDNTT	*The New International Dictionary of New Testament Theology*, ed. C. Brown, 3 vols. (Grand Rapids: Zondervan, 1975–78)
NIDNTTE	*New International Dictionary of New Testament Theology and Exegesis*, ed. M. Silva, 5 vols. (Grand Rapids: Zondervan, 2014)
NIV	New International Version (2011)
NLT	New Living Translation (1996)
nom.	nominative
NovT	*Novum Testamentum*
NovTSup	Supplements to Novum Testamentum
NT	New Testament
NTS	*New Testament Studies*
obj.	object(ive)
orig.	origin, original(ly)
OT	Old Testament
p(p).	page(s)
pass.	passive
periph.	periphrastic
pers.	person(al)
pf.	perfect
pl.	plural
Plummer	Alfred Plummer, *The Epistles of S. John*, The Cambridge Bible for Schools and Colleges (New York: Macmillan, 1894)
pluperf.	pluperfect, pluperfective
PNTC	Pillar New Testament Commentary
Porter, *Idioms*	S. E. Porter, *Idioms of the Greek New Testament*, 2nd ed. (Sheffield: JSOT, 1999)

Porter, *Verbal Aspect*	S. E. Porter, *Verbal Aspect in the Greek of the New Testament, with Reference to Tense and Mood* (New York: Lang, 1989)
poss.	possessive, possession
pred.	predicate, predicative
pref.	prefix
prep.	preposition(al)
pres.	present
prob.	probably
prog.	progressive
pron.	pronoun
prot.	protasis
ptc.	participle, participial(ly)
R	A. T. Robertson, *A Grammar of the Greek New Testament in the Light of Historical Research*, 4th ed. (Nashville: Broadman, 1934)
rdg(s).	(textual) reading(s)
ref.	reference
refl.	reflexive
rel.	relative
rev.	revised, revision
ResQ	*Restoration Quarterly*
Robertson, *Pictures*	A. T. Robertson, *Word Pictures in the New Testament*, 6 vols. (Nashville: Broadman, 1933)
Rogers and Rogers	Cleon L. Rogers Jr. and Cleon L. Rogers III, *The New Linguistic and Exegetical Key to the Greek New Testament* (Grand Rapids: Zondervan, 1998)
RSR	*Recherches de science religieuse*
Runge	S. E. Runge, *Discourse Grammar of the Greek New Testament: A Practical Introduction for Teaching and Exegesis* (Peabody, MA: Hendrickson, 2010)
SBJT	*The Southern Baptist Journal of Theology*
Schreiner, *NT Theology*	Thomas R. Schreiner, *New Testament Theology: Magnifying God in Christ* (Grand Rapids: Baker Academic, 2008)
Seifrid	Mark A. Seifrid, *Christ, Our Righteousness: Paul's Theology of Justification* (Downers Grove, IL: IVP Academic, 2000)
Sem.	Semitic, Semitism
sg.	singular
sim.	similar(ly)
SJT	*Scottish Journal of Theology*

Smalley	Stephen S. Smalley, *1, 2, and 3 John*, rev. ed., WBC (Grand Rapids: Zondervan, 2008)
Smyth	Herbert Weir Smyth, *Greek Grammar* (Cambridge: Harvard University Press, 1920)
SNTSMS	Society for New Testament Studies Monograph Series
Stott	John R. W. Stott, *The Letters of John*, TNTC 19 (Downers Grove, IL: IVP Academic, 1988)
Strecker	George Strecker, *The Johannine Letters: A Commentary on 1, 2, and 3 John*, trans. Linda M. Maloney, Hermeneia (Minneapolis: Fortress Press, 1996)
subj.	subject(ive)
subjunc.	subjunctive
subord.	subordinate, subordination
subst.	substantive, substantival(ly)
superl.	superlative
TDNT	*Theological Dictionary of the New Testament*, ed. G. Kittel and G. Friedrich, trans. G. W. Bromiley, 9 vols. (Grand Rapids: Eerdmans, 1964–74)
temp.	temporal(ly)
TNTC	Tyndale New Testament Commentary
tr.	translate(d), translator(s), translation(s)
Turner, *Style*	N. Turner, *Style*, vol. 4 of *A Grammar of New Testament Greek*, ed. J. H. Moulton (Edinburgh: T&T Clark, 1976)
Turner, *Syntax*	N. Turner, *Syntax*, vol. 3 of *A Grammar of New Testament Greek*, ed. J. H. Moulton (Edinburgh: T&T Clark, 1963)
Turner, *Words*	N. Turner, *Christian Words* (Edinburgh: T&T Clark, 1980)
TynBul	*Tyndale Bulletin*
UBS^4	*The Greek New Testament*, United Bible Society, 4th ed.
UBS^5	*The Greek New Testament*, United Bible Society, 5th ed.
v(v).	verse(s)
var.	variant (form or reading)
vb(s).	verb(s)
voc(s).	vocative(s)
vol(s).	volume(s)
Wallace	Daniel B. Wallace, *Greek Grammar beyond the Basics: An Exegetical Syntax of the New Testament* (Grand Rapids: Zondervan, 1996)
WBC	Word Biblical Commentary
WTJ	*Westminster Theological Journal*

WW	*Word and World*
Yarbrough	Robert W. Yarbrough, *1–3 John*, BECNT (Grand Rapids: Baker Academic, 2008)
Young	Richard A. Young, *Intermediate New Testament Greek: A Linguistic and Exegetical Approach* (Nashville: B&H, 1994)
Z	M. Zerwick. *Biblical Greek Illustrated by Examples*, trans. J. Smith (Rome: Pontifical Biblical Institute, 1963)
ZG	M. Zerwick, *A Grammatical Analysis of the New Testament*, trans. Mary Grosvenor, 5th ed. (Rome: Gregorian & Biblical Press, 2019)

Introduction for 1–3 John

AUTHORSHIP

The early church attributed authorship of 1 John and the Fourth Gospel to the apostle John, the son of Zebedee. Papias, a contemporary of Polycarp, represents the first to reference an epistle of John (Eusebius, *Hist. eccl.* 3.39.17). In the latter part of the second century, Irenaeus attributes 1 John and another letter (probably 2 John) to the apostle (*Haer.* 3.16.5). Clement of Alexandria refers to "the greater epistle" of John (*Strom.* 2.15.66). Origen (early third century) references all three letters, though his statement notes that the authenticity of 2 and 3 John was disputed by some (Eusebius, *Hist. eccl.* 3.25.3; 6.25.10). Elsewhere in his *Church History*, Eusebius quotes from a now lost work of Papias, whose words could be understood as referring to two Johns: John the apostle and the "John the elder" (*Hist. eccl.* 3.39.4). Eusebius cites this statement from Papias to support his attribution of Revelation to John the elder (a book Eusebius disliked and so preferred to distance from apostolic authority). Various modern scholars continue to view "John the elder" as the author of either some or all of the Johannine Letters. Yet, Papias's statement arguably refers to one individual, the apostle John, rather than to two separate individuals as held by Eusebius. Regardless, up through the Reformation the Letters were never explicitly attributed to anyone other than John the apostle, the son of Zebedee (although the authenticity of 2 and 3 John was debated, as noted above).

The author of 1 John does not identify himself. In 2 and 3 John, the author refers to himself only as ὁ πρεσβύτερος "the elder." The author of 1 John writes as an eyewitness of Jesus Christ (1:1–4) and, in all three letters, assumes a tone of authority consistent with that of an apostle. Furthermore, there are significant overlaps between 1 John and the Fourth Gospel, including similar themes, vocabulary, and syntax. Though there are notable differences in doctrine and wording, these differences can be attributed to their differences in genre, occasion, purpose, and intended audience. There are obvious similarities shared by 2 and 3 John. As Stott notes, their common authorship "is almost self-evident," and he adds that "the similarities between the greater [1 John] and the two lesser letters are striking" (28).

Most scholars today hold that 1, 2, and 3 John were written by the same author, though many argue for authorship other than the apostle John. Often, authorship is associated with a disciple or group of disciples of a Johannine community (e.g., Brooke, Brown, Smalley) though the existence of such a defined community is debatable. In agreement with many scholars, the internal and external evidence favors ascribing authorship to the apostle John, the son of Zebedee, for all three letters (among recent commentators, see Akin 27; Hiebert 16, 281; Kruse 14, 36, 42; Yarbrough 5).

GENRE

The book of 1 John lacks the expected greeting and closing salutation of a typical first-century, Greco-Roman letter. Scholarship reflects a variety of suggestions concerning the genre (e.g., a "paper" explaining the teaching of the Fourth Gospel, see Smalley xxv). Yet, the writing reflects aspects of a personal letter and was referenced as such by Irenaeus and Eusebius, among others. With this background in mind, it is reasonable to understand and speak of 1 John as a letter in broad terms. As Yarbrough notes, "That it should be understood as a letter of some kind can hardly be doubted" (16). In contrast, 2 and 3 John are clear examples of personal letters from the first-century Greco-Roman world.

DATE, PROVENANCE, AND DESTINATION

Evidence from church fathers suggests that John, the son of Zebedee, traveled to Ephesus before the destruction of Jerusalem (AD 70) and lived out his life there. If written after the Fourth Gospel (written AD 80–85 as assumed by many), the likely period of writing would have been just before or during the last decade of the first century. All three letters were likely written during this period, though there is not sufficient information to know with any degree of certainty the order in which the letters were written. A historical reconstruction that supports the canonical order is plausible if not likely (see Kruse 1–4). The letters, based on evidence of providence, were likely written to churches (1–2 John) and an individual (3 John) in the surrounding areas of Ephesus (possibly including the regions of the seven churches noted in Revelation 1–3).

OCCASION AND PURPOSE

First John was written by a pastor to a church (or group of churches) dealing with the effects of a schism. Certain members, holding to a false teaching, separated themselves from the church and left faithful members in need of assurance, encouragement, and guidance. The beliefs, actions, and words of the secessionists seeded doubts and questions among those who remained concerning their own beliefs and standing as children of God. John's purpose is to meet the remaining church members at their point of need, offering assurance and exhortation.

Scholars disagree as to the specifics of the false teaching of the opponents, though most would agree the teaching reflects a defective Christology of some type. The following three teachings are often proposed: (1) Proto-Gnosticism, an early manifestation of a broadly defined second-century teaching that viewed the material world as bad and the spiritual world as divine and good; (2) docetism, the belief that Jesus only appeared to be human; and (3) Cerinthianism, the teaching of Cerinthus who taught the Spirit came upon the man Jesus at his baptism and left him at the cross. Not every aspect of what is known about these teachings is reflected or aligns completely with what can be discerned about the false teaching from the letter. Caution is warranted in being too dogmatic in conclusions. Yet, it is reasonable to look to these influences as a likely background to the author's corrective teaching.

In response to the false teaching, the author emphasizes what is often referred to as three "tests" (see Law). John infuses and supports his words of assurance and exhortation with the following three emphases: (1) the theological dimension (belief in Jesus Christ, the Son of God, come in the flesh); (2) the moral dimension (obedience); (3) the relational dimension (loving one another). Carson and Moo capture well these emphases, writing that "John stresses the truth that Jesus is the Christ come in the flesh and that genuine belief in this Jesus works itself out in obedience to the commands of God and in love for God's people" (Carson and Moo 681). Additionally, John seeks to assure his readers of their standing as children of God by pointing them to the objective reality of the historical fact of Jesus's ministry as well as the subjective reality of their own transformative experience as believers.

Recent scholarship has suggested a nonpolemical reading of 1 John (See Lieu, *I, II, & III John*; Griffith, "Non-Polemical Reading"). While aspects of this scholarship are helpful, the conclusion that 1 John was written to a specific community affected by a false teaching and church schism is a more productive basis for interpretation. The letter should be read in light of this reconstructed background, though with discernment and sensitivity to the text. As Marshall notes, "We should beware of supposing that every attitude which John condemns must necessarily be attributed to the false teachers, or that their teaching formed a coherent complete system of thought" (15).

The author of 2 John refers to himself as "the elder" and writes to "the chosen lady and her children," which refers to a church and its body of believers. The author exhorts the church to walk in obedience and warns the church about the danger of receiving traveling preachers who do not abide in the teaching of Jesus Christ, who "do not confess the coming of Jesus Christ in the flesh." The author of 3 John again refers to himself as "the elder" and writes to a fellow believer named Gaius. The author seeks to address an issue with a certain Diotrephes, who has rejected the elder's authority and is forbidding those in the church to show hospitality to traveling missionaries.

LINGUISTIC CONSIDERATIONS

John's Style

In the context of the Greek of the NT as a whole, 1–3 John reflects fairly straightforward syntax and vocabulary. Yet, this relatively simple representation of Koine Greek provides the author the pallet to convey the rich and complex theological truths that will meet believers at their point of need. Like all NT authors, John's writing style has its own unique features, such as John's tendency for stylistic variation, the oft-used subst. ptc. (i.e., ὁ λέγων . . . ; for a helpful discussion on John's style and vocabulary, see Bateman and Peer 54–59).

Accentuation Pattern of εἰμί

All the present indicative forms of εἰμί except the second person sg. (εἶ) are enclitic, meaning that the vb. will shift its accent to the preceding word. An exception is when ἐστίν either begins a sentence or clause or is preceded by καί or οὐκ. In these cases, ἐστίν becomes ἔστιν (accent shifts to the first syllable). Lastly, note that εἰμί, ἐστίν, ἐσμέν, ἐστέ, and εἰσίν will retain their accent if the preceding word has an acute accent on the penult (next to last syllable). Only rules significant to our text are noted (for a full discussion on enclitics and proclitics, see Carson, *Greek Accents*, 47–51; see also the helpful discussion in Culy 10–12).

Verbal Aspect

The scholarship on verbal aspect continues to advance and deepen our understanding of the Greek verbal system. In the following commentary, various observations are noted as needed, but the reader is encouraged to pursue further study of the topic to appreciate its appropriate application in exegesis, teaching, and preaching. (As of the date of the writing of this EGGNT volume [2023], helpful resources include Picirilli, "Meaning of the Tenses"; Campbell, *Study of Greek*, 105–33; Campbell, "Aspect and Tense"; Andreas J. Köstenberger, Benjamin L. Merkle, and Robert L. Plummer, *Going Deeper with New Testament Greek: An Intermediate Study of the Grammar and Syntax of the New Testament*, rev. ed. (Nashville: B&H Academic, 2020), chap. 2, "Nominative, Vocative & Accusative Cases" (51–85).

Supplementary Participles

A repeated use of the ptc. in John's Letters warrants further introductory comments. First John 3:17 provides an example of this usage. The text reads: ὃς δ' ἂν ἔχῃ τὸν βίον τοῦ κόσμου καὶ θεωρῇ τὸν ἀδελφὸν αὐτοῦ χρείαν ἔχοντα "Whoever has the life of the world and sees his brother having need." Τὸν ἀδελφόν is the acc. dir. obj. of θεωρῇ, but how should we label the function of the ptc. ἔχοντα? Several times in the Johannine Epistles (1 John 3:15, 17; 4:2; 5:16; 2 John vv. 4, 7; 3 John v. 4) and hundreds of times throughout the GNT, we find a similar construction with a verb of perception or communication followed by a dir. obj. in the acc. case (usually articular) and an anarthrous ptc. (also in the acc. case). At one level, the meaning of these constructions is obvious. The ptc. is describing an activity that the dir. obj. is doing and the subj. of the (main) verb is seeing, hearing, or knowing about that reality. With the influence of Dan Wallace's *Greek Grammar beyond the Basics* and the Baylor Handbook on the Greek New Testament series, these constructions are usually labeled "double accusative" constructions with the acc. noun considered the "object" and the ptc. labeled as the "complement" (Culy 88; Wallace 182–89). Wallace explains: "An object-complement double accusative is a construction in which one accusative substantive is the direct object of the verb and the other accusative (either noun, adjective, participle, or infinitive) complements the object in that it predicates something about it. The complement may be substantive or adjectival (182)."

This description is understandable, but we wonder if it is misleading to include the ptc. as a "complement" alongside substantival/nominal "complements." For example, Wallace labels 1 John 4:14b as a double accusative object-complement construction. First John 4:14 says: *ὁ πατὴρ ἀπέσταλκεν τὸν υἱὸν σωτῆρα τοῦ κόσμου*. According to Wallace's schema, *τὸν υἱόν* is the object and *σωτῆρα* is the complement (186). Indeed, this seems a useful grammatical label, but when we compare 1 John 4:14 with 3:17 above, the relationship between the supposed object and complement are markedly different. In 1 John 4:14, there is an implied equative sense. The Son *is* the Savior of the world. In 1 John 3:17, John is not so much asserting, "The brother is the one having need," as he is saying that a brother is in a state of having need. Χρείαν ἔχοντα "having need," is a verbal reality predicated/asserted about the brother, not a substantive/nominal expression in an implied equative sense. Indeed, in both English and Latin grammars this use of the ptc. is usually labeled a "predicate" use of the ptc., a label sometimes found in classical Greek grammars as well (e.g., Goodell §586).

The majority of classical Greek grammars and older grammars of the GNT specifically discuss this use of the ptc. under the category of the "supplementary ptc." (sometimes called the complementary ptc.). The term "supplementary" implies that the activity of the main verb is not complete until it is *supplemented* by taking into account the action of the ptc.

So, in the example we began with from 1 John 3:17, the person who has the life of the world does not just see his brother (the activity of seeing is not fully complete in such a partial description); that person sees his brother *having need*. If we do not have the ptc. construction further supplementing the dir. obj.—predicating something about it—then the activity of θεωρῇ "sees," is incomplete. *The Cambridge Grammar of Classical Greek* (2019) also labels this type of ptc. as supplementary, "to complement verbs expressing direct sensory perception ('see,' 'hear'), verbs expressing some phase of action ('begin,' 'continue,' 'stop'), and vbs. meaning to 'endure,' 'persist,' etc." (610). Blass and Debrunner similarly categorize this use of the ptc. as "the supplemental participle with verbs of perception and cognition" (BDF §416). One should note that a major subcategory of the supplementary ptc. is to express indir. discourse (e.g., 1 John 4:2; 2 John 1:7; see Robertson 1122–24; KMP 343). William Goodwin divides supplementary ptcs. into two categories, "Participles Not in Indirect Discourse" (§§1580–87) and "Participles in Indirect Discourse" (§§1588–93). H. W. Smyth follows a similar division in his discussion of the supplementary ptc. (§§2094–105; §§2106–22). In assessing this scholarly discussion, we judge that both the clarity of explanation and the weight of tradition are on the side of labeling the ptcs. in question as "supplementary ptcs." We shall use that label in this commentary.

STRUCTURE OF 1, 2, AND 3 JOHN

There is no consensus on the structure of 1 John (for discussion on the various approaches to the structure see the classic study by Hershael York, "Exegetical Methods of Rhetorical Criticism"; Akin 37–47; Marshall 22–27). We agree fundamentally with Marshall, who notes that "it seems preferable to regard the Epistle as being composed of a series of connected paragraphs whose relation to one another is governed by association of ideas rather than by a logical plan" (26). The outline of 1 John is offered as a helpful guide for analysis, teaching, and preaching. As noted above under "Genre," 2 and 3 John are clear examples of the letter genre of the first-century Greco-Roman world. Their structures are relatively straightforward as reflected by their outlines.

Exegetical Outlines

1 JOHN

I. Prologue (1:1–4)

- A. Eyewitness to the Eternal Word of Life (1:1)
- B. Revelation and Declaration of the Word of Life (1:2)
- C. Intention of Fellowship and Completed Joy (1:3–4)

II. Relationship with a Holy God: Claim versus Reality (1:5–10)

- A. God Is Light (1:5)
- B. Walking in Darkness versus Walking in Light (1:6–7)
- C. Denying Sin versus Confessing Sin (1:8–10)

III. Sin and the Believer (2:1–6)

- A. Christ Our Advocate (2:1)
- B. Christ the Propitiation for Our Sins (2:2)
- C. Knowing God Means Obeying Him and Keeping His Commands (2:3–6)

IV. An Old and New Commandment in the Light of the New Age (2:7–11)

- A. The Old Command Had from the Beginning (2:7)
- B. Yet, a New Command as the Light Breaks into the Darkness (2:8)
- C. Loving versus Hating One Another (2:9–11)

V. Encouragement to the Church (2:12–14)

- A. Children, Fathers, Young Men (2:12–13b)
- B. Children, Fathers, Young Men (2:13c–14)

VI. Warning about the World (2:15–17)

- A. Do Not Love the World (2:15)
- B. The Things of the World Are Not from the Father (2:16)
  1. The Evil Desire of the Flesh
  2. The Evil Desire of the Eyes
  3. The Boasting in One's Possessions

- C. The World Is Passing Away; Obedient Living Means Eternal Life (2:17)

VII. Warning against the Antichrists (2:18–27)

- A. Many Antichrists Have Come (2:18–19)
  1. The Group's Departure Reveals They Did Not Belong to the Community (2:19)
  2. If They Were True Members of the Community of Faith, They Would Have Stayed (2:19)
- B. The Community Members Have an Anointing and Knowledge of the Truth (2:20–21)
- C. The Antichrist Denies the Father and the Son (2:22–23)
- D. Imperative to Abide and Promise of Eternal Life (2:24–27)

VIII. The Children of God and the Children of the Devil (2:28–3:10)

- A. Living as a Child of God (2:28–3:1)
- B. Eschatological Hope and Christ's Future Appearance (3:2–3)
- C. Children of God Do Not Make a Practice of Sin (3:4–6)
- D. Children of God Contrasted with Children of the Devil (3:7–10)

IX. Love One Another (3:11–18)

- A. Reminder of the Message Heard from the Beginning: Love One Another (3:11)
- B. The Way of the World (3:12–13)
- C. The Consequences of Loving versus Hating a Brother (3:14–15)
- D. Loving in Deed and Truth (3:16–18)

X. Assurance and the Condemning Heart (3:19–24)

- A. God is Greater than Our Hearts (3:19–20)
- B. Relationship between Confidence before God and Obedience to Him (3:21–22)
- C. God's Command: Believe in the Name of Jesus Christ and Love One Another (3:23)
- D. The One Who Obeys God's Commands Abides in Him and God in Him (3:24)

XI. The Spirit of Truth and the Spirit of Deception (4:1–6)

- A. Test the Spirits by the Confession of Christ (4:1–3)
  1. The Spirit of God (4:1–2)
  2. The Spirit of the Antichrist (4:3)
- B. Note Who Listens: Those from the World and Those from God (4:4–6)
  1. Those from the World Are Listened to by the World (4:5)
  2. Those from God are Listened to by Those Who Know God (4:6)

C. By This, the Spirit of Truth and the Spirit of Deception Are Recognized (4:6)

XII. The Love of God (4:7–12)

A. Command to Love One Another (4:7–8)

1. The One Who Loves Has Been Born of God (4:7)
2. The One Who Does Not Love Does Not Know God (4:8)

B. The Revelation of God's Love in His Son (4:9–10)
C. Loving One Another as a Response to God's Divine Love (4:11–12)

XIII. Assurance for Believers and the Love of God (4:13–21)

A. Basis of Assurance for Believers (4:13–16)
B. Perfected Love for God (4:17–21)

1. Confidence before God (4:17–18)
2. Love for One Another (4:19–21)

XIV. Belief, Love, Obedience (5:1–5)

A. A Child of God Believes Jesus Is the Christ (5:1, 5)
B. A Child of God Loves God's Children (5:1–2)
C. A Child of God Obeys His Commandment (5:2–3)
D. A Child of God Overcomes the World (5:4–5)

XV. Eternal Life and God's Testimony concerning His Son (5:6–12)

A. Testimony to Christ (5:6–8)
B. The Testimony of God Is Greater than the Testimony of Man (5:9–10)
C. Eternal Life Is in the Son of God (5:11–12)

XVI. Conclusion (5:13–21)

A. Purpose of Letter: Assurance of Eternal Life (5:13)
B. Confidence in Prayer (5:14–17)
C. Three Things Known (5:18–20)
D. Warning against Idolatry (5:21)

2 JOHN

I. Opening Greeting (1–3)
II. A New Command: Love One Another (4–6)
III. Beware of False Teachers (7–11)

A. Deceivers in the World (7)
B. Be on Guard in Order to Receive a Full Reward (8)
C. The One Abiding in the Teaching of Christ Has Both the Father and the Son (9)
D. Exhortation to Not Receive Such Traveling False Teachers (10–11)

IV. Final Greetings (12–13)

3 JOHN

I. Opening Greeting (1–4)

   A. Sender-Recipient (1)
   B. Prayer for Gaius (2)
   C. Rejoicing in News of Gaius's Faithfulness (3–4)

II. Affirmation and Exhortation (5–8)

   A. Affirming of Gaius's Support for Traveling Believers (5)
   B. Exhortation to Support Such Persons (6–8)

III. Conflict with Diotrephes (9–10)
IV. Commendation of Demetrius (11–12)
V. Final Greeting (13–15)

RECOMMENDED COMMENTARIES AND OTHER CITED SOURCES

Throughout this volume of the EGGNT, reference is made to a number of commentaries. Seven commentaries serve as primary references because of their engagement with the Greek text and/or their insights for the reader. They are:

Culy, Martin M. *I, II, III John: A Handbook on the Greek Text*. BHGNT. Waco: Baylor University Press, 2004.
Jobes, Karen H. *1, 2, 3 John*. ZECNT. Grand Rapids: Zondervan, 2014.
Kruse, Colin G. *The Letters of John*. PNTC. Grand Rapids: Eerdmans, 2000.
Marshall, I. Howard. *The Epistles of John*. NICNT. Grand Rapids: Eerdmans, 1978.
Smalley, Stephen S. *1, 2, 3 John*. Rev. ed. WBC. Grand Rapids: Zondervan, 2008.
Stott, John R. W. *The Letters of John*. 2nd ed. TNTC. Downers Grove, IL: IVP Academic, 1988.
Yarbrough, Robert W. *1–3 John*. BECNT. Grand Rapids: Baker Academic, 2008.

The following secondary commentaries are also referenced throughout the volume for their lexical, grammatical, and theological insights:

Akin, Daniel L. *1, 2, 3 John*. NAC 38. Nashville: B&H, 2001.
Brown, Raymond E. *The Epistles of John*. Anchor Bible. New York: Doubleday, 2008.
Hiebert, D. Edmond. *The Epistles of John: An Expositional Commentary*. Greenville, SC: Bob Jones University Press, 1991.
Law, Robert. *The Tests of Life: A Study of the First Epistle of St. John, Being the Kerr Lectures for 1909*. Edinburgh: T&T Clark, 1909.
McGaughy, Lane C. *Toward a Descriptive Analysis of Εἶναι as a Linking Verb in New Testament Greek*. SBL Dissertation Series 6. Atlanta: Society of Biblical Literature, 1972.

Marshall's NICNT commentary (1978) has remained a solid reference on John's Letters for decades, offering a balanced and informed assessment of the text. The more technical analysis, including that of significant points in the Greek text, is developed in footnotes. Stott's TNTC commentary (1988), another standard resource, is both accessible and exegetically sound; his voice is a welcome companion for the Bible student, teacher, or preacher. Brown's Anchor Bible commentary (1982) is an exhaustive work and was used with great benefit. Though speculative at times in its historical reconstruction of the Johannine community, the body of the commentary, along with its five appendices, is a wealth of information reflecting years of study from a significant Johannine scholar. Smalley's WBC commentary (2008) is quite thorough in nature. This well-respected commentary reflects broad engagement with scholarship on interpretive issues and helpful analysis of significant points in the Greek text and its variants. Though less "user-friendly" in format, the work is among the top resources on John's Letters. Kruse's Pillar commentary (2000) is a less technical commentary offering clear and accessible analysis. His insights provide a complement to other resources, and his twenty-four excurses on key topics in the letters are a distinctive and helpful contribution. Jobes's ZECNT commentary (2014), true to the intent of the series, guides the reader through interpretive issues with a solid engagement with the Greek text. Jobes offers thoughtful analysis throughout, highlighting the major interpretive issues of each section. The "Theology in Application" sections offer insightful observations. Culy's commentary in the BHGNT series (2004) offers, by its design, a skilled, verse-by-verse analysis of the Greek text. His commentary would be a helpful dialogue partner for any student of the Bible working with the Greek text of John's Letters. Lastly, Bateman and Peer in the Big Greek Idea Series offer the reader detailed exegetical analysis on the Greek text of John's Letters.

Additional research publications that are cited in short form in this volume include:

Campbell, Constantine R. *Advances in the Study of Greek*. Grand Rapids: Zondervan, 2015.

———. "Aspect and Tense in New Testament Greek." Pages 37–53 in *Linguistics and New Testament Greek: Key Issues in the Current Debate*. Edited by D. A. Black and B. L. Merkle. Grand Rapids: Baker Academic, 2020.

Carson, D. A. "Syntactical and Text-Critical Observations on John 20:30–31." *JBL* 124, no. 4 (2005): 693–714.

Griffith, Terry. "A Non-Polemical Reading of 1 John: Sin, Christology, and the Limits of Johannine Christianity." *TynBul* 49, no. 2 (1998): 253–76.

Lieu, Judith M. *I, II, & III John: A Commentary*. Louisville: Westminster John Knox, 2008.

Picirilli, Robert E. "The Meaning of the Tenses in New Testament Greek: Where Are We?" *JETS* 48 (2005): 535–36.

Tan, Randall K. J., "Should We Pray for Straying Brethren? John's Confidence in 1 John 5:16." *JETS* 45 (2002): 599–609.

York, Hershael. "An Analysis and Synthesis of the Exegetical Methods of Rhetorical Criticism and Discourse Analysis as Applied to the Structure of First John." ThD diss., Mid-America Baptist Theological Seminary, 1993.

1 JOHN

I. Prologue (1:1–4)

John begins his letter with a striking series of headless rel. clauses (i.e., rel. clauses that lack an explicit antecedent). Writing as a representative of the apostolic witness (note the first-person plural vbs.), he proclaims that which he has witnessed, Jesus Christ, the Son of God. The opening verses are textured with perception verbs, underscoring the authority of the testimony and the historical reality of the person and work of Christ. It is not until v. 3, after a parenthetical note in v. 2, that the main vb. is encountered (ἀπαγγέλλομεν). The ἵνα clause denotes the purpose of the proclamation: that the readers may have fellowship with him who has fellowship with the Father and the Son. His proclamation of Christ is written to a church in need of encouragement and exhortation. These initial verses powerfully begin the task of strengthening and affirming their fellowship with God.

1 Ὃ ἦν
ἀπ᾽ ἀρχῆς,
ὃ ἀκηκόαμεν,
ὃ ἑωράκαμεν
τοῖς ὀφθαλμοῖς ἡμῶν,
ὃ ἐθεασάμεθα καὶ
αἱ χεῖρες ἡμῶν ἐψηλάφησαν
περὶ τοῦ λόγου τῆς ζωῆς—

2 καὶ ἡ ζωὴ ἐφανερώθη,
καὶ ἑωράκαμεν
καὶ μαρτυροῦμεν
καὶ ἀπαγγέλλομεν
ὑμῖν τὴν ζωὴν τὴν αἰώνιον
ἥτις ἦν πρὸς τὸν πατέρα
καὶ ἐφανερώθη ἡμῖν—

3 ὃ ἑωράκαμεν καὶ
ἀκηκόαμεν,
ἀπαγγέλλομεν
καὶ ὑμῖν,
ἵνα καὶ ὑμεῖς κοινωνίαν ἔχητε
μεθ᾽ ἡμῶν.

καὶ ἡ κοινωνία δὲ
ἡ ἡμετέρα [ἐστιν] μετὰ τοῦ πατρὸς
καὶ μετὰ τοῦ υἱοῦ αὐτοῦ = Ἰησοῦ Χριστοῦ.

4 καὶ ταῦτα γράφομεν ἡμεῖς,
ἵνα ἡ χαρὰ ἡμῶν ᾖ πεπληρωμένη.

VERSE 1

Ὃ ἦν ἀπ' ἀρχῆς
What was from the beginning

The first in a staccato pattern of five headless rel. clauses, the apostle's words here allude to both Gen 1:1 and John 1:1. The repeated neut. rel. pron. ὅ (here nom., but acc. in the other four instances) refers to the incarnate Second Person of the triune God, the neuter likely being chosen not as a broader reference to Jesus's attributes, words, and works (contra BDF §138[1]; Brown 154; Culy 2; A. Plummer 72) but as a matter of John's idiolect, with the apostle sometimes using neut. forms where masc. forms are expected (e.g., John 3:6; 4:22; 6:37, 39; 17:2, 10; 1 John 5:4). (For other commentators who view the rel. pron. reflecting both the person and message of Christ, cf. Akin 51, "the person and message of Jesus"; Jobes 44, "the gospel message centered on Jesus"; Marshall 101 n. 6, "the Christian message incarnated in Jesus.") The 3rd per. sg. impf. of εἰμί (ἦν) points to the ongoing existence of the preincarnate Christ in eternity past. It is noteworthy that John does not use a form of γίνομαι as he does in reporting the incarnation in John 1:14. The phrase ἀπ' ἀρχῆς "from the beginning," is used eight times in 1 John (18× in the NT) to communicate a variety of disparate durations (2:7, the community's reception of the love command; 2:13–14 [2×], references to the eternal existence of the Son, alluding back to the beginning of the letter; 2:24 [2×] the reception of the gospel by the community; 3:8, a reference to the devil's rebellion; 3:11, another reference to the community's reception of the love command). Perhaps only the gloss "all along" is sufficient to cover these dissimilar referents (for an overview of interpretive options of the phrase, see Jobes 45–46). The Son of God "was [existing] all along" (cf. Exod 3:14–15). This early Christian community, in contrast, had the love command from their founding until the time of John's composition (i.e., also "all along"). The def. obj. of prep. frequently appears without the art. (Porter, *Idioms*, 113), but context here strongly favors a def. sense, alluding to a known eternity past ("from *the* beginning," most EVV; see Hong). Regarding the staccato style of headless rel. clauses, Marshall notes, "The result—which is important—is that the opening emphasis falls on the nature of the object which is proclaimed rather than on the activity of proclaiming it. The writer's purpose is to remind his readers of the character of the Christian message rather than drawing attention to the actual act of preaching it" (100).

ὃ ἀκηκόαμεν
what we have heard

Ἀκηκόαμεν is 1st pl. pf. act. indic. of ἀκούω, "hear, exercise the faculty of hearing" (BDAG 37c). The rel. pron. ὃ is in the acc. because it functions as the object of the vb. Wallace suggests the 1st pers. pl. forms here are debatable illustrations of the epistolary plural (396). More likely, John uses a 1st pers. plural to reference himself as the spokesman for the totality of the apostles in their eyewitness role (cf. Akin 60 n. 54; Culy 3; Jobes 49; Stott 31; Yarbrough 33; see Wallace 397–99 on "inclusive" [the author and audience] vs. "exclusive" ["we," the author and those with him]). In Koine Gk., the pf. tense often speaks to an ongoing relevance for a prior action, as it does here undergirding John's current role of announcing and bearing witness (1:2). Kruse notes the pf. emphasizes the "status of the author as one of the eyewitnesses" (52). John and the other apostles, in space and time, on a hillside in Galilee, heard "the one who was from the beginning" speaking. Stott has rightly noted that this section of 1 John teaches "the historical, audible, visible, tangible manifestation of the eternal" (30).

ὃ ἑωράκαμεν τοῖς ὀφθαλμοῖς ἡμῶν
what we have seen with our eyes

The sensory nature of the apostles' eyewitness testimony is further concretized. John leaves no doubt that this seeing was not visionary, for it was done "with our eyes." Ἑωράκαμεν is 1st pl. pf. act. indic. of ὁράω, the pf. tense again points to both the historical act of seeing and its ongoing role in undergirding John's proclamatory eyewitness ministry. Τοῖς ὀφθαλμοῖς is an instr. dat. (Robertson, *Pictures* 6:204; Rogers and Rogers 591). Ἡμῶν is a poss. 1st pl. pers. pro. Head nouns qualified by gen. pers. pron. are usually art. (Baugh 85). Both the art. and the qualifying pron. communicate the specificity or definiteness of the noun.

ὃ ἐθεασάμεθα καὶ αἱ χεῖρες ἡμῶν ἐψηλάφησαν
what we observed and our hands touched

In John's continuing list of eyewitness sensory experiences, he shifts to two aor. tense vbs. of rarer occurrence. Ἐθεασάμεθα is an 1st pl. aor. mid. indic. of θεάομαι "to take someth[ing] in with one's eyes, with implication that one is esp. impressed" (BDAG 445c–d); "see, behold, look at; consider" (C. H. Peisker, *EDNT* 2:136c). Perhaps this vb. prefers the mid. voice because of the heightened sense of emotion that usually accompanies the observation reported (LN §24.14). Ἐψηλάφησαν is a 3rd pl. aor. act. indic. of ψηλαφάω, "to touch by feeling and handling" (BDAG 1097d–98a; see LN §24.76). The word only occurs four times in the GNT. John's shift to both a different tense (aor. rather than pf.) and rarer verbal forms likely alludes to known resurrection appearances of Jesus (John 20:19–29).

περὶ τοῦ λόγου τῆς ζωῆς
concerning the word of life

Λόγος likely does not refer here to the preincarnate Second Person of the triune God, as it does in the prologue to John's Gospel (John 1:1–5). Arguments against a reference here to Jesus as the λόγος include (1) the genitive qualifier τῆς ζωῆς; and (2) no other instance in John's Letters where λόγος refers to the Son. Culy notes, "There are no clear examples of a personified λόγος modified by an attributive genitive elsewhere in the NT, and there are no clear contextual markers pointing to personification here" (Culy 5; contra ZG 726; see Brown 164–66 for a developed argument against the personal interpretation of λόγος). Τῆς ζωῆς should be understood as a gen. of content, giving the content or subject of the gospel proclamation (see Stott 64–65, 72; for varied understandings of gen. here, see also Jobes 51; Smalley 5–6; Yarbrough 38n24; Turner, *Style*, 135). The "word of life" is used by Paul in Phil 2:16 as shorthand for the gospel. We see in τοῦ λόγου τῆς ζωῆς an example of Apollonius's Canon (see KMP 163–64; Moule 114–15), a relatively strong pattern in Koine Gk. whereby both the head noun and any attached gens. share in being art. or anar. The prep. phrase περὶ τοῦ λόγου τῆς ζωῆς appears a bit awkwardly at this point. The prep. phrase likely anticipates the vbs. of "witnessing" and "announcing" we find nearby (1:2–3). John would thus be saying that his strong affirmations of "the historical manifestation of the eternal" (Stott 93) are made with reference to the apostolic proclamation of the gospel. The eternality of the Son of God and the reality of his incarnation are the *sine qua non* of any true gospel proclamation.

VERSE 2

καὶ ἡ ζωὴ ἐφανερώθη
that life was revealed

The content of the gospel proclamation is life ("the word of life"; see v. 1). Now John reminds us that this life became climactically visible in one who can himself be called "life" (cf. John 14:6). Jesus both proclaimed the way to life and was himself the manifestation of life from God. Ἐφανερώθη is a 3rd sg. aor. pass. indic. of φανερόω ("reveal," CSB; "manifest," ESV). The aor. pass. form here could convey a mid. idea ("appeared," NIV), but perhaps more likely a divine pass. is intended (i.e., the life was revealed [by God]).

καὶ ἑωράκαμεν καὶ μαρτυροῦμεν καὶ ἀπαγγέλλομεν ὑμῖν τὴν ζωὴν τὴν αἰώνιον
and we have seen it and we testify and declare to you the eternal life

Ἑωράκαμεν, 1st pl. pf. act. indic. of ὁράω, asserts again the historical eyewitness experience of the apostles. The pf. tense both speaks of the historical event of seeing as well as asserts that seeing is the conceptual undergirding for the following vbs. That is, only *as eyewitnesses* can John and the other apostles now authoritatively testify and announce the message about what God has done in Christ. Μαρτυροῦμεν is a 1st pl. pres. act. indic. of μαρτυρέω ("testify, bear witness"). Ἀπαγγέλλομεν is a 1st pl.

pres. act. indic. of ἀπαγγέλλω ("declare, proclaim"). Ὑμῖν is a dat. indir. obj. Τὴν ζωὴν τὴν αἰώνιον is the acc. direct obj. of both μαρτυροῦμεν and ἀπαγγέλλομεν. The adj. αἰώνιος is one of 322 two-termination adjs. (with 944 total occurrences) in the GNT (MNTG 89–92), occurring six times in 1 John (1:2; 2:25; 3:15; 5:11, 13, 20). Two-termination adjs. follow 2nd decl. endings, even when modifying a fem. noun (BDF §59[1]; Decker 95; R 272–73). Αἰώνιος is an unusual two-termination adj. in that 1st decl. endings are intermittently affixed to the stem (e.g., 1 Macc 2:54). As "life" is the content of the gospel message (περὶ τοῦ λόγου τῆς ζωῆς), "eternal/never-ending life" is fittingly described as the subject of the apostles' proclamation and witness (see 1:1).

ἥτις ἦν πρὸς τὸν πατέρα καὶ ἐφανερώθη ἡμῖν
that was with the Father and was revealed to us—

Ἥτις is an alternate form of the fem. rel. pron., sometimes having a qualitative sense ("who is of such a sort that"; BDAG 729d–30a; Brown 168–69), but more commonly indistinguishable in sense from the regular rel. pron. (ἥ), as here (see BDF §§64[3]; 293[2]). The antecedent of ἥτις is τὴν ζωὴν τὴν αἰώνιον "eternal life," of which John now declares the ongoing existence with the Father and historical appearance to the apostles. While it is possible that John refers to the abstract sense of "life," the literary context strongly favors taking "eternal life" here as a reference to the Second Person of the triune God (see Kruse 57; Jobes 53). He was with (πρός; see BDAG 875b–c) the Father (in eternity past) and has now been revealed to us. That is, he has been revealed as the audible, visible, palpable incarnate Son to the apostles, who are then entrusted with the task of testifying to him.

VERSE 3

ὃ ἑωράκαμεν καὶ ἀκηκόαμεν
what we have seen and have heard

Ἑωράκαμεν is 1st pl. pf. act. indic. of ὁράω. Ἀκηκόαμεν is 1st pl. pf. act. indic. of ἀκούω. The repetition of the pf. tense stresses both the historical fact of the apostles' sensory eyewitness experiences as well as the immediate relevance and conceptual undergirding which those experiences provide for the apostolic tasks of witnessing/proclaiming/announcing.

ἀπαγγέλλομεν καὶ ὑμῖν
we also declare to you

Ἀπαγγέλλομεν is 1st pl. pres. act. indic. of ἀπαγγέλλω. Καί here is best translated as "also," (most EVV, e.g., CSB, NASB; though omitted by KJV, NIV) with ὑμῖν serving as indir. obj.

ἵνα καὶ ὑμεῖς κοινωνίαν ἔχητε μεθ' ἡμῶν
so that you may also have fellowship with us

Ἵνα introduces a purpose clause (see R 982; Wallace 472) with ἔχητε as the 2nd pl. pres. act. subj. of ἔχω. Κοινωνίαν (κοινωνία, -ας, ἡ, "association, communion, fellowship, close relationship"; BDAG 552d–53c; on the term, see also *NIDNTTE* 2:706–13; J. Hainz, *EDNT* 2.303–5; LN §34.5) is the acc. dir. obj. of ἔχητε. The prep. μετά in this phrase and the next (here appearing as μεθ' because it is immediately followed by a vowel with a rough breathing mark) conveys the idea of association, "together with, in the company of" (Harris 163; Wallace 377; BDAG 636b–c).

καὶ ἡ κοινωνία δὲ ἡ ἡμετέρα μετὰ τοῦ πατρὸς καὶ μετὰ τοῦ υἱοῦ αὐτοῦ Ἰησοῦ Χριστοῦ.
and, indeed, our fellowship is with the Father and with his Son, Jesus Christ.

Greek sometimes employs more connecting particles than English, as is the situation here, with both καί and δέ stitching this clause to the previous one. Perhaps an intensive sense is conveyed by the pleonastic δέ ("indeed," ESV, CSB, NASB, NET; Moule 165; cf. BDF §285[1]), a nuance further supported by the choice of the rare pronominal adj. (ἡμέτερος, 7× in GNT), rather than simply a gen. poss. pron. (ἡμῶν). The vb. ἐστίν is implied (on the twice-repeated prep. μετά see commentary on the phrase above). As a monadic noun (BW 73–74; KMP 158), πατήρ has an art. Likewise, υἱός stands with an art. and highlights the Son's distinct and unique filial status. Moreover, it should be noted that as a stylistic feature, nouns with poss. gen. pron. (as here, τοῦ υἱοῦ **αὐτοῦ**) frequently appear with an art. (Baugh 85). This pattern should not surprise the reader as both the poss. gen. pron. and presence of the art. highlight the same thing—specificity.

VERSE 4

καὶ ταῦτα γράφομεν ἡμεῖς
We are writing these things

In classic paratactic style, John begins many of his clauses with καί. This pattern perhaps reflects an underlying Semitic idiom. The *vav* consecutive "and . . ." begins many clauses in the Hebrew Bible. Culy notes, "While the specific semantic relationship between clauses or sentences linked by καί will vary, clause-initial conjunctive uses of καί generally highlight both thematic continuity and progression of thought" (5; on the frequent use of καί in 1 John, see Bateman and Peer 34). Γράφομεν is 1st pl. pres. act. indic. of γράφω. Ἡμεῖς is the nom. pron. functioning as the subj. of γράφομεν. Grammatically unnecessary (as the ending of γράφομεν conveys the person and number of the vb.), ἡμεῖς is perhaps emphatic or contrastive (see Smalley 12, who notes "deliberately emphatic"). Some ancient mss. (A^c C K et al.) read ὑμῖν, but ἡμεῖς is well attested (א B P Ψ 33 it^z $cop^{sa\ (mss)}$) and is almost certainly original. UBS^5 editors give ἡμεῖς a "B" rating (almost certain). The acc. neut. pl. dem. pron. ταῦτα "these things," acts as the dir. obj. of the vb.

ἵνα ἡ χαρὰ ἡμῶν ᾖ πεπληρωμένη
so our joy may be complete.

Ἵνα introduces a purpose clause followed by the 3rd sg. pres. subj. of εἰμί (ᾖ). Πεπληρωμένη is a fem. sg. nom. of pf. pass. ptc. of πληρόω (gender agrees with the fem. noun χαρά). The ptc. is employed in a periph. cstr. (εἰμί + ptc.; on this topic, see Turner, *Syntax*, 88–89; KMP 345–46). The pf. ptc. conveys the idea that the action (i.e., to complete or perfect) is finished and an ongoing state continues ("May be [made] complete," e.g., CSB, ESV, NASB; LN §13.1). We might *overtranslate* this clause, "that our joy may reach a state of lasting completion" (cf. Porter, *Verbal Aspect*, 486). UBS[5] editors note that the ms. evidence between ἡμῶν (א B L Ψ 322 436 1067 1175 1241 1409 *Lect* it[ar, z] vg[ww, st] cop[sa] geo) and ὑμῶν (A C 33 81 945 1243 1292 1505 1611 1735 1739 1844 1852 1881 2138 2298 2344 2464 *Byz* [K P] *l* 1021 vg[cl] syr[h, pal] cop[bo] arm eth slav Augustine Bede) is so evenly divided, that "the two different variants could equally well be adopted as the reconstructed initial text" (UBS[5] 7*). Smalley (3) notes, "Both readings make sense in the context, but the writer's identification with his readers in terms of 'fellowship' suggests that a mutual 'joy' (ἡ χαρὰ ἡμῶν, 'our joy') is in view at this point also" (3). Ἡμῶν then would be a subj. gen. (on topic, see KMP 99–100). We note again how head nouns followed by poss. gen. pron. usually are art. (Baugh 85). Anything possessed by us (i.e., "our") is going to be something specific, so it is natural to expect the noun possessed to appear with an art. Likewise, it is worth noting that abstract nouns in Gk. (e.g., ἡ χαρά) usually are art. (BW 74; R 758). Marshall notes, "John's prologue highlights two dangers which still confront the church. The one is the assumption that Christian fellowship is possible other than on the basis of common belief in Christ. . . . The other danger is the assumption that it is possible to have a true relationship with God while rejecting Jesus Christ as the way, the truth and the life. As the Epistle will go on to make clear, the Father can be known only through the Son. There is 'no other name'" (107–8).

FOR FURTHER STUDY

1. Prologue of 1 John (1:1–4)

Brickle, Jeffrey E. *Aural Design and Coherence in the Prologue of First John*. LNTS 465. Bloomsbury: T&T Clark, 2013.

2. Proclamation Language (1:2–3)

Beutler, J. *EDNT* 2:389–91, 391–93.
Broer, I. *EDNT* 1:12–13.
Houlden, James Leslie. "Salvation Proclaimed Pt 2, 1 John 1:5–2:6: Belief and Growth." *ExpTim* 93.5 (1982): 132–36.
Graham, D. J. *DLNT*, 1204–5.
Joüon, P. "Le verbe ἀναγγέλλω dans Saint Jean." *RSR* 28 (1938): 234–35.
Kaiser, Walter C., Jr. "The Old Testament and the Proclamation of the Gospel." *JETS* 17, no. 2 (1974): 124–26.
Kruse, 183 (see "A Note on Witness").
Maccini, R. G. *NDBT*, 811–14.

McDonald, James I. H. *Kerygma and Didache: The Articulation and Structure of the Earliest Christian Message*. SNTSMS 37. Cambridge: Cambridge University Press, 1980.
NIDNTTE 1:116–20.
Olagunju, Olugbenga. "Apostolic Witness of Jesus Christ in 1 John 1:1–4 and Its Relevance to Combating Contemporary Heretical Teaching about the Person of Jesus Christ." *JBT* 3, no. 1 (2020): 70–133.
Schniewind, J. *TDNT* 1:56–73.
Trites, A. A. *DPL*, 973–75.
———. *The New Testament Concept of Witness*. SNTSMS 31. Cambridge: Cambridge University Press, 1977.

3. Fellowship (1:3)

Casurella, A. *DLNT*, 373–74.
Combs, William W. "The Meaning of Fellowship in 1 John." *Detroit Baptist Seminary Journal* 13 (2008): 3–16.
Frame, 1050–52.
Hainz, J. *EDNT,* 2:303–5.
Hauck, F. *TDNT,* 3:789–809.
Kloha, Jeffrey J. "Koinonia and Life Together in the New Testament." *CJ* 38, no. 1 (2012): 23–32.
Kruse, 59–61 (see "A Note on the Meaning of 'Fellowship'").
McDermott, John M. "Biblical Doctrine of Koinōnia." *Biblische Zeitschrift* 19, no. 2 (1975): 219–33.
Panikulam, George. *Koinōnia in the New Testament: A Dynamic Expression of Christian Life*. Rome: Biblical Institute Press, 1979.
Perkins, Pheme. "Koinōnia in 1 John 1:3–7: The Social Context of Division in the Johannine Letters." *CBQ* 45, no. 4 (1983): 631–41.

4. Joy (1:4)

Berger, K. *EDNT,* 3:454–55.
Conzelmann, H. *TDNT,* 9:359–415.
*Hawthorne, G. F. *DLNT*, 600–605.
Moltmann, J. *Theology and Joy*. London: SCM, 1971.
Morrice, William G. *Joy in the New Testament*. Exeter: Paternoster, 1984.
NIDNTTE 4:644–49.
Smalley, S. S. *NDBT*, 608–10.

HOMILETICAL SUGGESTIONS

Witness to Eternal Life (1:1–4)

1. The historical reality of the eternal Son of God (vv. 1–2a)
2. The proclamation of the eternal Son of God (vv. 2–3a)
3. Fellowship in the eternal Son of God (vv. 3–4)

II. A Relationship with a Holy God: Claim versus Reality (1:5–10)

This section begins with the statement of the message (ἀγγελία) which John, in company with the other apostles, heard from the Lord and now declares to the recipients of this letter—that God is light and that there is no darkness in him at all (v. 5). This affirmation of God as light seems to be primarily a declaration of God's holiness or moral purity (note the repetition of vocabulary dealing with sin). In vv. 6–10, John evaluates claims to know God on the basis of the claimant's behavior (note the repetition, "If we say . . ."). To come into relationship with a holy God means that there will be a reflection of that divine holiness in the lives of his people.

5 Καὶ ἔστιν αὕτη ἡ ἀγγελία
ἣν ἀκηκόαμεν
ἀπ' αὐτοῦ
καὶ ἀναγγέλλομεν
ὑμῖν
ὅτι ὁ θεὸς φῶς ἐστιν καὶ σκοτία
ἐν αὐτῷ
οὐκ ἔστιν οὐδεμία.

6 Ἐὰν εἴπωμεν
ὅτι κοινωνίαν ἔχομεν
μετ' αὐτοῦ,
καὶ περιπατῶμεν
ἐν τῷ σκότει
ψευδόμεθα καὶ οὐ ποιοῦμεν τὴν ἀλήθειαν·

7 ἐὰν ἐν τῷ φωτὶ περιπατῶμεν
ὡς αὐτός ἐστιν ἐν τῷ φωτί,
κοινωνίαν ἔχομεν
μετ' ἀλλήλων
καὶ τὸ αἷμα Ἰησοῦ τοῦ υἱοῦ αὐτοῦ καθαρίζει ἡμᾶς
ἀπὸ πάσης ἁμαρτίας.

8 ἐὰν εἴπωμεν
ὅτι ἁμαρτίαν οὐκ ἔχομεν,
ἑαυτοὺς πλανῶμεν καὶ ἡ ἀλήθεια οὐκ ἔστιν
ἐν ἡμῖν.
9 ἐὰν ὁμολογῶμεν τὰς ἁμαρτίας ἡμῶν,
πιστός ἐστιν καὶ δίκαιος,
ἵνα ἀφῇ ἡμῖν τὰς ἁμαρτίας
καὶ καθαρίσῃ ἡμᾶς
ἀπὸ πάσης ἀδικίας.
10 ἐὰν εἴπωμεν ὅτι οὐχ ἡμαρτήκαμεν,
ψεύστην ποιοῦμεν αὐτὸν καὶ ὁ λόγος αὐτοῦ οὐκ ἔστιν.
ἐν ἡμῖν

VERSE 5

Καὶ ἔστιν αὕτη ἡ ἀγγελία
And this is the message

The word ἀγγελία, -ας, ἡ, "message, announcement" (LN §33.193; see also BDAG 8a) only occurs two times in the NT, here and in 1 John 3:11, though there are many words in the NT built off the same root (e.g., ἀπαγγέλλομεν, 1 John 1:3, which is likely intentionally echoed here). The NET rendering of ἀγγελία as "gospel message," based on the soteriological context, is perhaps an overtranslation, for the apostle seems to be picking up only one dimension of the gospel (i.e., the holiness of God; cf. Akin 63 n. 73; Kruse 52 n. 13). Αὕτη "this," is the nom. sg. fem. dem. pron., used cataphorically by looking forward to the coming ὅτι clause (Culy 11; Smalley 17–18; Yarbrough 47; Young 190). Virtually all EVV translate αὕτη as the subj. nom. and ἡ ἀγγελία as the pred. nom., "This is the message," though this phrasing may simply be an accommodation to normal English style. Culy, citing Wallace (42–44), argues that the ἡ ἀγγελία is the subj. and αὕτη is the pred. nom., "The message is this" (11). Baugh (9) points out that the word order in 1:5 (cf. 1 John 2:25; 3:23; 5:4, 11, 14; 2 John 6) favors seeing αὕτη as an attrib. adj. modifying ἡ ἀγγελία, resulting in a formally equivalent translation, "This message is (that) which we have heard."

ἣν ἀκηκόαμεν ἀπ' αὐτοῦ καὶ ἀναγγέλλομεν ὑμῖν
that we have heard from him and declare to you,

Ἥν is the acc. sg. fem. rel. pron., functioning as the object of the following two vbs. Ἀκηκόαμεν "we have heard" is the 1st pl. pf. act. indic. of ἀκούω. The prep. phrase ἀπ' αὐτοῦ "from him," functions to communicate source/origin (BDAG 105d–6a, Harris 63, R 579). The antecedent of αὐτοῦ is most likely Jesus Christ (Akin 63; Culy 11; Marshall 108 n. 1). Ἀναγγέλλομεν "we announce," is the 1st pl. pres. act. indic. of ἀναγγέλλω, "disclose, announce, proclaim, teach" (BDAG 59c–d; I. Broer, *EDNT* 1:12d–13b; *NIDNTTE* 1:118; Schniewind, *TDNT* 1:56–73). Notice the slight difference in wording (ἀπαγγέλλομεν, 1 John 1:3) for *variatio* or stylistic reasons (Baugh 9). Ὑμῖν is a dat. indir. obj.

ὅτι ὁ θεὸς φῶς ἐστιν καὶ σκοτία ἐν αὐτῷ οὐκ ἔστιν οὐδεμία.
that God is light, and there is absolutely no darkness in him.

Ὅτι introduces a content clause, providing the content of the apostolic proclamation (Baugh 9; BDF §397[3]; BW 179–80; Porter, *Idioms*, 238; R 1033; Wallace 458–59 labels this particular use of ὅτι as the appos. function "namely, that"; BDAG 732a more broadly labels this use of ὅτι as the "marker of an explanatory clause"). Ὁ θεός functions as the subj., as is both clear from context and favored by the presence of the art. (Young 65). Φῶς, the pred. nom., perhaps lacks the art. as a qualitative assertion (i.e., God is, in essence, light or holy), or simply to mark it as the non-subject. The affirmation of God as light could mean several things:

*1. God is holy. Marshall, while highlighting the illumination symbolism, writes that "living in the darkness is incompatible with fellowship with God. This makes it clear the writer is thinking of light and darkness in predominantly ethical terms" (109). See also Jobes, who notes this initial phrase of v. 5a is "a definition of ethical and moral goodness" (63–65; so too Yarbrough 48–50).
2. God is a revealer of truth—light as a metaphor for revelation (Brown 229: "'light' refers to the knowability of God"). See also Kruse, who notes the author "does not intend to define what God is in himself, but to provide a basis for ethical application" (62).
3. God is both holy and revealer of truth (Hiebert 57–58; Smalley 20; Stott 70–72).

The continued prominence of the category of sin, as seen above, favors seeing option 1 as most likely.

Σκοτία, -ας, ἡ, "darkness," nom. sg. fem., functioning as the subj. of the second ἔστιν in v. 5, is used interchangeably with σκότος, -ους, τό ("darkness," v. 6). The nom. sg. fem. adj. οὐδεμία "none," modifies σκοτία. A literal rendering is: "None darkness is not in him." EVV bring out this emphatic negation in a variety of ways (e.g., "there is absolutely no darkness in him," CSB; "in him there is no darkness at all," NIV). The prep. phrase ἐν αὐτῷ communicates location ("locatival," Harris 118) in a metaphorical sense (i.e., in the person of God the Father, there is found no wickedness).

VERSE 6

Ἐὰν εἴπωμεν ὅτι κοινωνίαν ἔχομεν μετ' αὐτοῦ καὶ ἐν τῷ σκότει περιπατῶμεν
If we say, "We have fellowship with him," and (yet) walk in darkness

Ἐάν introduces a third class cond. clause, presenting the prot. for hypothetical consideration (BW 183; Porter, *Idioms*, 262; Young 228; Moule 148–52; Z §320; Wallace 696–99; KMP 447–48). The clause is the first of a series in vv. 6–10, three beginning with ἐὰν εἴπωμεν (vv. 6, 8, 10). Perhaps John uses the more remote third class cond.

because the 1st pl. (εἴπωμεν, 1st pl. aor. act. subj. of λέγω) ostensibly includes himself and his hearers in considering a false claim to faith—something belied by affirmations later in the letter (1 John 5:13). The exact mng. of any third class cond. is best determined by context. Wallace remarks, "In the *third class condition* there is a wide variety of nuances found in the protasis, from hypothetical to probable. Some examples also involve a 'present general' reality" (663).

Ὅτι introduces the content of the verbal claim (dir. discourse; see BDAG 731d; R 1034–35). Κοινωνία, -ας, ἡ, "fellowship" (see 1:3), here acc., functions as the direct object of ἔχομεν. The prep. phrase μετ' αὐτοῦ communicates association, "with, together with" (Harris 163).

Many EVV add "yet" or "but" before the final phrase in v. 6a (CSB, NAS, NET, NIV). Some grammarians label the καί that begins this phrase as an "adversative καί," possibly reflecting Semitic influence (Moule 178). Regardless of what one labels καί, it is consideration of the broader context (pragmatics), not the word καί itself, that results in the English translation "yet" (Culy 15).

Σκότει is dat. sg. neut. of σκότος, -ους, τό, "darkness," here as the dat. obj. of ἐν and communicating location/sphere. The metaphorical sense of darkness is intended—"realm of evil, evil world" (LN §88.125) or "the state of spiritual or moral darkness, of the state of unbelievers and of the godless" (BDAG 932c; see also *NIDNTTE* 4:319–25). Abstract nouns normally include the art. (Baugh 11), but perhaps a more specific sense is present—walking in *the* realm of darkness (some EVV leave art. untranslated [e.g., CSB] while others include it [e.g., NASB, NIV, NET]). Περιπατῶμεν, 1st pl. pres. act. subj. of περιπατέω, "walk," here conveys the metaphorical sense of "to conduct one's life, live" (BDAG 803c–d; "living," NLT; "habitually live," Stott 78).

Verbs describing human behavior in this section are in the present tense and contrast with the verbal claims in the aor. (Porter, *Idioms*, 263). Emphasis is directed toward a pattern of behavior (imperfective aspect), which is the test of one's claim. About the pres. tense of περιπατῶμεν, the NET Translation Notes read, "The context . . . indicates clearly that the progressive (continuative or durative) aspect of the present tense must be in view here." Of course, the procedural nature of the activity of walking (most naturally conceived without reference to a beginning or ending) is best conveyed via imperfective aspect.

ψευδόμεθα καὶ οὐ ποιοῦμεν τὴν ἀλήθειαν·
we are lying and are not practicing the truth.

The apod. provides a stark negative evaluation of the claim to be in relationship with a holy God and yet walk around in darkness. Ψευδόμεθα is 1st pl. pres. mid. indic. of ψεύδομαι, "lie" (BDAG 1096d–97a). Ποιοῦμεν is 1st pl. pres. act. indic. of ποιέω, with the dir. obj. τὴν ἀλήθειαν. "To do the truth" reflects a literal rending of a Hebraic idiom (Gen 32:11 [LXX]; 47:29; Isa 26:10; T. Reu. 6:9; T. Benj. 10:3; 1QS I, 5), mng. to live in accord with the truth or to put the truth into practice (BDAG 42d; Baugh 11; Harris 134; LN §41.7). ZG renders it, "do the deeds that truth demands" (726). The NEB translates v. 6b "our words and our lives are a lie." Culy, drawing upon Longacre, points out that the cond. statement in v. 6 functions as a mitigated exhortation: "Do not claim to have fellowship with him and continue to walk in darkness" (14; see xxv–xxvii for brief discussion on mitigated or "softened" exhortations in 1 John).

VERSE 7

ἐὰν ἐν τῷ φωτὶ περιπατῶμεν ὡς αὐτός ἐστιν ἐν τῷ φωτί,
If we walk in the light as he himself is in the light

This prot. of a third class cond. (a "hypothetical projection," see 1:6) describes the appropriate response of a person living in relationship with the God who is light (holy, pure); such a person should "walk in the light." Editors of the NA[28]/UBS[5], following the *Editio Critica Maior*, have concluded that the δέ (following ἐάν in some mss.) is not original, thus differing from the NA[27]/UBS[4]. The art. with τῷ φωτί is perhaps anaphoric, referring to the (previously mentioned) realm of God's light (v. 5), "the element and sphere of the divine" (BDAG 1072d). Note the fluid, metaphorical nature of light. God is both described as light (v. 5) and being in the light (v. 7; cf. 1 Tim 6:16). Περιπατῶμεν is 1st pl. pres. act. subj. of περιπατέω, "walk" (see v. 6 for description of metaphorical use). The prep. phrase ἐν τῷ φωτί expresses location/sphere. The subj. pron. αὐτός occurs here without emphasis, as it does frequently with εἰμί (Baugh 12; constr. occurs 20× in NT, incl. 1 LXX citation in Heb 1:5).

κοινωνίαν ἔχομεν μετ' ἀλλήλων
we have fellowship with one another

This phrase begins the apod. of the third class cond. sentence in v. 7. Κοινωνία, -ας, ἡ, "fellowship" (see v. 3), is acc., functioning as dir. obj. of ἔχομεν. The prep. μετά, followed by the gen. obj. ἀλλήλων (reciprocal pron.), communicates association, "with one another" (most EVV; Young 79).

καὶ τὸ αἷμα Ἰησοῦ τοῦ υἱοῦ αὐτοῦ καθαρίζει ἡμᾶς ἀπὸ πάσης ἁμαρτίας.
and the blood of Jesus his Son cleanses us from all sin.

Ἰησοῦ is a gen. of poss., referring to the blood that belongs to Jesus and was shed at the crucifixion—here functioning metonymically to refer to his atoning death/sacrifice (Harris 79). Robertson remarks, "John is not ashamed to use this word [i.e., αἷμα]. It is not the mere 'example' of Jesus that 'cleanses' us from sin. It does cleanse the conscience and life and nothing else does (Heb. 9:13f.; Titus 2:14)" (Robertson, *Pictures* 6:207). Τοῦ υἱοῦ is a gen. of appos., restating the gen. noun Ἰησοῦ. Nouns that occur with a poss. gen. pron., such as υἱοῦ in this verse, usually are art. (Baugh 85). Αὐτοῦ is a gen. of relationship (see BW 9; KMP 94–95, 108), the antecedent being God the Father (v. 5).

Καθαρίζει (vb. found only here and 1:9 in the writings of John) is the 3rd sg. pres. act. indic. of καθαρίζω, "purify, cleanse, make pure" (H. Thyen, *EDNT* 2:218a; BDAG 488d–89a) with τὸ αἷμα as the subj. nom. and ἡμᾶς as the acc. dir. obj. Marshall writes, "To say that the blood of Jesus purifies us is to say that our sin is removed and forgiven; its defiling effects no longer condemn us in the sight of God" (112).The prep. phrase ἀπὸ πάσης ἁμαρτίας communicates disassociation (LN §89.122; R 518). The anar.

const. πάσης ἁμαρτίας could be understood distributively (i.e., "from *every* sin") with the focus on individual believers or for the class as a whole (from *all* sin). Yarbrough writes, "Perhaps whichever rendering be followed, it cannot rule out all aspects of the sense of the other rendering" (58). (On const., see Moule 93–95; Turner, *Syntax* 199–200; Wallace 253.) Jobes summarizes, "Christ's atonement for sin achieves a reconciliation with God that restores fellowship" (70). On the topic of "sin," see For Further Study 11 "Sin."

VERSE 8

ἐὰν εἴπωμεν ὅτι ἁμαρτίαν οὐκ ἔχομεν,
If we say, "We have no sin,"

Verse 8 is the third of five third class cond. sentences (see 1:6 on third class cond. sentences) in which the apostle John considers the life of a person who *claims* to be in relationship with a holy God. Εἴπωμεν is a 1st pl. aor. act. subj. of λέγω. Ὅτι introduces the content of the verbal claim (see BDAG 731d; R 1034–35). Ἁμαρτίαν is the acc. dir. obj. of the negated vb. ἔχομεν, 1st pl. pres. act. indic. of ἔχω.

Scholars debate the exact claim that John addresses. Possibilities include:

1. A claim to ontological sinlessness (i.e., one is sinless in nature; Hiebert 64; Stott 81). The pl. τὰς ἁμαρτίας in the corrective parallel in v. 9 argues against the ontological interpretation.

*2. A claim that one's immoral behavior (however clearly it might be condemned in Scripture) did not, in fact, separate the sinner from God (i.e., a claim to freedom from the culpability for sins committed; cf. John 9:41; 15:22, 24; 19:11; Akin 74 n. 129; Brown 205–6; Kruse 66; Law 130). The NET Translation Notes read, "Where ἔχω governs an abstract noun (e.g., 1 John 1:3, 6, 7; 2:28; 3:3, 15, 21; 4:16, 17; 5:12–13), it indicates that a *state* is involved, which in the case of ἁμαρτία would refer to *a state of sin*." Brown notes that "their (the secessionists') claim may have reflected the thesis that actions committed by the believer were not important enough to be sins that could challenge the intimacy with God acquired through belief" (206). Sim., Marshall argues the opponents of the author did not view the actions they were doing as being sinful (113).

3. A claim to freedom from ongoing sins. Though reflecting aspects of option 1 above, Cox notes they claimed they "neither had sin nor committed sin" (325).

In light of usage of the vb. ἔχω in combination with the singular direct object ἁμαρτίαν, a Johannine cstr. found only here and in John's Gospel (e.g., John 9:41; 15:22, 24; 19:11), option 2 seems more likely. Yet, without knowing the exact nature of the deviant theology John addresses, one cannot be dogmatic. Regardless of the exact error, we note a person's failure to recognize his sinfulness exposes the fact that he has not come into relationship with God who is completely morally pure.

ἑαυτοὺς πλανῶμεν καὶ ἡ ἀλήθεια οὐκ ἔστιν ἐν ἡμῖν.
we are deceiving ourselves, and the truth is not in us.

This is the apod. of the third class cond. sentence that starts at the beginning of v. 8. John offers two damning evaluations of persons who do not recognize their sinfulness: (1) They are self-deceived (in both their evaluation of themselves and their presumption in claiming to know God); and (2) objectively, the truth (of the gospel) is absent from their lives. Πλανῶμεν is a 1st pl. pres. act. indic. of πλανάω, which has the reflexive pron. ἑαυτούς, "ourselves," as its acc. dir. obj. Robertson insightfully comments, "We do not deceive others who know us" (Robertson, *Pictures* 6:208). The prep. phrase ἐν ἡμῖν communicates sphere/location in a metaphorical sense (LN §83.13).

VERSE 9

ἐὰν ὁμολογῶμεν τὰς ἁμαρτίας ἡμῶν,
If we confess our sins,

Verse 9 is the fourth of five third class cond. sentences in vv. 6–10 (on third class cond., see 1:6). Ὁμολογῶμεν is 1st pl. pres. act. subj. of ὁμολογέω (cf. 2:23; 4:2, 3, 15; 2 John 7). The confession here is with a "focus on admission of wrongdoing" (BDAG 708c). Τὰς ἁμαρτίας is a dir. obj. and appears with the art., as is common with nouns modified by a pers. poss. pron. Culy notes, "The plural form of the noun probably points to confession of specific sins rather than confession of sinfulness in general" (18). Ἡμῶν functions as subj. gen. (on gen. use, see KMP 99–100).

πιστός ἐστιν καὶ δίκαιος,
he is faithful and righteous

Πιστός and δίκαιος are pred. adj. appearing with the copulative vb. ἐστιν. How are God's πιστός, "faithfulness," and δίκαιος, "righteousness," of comfort to the believer in the confession of sin? God is faithful in keeping his promise to forgive. Here, the term δίκαιος is probably not best understood as focusing on an abstract moral quality of God (cf. 1 John 3:7), but on his powerful, saving actions on behalf of those who call out to him (*NIDNTTE* 1:739–40; Seifrid 178). Alternately, the word may focus on the "justice" or "fairness" of God (BDAG 246d; Culy 19; Jobes 71; Marshall 114; Stott 82), in that God will not provide a way of salvation and then not welcome those who approach him in that way. Most EVV render the word as "just" (ESV, NIV, KJV) or "righteous" (NASB, NET, CSB). On the term, see G. Schneider, *EDNT* 1:324b–25b; see also For Further Study 13 "Righteous/Righteousness Word Study."

ἵνα ἀφῇ ἡμῖν τὰς ἁμαρτίας καὶ καθαρίσῃ ἡμᾶς ἀπὸ πάσης ἀδικίας.
so that he forgives us our sins and cleanses us from all unrighteousness.

Ἵνα presents the result (BDF §391; Baugh 13; DM 249; Moule 142; NET Translation Notes; Porter, *Idioms*, 235; R 961, 998; Z §352) of one confessing sin to the God who is faithful and righteous—God forgives the sin ("cancels their 'debt,'" Kruse 69), and cleanses the sinner's inner evil inclinations (see Marshall 114 n. 14). Wallace says this ἵνα clause is difficult to label and suggests result, purpose, purpose-result, or explanatory (Wallace 474, 476). Ἀφῇ is the 3rd sg. aor. act. subj. of ἀφίημι "forgive" (used here and 2:12) with ἡμῖν as a dat. of advantage (on this topic, see BW 33–34; KMP 126; Wallace 142–44) and τὰς ἁμαρτίας as the dir. obj. The poss. idea "*our* sins," is implied, and in such cases of implied poss. the Gk. art. is usually present. Καθαρίσῃ is 3rd sg. aor. act. subj. of καθαρίζω (see 1:7), with ἡμᾶς as the dir. obj. The prep. phrase ἀπὸ πάσης ἀδικίας communicates disassociation/separation (LN §89.122; Harris 60–61; Culy 19). The paronomasia in the original Gk. is often lost in EVV. The one who is δίκαιος "righteous" (see above) cleanses us from all ἀδικίας "unrighteousness" (BDAG 20c–d; Schrenk, *TDNT* 1:153–57).

VERSE 10

ἐὰν εἴπωμεν ὅτι οὐχ ἡμαρτήκαμεν,
If we say, "We have not sinned,"

Verse 10 begins the last of five third class conds. (on third class cond, see 1:6) that consider the claims of those who know God versus the reality of their lives and self-awareness of their sinfulness. Ὅτι introduces the content of the verbal claim (see BDAG 731d; R 1034–35). Εἴπωμεν is a 1st pl. aor. act. subj. of λέγω. Ἡμαρτήκαμεν is 1st pl. pf. act. indic. of ἁμαρτάνω. Wallace labels ἡμαρτήκαμεν as an extensive or consummative pf., with the emphasis on the completion of the action (577). There are several ways to understand this reference to sin in the pf.:

*1. This is simply a restatement, with minor stylistic variation, of the earlier claim to sinlessness in v. 8 (Akin 74; Yarbrough 66, although he notes the pf. "may call special attention to the stative aspect of the verbal action").
2. This second assertion is a claim to be free from sinful behavior alongside the earlier assertion to be free from the ontological nature of sin (Hiebert 67–68; Stott 82; cf. Smalley 27, 31).
3. This verse records the claim that one is not only free from the current guilty effects of present sin but has never been tainted by sin (cf. Marshall 115, who notes that possibly v. 8 reflects a denial of present sinfulness and v. 10 reflects past acts of sin).
4. This change in wording now directs attention to discrete acts of sin (Baugh 14; Brown 211; Robertson, *Pictures* 6:208)

ψεύστην ποιοῦμεν αὐτὸν καὶ ὁ λόγος αὐτοῦ οὐκ ἔστιν ἐν ἡμῖν.
we make him a liar, and his word is not in us.

The vb. ποιοῦμεν, 1st pl. pres. act. indic. of ποιέω, is followed by a double accusative (BDAG 840c) object-complement cstr. Αὐτόν "him" (i.e., God) is the object and ψεύστην (ψεύστης, -ου, ὁ, "liar," LN §33.255) is the complement. Most EVV read, "We make him a liar." In other words, because God has declared us sinful, "we make him out to be a liar" (NIV) when we say we are not sinners. Culy (13–14) notes the *inclusio* of ψευδόμεθα (v. 6) and ψεύστην (v. 10).

John does not mince words. The person who denies their sinfulness is not indwelt by the saving word of God (i.e., the gospel message).

Ὁ λόγος is the nom. subj. Αὐτοῦ is the gen. of source, that is, the word (gospel) that comes from God, "the divine revelation through Christ and his messengers" (BDAG 599d). ZG describes ὁ λόγος αὐτοῦ as "the word of truth revealed as the norm for judgement and for action" (727). The prep. phrase ἐν ἡμῖν communicates sphere/location (LN §83.13) in a metaphorical sense, that is, the divine word so filling people as to characterize and determine their lives (BDAG 327d).

FOR FURTHER STUDY

5. Holiness of God (1:5)

Alexander, T. Desmond. *From Eden to the New Jerusalem: An Introduction to Biblical Theology*. Grand Rapids: Kregel, 2013 (See 138–55).
Bavinck, 2:216–21.
Bloesch, Donald G. *God the Almighty: Power, Wisdom, Holiness, Love*. Downers Grove, IL: IVP Academic, 1995.
Frame, 276–79.
Gentry, Peter J. "The Meaning of 'Holy' in the Old Testament." *BSac* 170 (2013): 400–417.
Grudem, 202–3.
Harrison, E. F. *ISBE,* 2:725–26.
Hawthorne, G. F. *DLNT*, 485–89.
Lösel, Steffen. "Church, Theology and the Holiness of God." *SJT* 72, no. 2 (2019): 207–26.
Newman, C. C. *DLNT*, 423, 425–26.
Peterson, D. G. *NDBT*, 544–50.
Sproul, R. C. *The Holiness of God*. Rev. ed. Carol Stream, IL: Tyndale Momentum, 2000.
Webster, J. B. "The Holiness and Love of God." *SJT* 57, no. 3 (2004): 249–68.
Willis, David. *Notes on the Holiness of God*. Grand Rapids: Eerdmans, 2002.

6. Light and Darkness (Johannine Dualism) (1:5–7)

Achtemeier, Elizabeth. "Jesus Christ the Light of the World: The Biblical Understanding of Light and Darkness." *Int* 17, no. 4 (1963): 439–49.
Baylis, Charles P. "The Meaning of Walking 'in the Darkness' (1 John 1:6)." *BSac* 149 (1992): 214–22.
Conzelmann, H. *TDNT,* 7:423–45.
———. *TDNT,* 9:310–58.
Hunt, S. A. *DLNT*, 657–59.
Jobes, 65–67 (see "IN DEPTH: The Johannine Dualistic Framework).
Köstenberger, *Theology*, 282–92.
Kruse, 65–66 (see "A Note on Light and Darkness").
NIDNTTE 4:319–25, 637–43.
Paddison, Angus. "Walking in the Light." *ExpTim* 123, no. 6 (2012): 287–89.

7. Obedience/Christian Growth (1:6–7)

Bock, Darrell L. *Cultural Intelligence: Living for God in a Diverse, Pluralistic World.* Nashville: B&H Academic, 2020.

Bonhoeffer, Dietrich. *The Cost of Discipleship*. New York: Touchstone, 1995.

Callen, Barry L. *Authentic Spirituality*. Lexington, KY: Emeth, 2006.

Chan, Simon. *Spiritual Theology: A Systematic Study of the Christian Life*. Downers Grove, IL: IVP Academic, 1998.

Goodrich, John, and Mark Strauss, eds. *Following Jesus Christ: The New Testament Message of Discipleship for Today*. Grand Rapids: Kregel Academic, 2019.

Inrig, Gary. *A Call to Excellence*. Wheaton: Scripture Press, 1985.

Packer, J. I. *NDBT*, 680–81.

Peterson, Eugene H. *A Long Obedience in the Same Direction: Discipleship in an Instant Society*. Downers Grove, IL: IVP, 2000.

8. Christian Ethics (1:6–7)

Bennema, C. *Mimesis in the Johannine Literature: A Study in Johannine Ethics*. London: Bloomsbury T&T Clark, 2017.

Brawley, Robert L., ed. *Character Ethics and the New Testament: Moral Dimensions of Scripture*. Louisville: Westminster John Knox, 2007.

Brown, Sherri, and Christopher W. Skinner, eds. *Johannine Ethics: The Moral World of the Gospel and Epistles of John*. Minneapolis: Fortress, 2017.

*Burridge, Richard A. *Imitating Jesus: An Inclusive Approach to New Testament Ethics*. Grand Rapids: Eerdmans, 2007.

Hays, Richard B. *The Moral Vision of the New Testament: A Contemporary Introduction to New Testament Ethics*. San Francisco: HarperOne, 1996.

Loader, William, R. G. "The Significance of 2:15–17 for Understanding the Ethics of 1 John." Pages 223–36 in *Communities in Dispute: Current Scholarship on the Johannine Epistles*. Edited by R. Alan Culpepper and Paul N. Anderson. Atlanta: SBL Press, 2014.

Pregeant, Russell. *Knowing Truth, Doing Good: Engaging New Testament Ethics*. Minneapolis: Fortress, 2008.

Verhey, A. *DLNT*, 351.

Watt, J. G. van der. "Ethics in First John: A Literary and Socioscientific Perspective." *CBQ* 61, no. 3 (1999): 491–511.

9. Truth (1:6, 8)

Bultmann, R. et al. *TDNT,* 1:232–51.

Hübner, H. *EDNT,* 1:57–60.

Jobes, 69 (see "IN DEPTH: 'Truth' in John's Letters").

Kruse, 67 (see "A Note on Truth").

NIDNTTE 1:222–42.

Potterie, Ignace de la. *La vérité dans saint Jean*. Analecta Biblica 73–74. Rome: Biblical Institute, 1977.

Reed, J. T. *DLNT*, 1184–87.

10. Atonement (1:7, 9)

Allen, David L. *The Atonement: A Biblical, Theological, and Historical Study of the Cross of Christ*. Nashville: B&H, 2019.

Allison, Gregg R. "A History of the Doctrine of the Atonement." *SBJT* 11, no. 2 (2007): 4–19.

Armitage, Christopher. *Atonement and Ethics in 1 John: A Peacemaking Hermeneutic*. London: Bloomsbury, 2021.

Beilby, James K., and Paul R. Eddy, eds. *The Nature of the Atonement: Four Views*. Downers Grove, IL: IVP Academic, 2006.

Bromiley, G. W. *ISBE,* 1:353–60.

Craig, William Lane. *Atonement and the Death of Christ: An Exegetical, Historical, and Philosophical Exploration*. Waco: Baylor University Press, 2020.

Gathercole, Simon J. "The Cross and Substitutionary Atonement." *SBJT* 11, no. 2 (2007): 64–73.

Green, Joel B. *NIDB,* 1:344–48.

Grudem, 568–607.

Jeffery, Steve, Michael Ovey, and Andrew Sach. *Pierced for Our Transgressions: Rediscovering the Glory of Penal Substitution*. Wheaton, IL: Crossway, 2007.

Kim, Jintae. "The Concept of Atonement in Hellenistic Thought and 1 John." *Journal of Greco-Roman Christianity and Judaism* 2 (2001): 100–116.

Kleinig, John W. "Sacrificial Atonement by Jesus and God's Wrath in the Light of the Old Testament." *CTQ* 84, no. 3 (2020): 195–208.

Morris, Leon. *The Apostolic Preaching of the Cross*. 3rd ed. Grand Rapids: Eerdmans, 1965.

———. *The Atonement: Its Meaning and Significance*. Leicester: IVP, 1983.

*Rutledge, Fleming. *The Crucifixion: Understanding the Death of Jesus Christ*. Grand Rapids: Eerdmans, 2017.

Seifrid, Mark. *DLNT*, 267–86 (see esp. 281–82).

Sproul, R. C. *The Truth of the Cross*. Orlando: Reformation Trust, 2007.

Stott, John R. W. *The Cross of Christ.* Leicester: IVP, 1986.

Tuckett, C.M. *ABD,* 1:518–22.

Yarbrough, R. W. *NDBT*, 388–92.

11. Sin (1:8)

Anderson, Gary A. *Sin: A History*. New Haven: Yale University Press, 2009.

Bavinck, 3:126–57.

Berkouwer, G. C. *Sin*. Translated by P. C. Holtrop. Grand Rapids: Eerdmans, 1971.

Biddle, Mark E. *Missing the Mark: Sin and Its Consequences in Biblical Theology*. Nashville: Abingdon, 2005.

Blocher, H. A. G. *NDBT*, 781–88.

Bridges, Jerry. *Respectable Sins: Confronting the Sins We Tolerate.* Colorado Springs: NavPress, 2007.

Grudem, 490–514.

Jobes, 341–42 (see "Sin and Atonement").

Köstenberger, *Theology*, 466–68.

Murray, John. *The Imputation of Adam's Sin.* Phillipsburg: P & R, 1977.

NIDNTTE 1:255–63.

Plantinga, Cornelius. *Not the Way It's Supposed to Be: A Breviary of Sin*. Grand Rapids: Eerdmans, 1996.
*Porter, S. E. *DLNT*, 1095–98.
Quell, G. et al. *TDNT,* 1:267–335.
Schneider, J. *TDNT,* 5:736–44.
Scholer, David M. "Sins within and Sins without: An Interpretation of 1 John 5:16–17." 230–46 in *Current Issues in Biblical and Patristic Interpretation: Studies in Honor of Merrill C Tenney Presented by His Former Students*. Edited by Gerald F. Hawthorne. Grand Rapids: Eerdmans, 1975.
Smith, C. R. *The Bible Doctrine of Sin*. London: Epworth, 1953.
Swadling, Harry C. "Sin and Sinlessness in 1 John." *SJT* 35, no. 3 (1982): 205–11.
Vitrano, Steven P. "The Doctrine of Sin in 1 John." *Andrews University Seminary Studies* 25, no. 1 (1987): 123–31.

12. Confession of Sin (1:9)

Allman, James E. "First John 1:9: Confession as a Test, but of What?" *BSac* 172 (2015): 203–21.
Glasscock, Ed. "Forgiveness and Cleansing According to 1 John 1:9." *BSac* 166 (2009): 217–31.
Michel, O. *TDNT,* 5:199–220.
NIDNTTE 3:505–10.
Stott, John. *Confess Your Sins: The Way of Reconciliation*. Grand Rapids: Eerdmans, 2017.

13. Righteous/Righteousness Word Study (1:9)

BDAG 246b–49a.
Brown, C., and H. Seebass. *NIDNTT,* 3:360–73.
Brown, 209–10.
Grudem, 204–5.
Jobes, 71–72.
Kelly, R. A. *ISBE,* 4:192–95.
Kertelge, K. *EDNT,* 1:325–34.
Kruse, 69–70.
Lieu, Judith. "What Was from the Beginning: Scripture and Tradition in the Johannine Epistles." *NTS* 39, no. 3 (1993): 458–77.
Newman, C. C. *DLNT*, 1053–59.
NIDNTTE 1:723–41.
Schrenk, G., and G. Quell. *TDNT,* 2:182–225.
Scullion, J. J., and J. Reumann. *ABD,* 5:724–73.

See also For Further Study 2 "Proclamation Language"

HOMILETICAL SUGGESTIONS

Fellowship with a Holy God (1:5–10)

1. God is light: comprehending the holiness of God (v. 5)
2. Walking in darkness versus the light (vv. 6–7)
3. Denying versus confessing our sins (vv. 8–10)

A Relationship with a Holy God: Claim versus Reality (1:5–10)

God is completely pure, and those who know him will reflect that purity

1. A false claim to a relationship with God will be revealed by our deeds
   a. If we wallow in unconfessed impurity, we do not know God (v. 6)
   b. If we deny the sin in our lives, we show we are self-deceived non-Christians (v. 8)
   c. If we deny that we are sinners, we deny God's true judgment of us, and so show his word does not indwell us (v. 10)
2. A true claim to a relationship with God will be revealed by our deeds
   a. If we confess our sins and reflect God's purity in our lives, we show we are part of God's people and are experiencing the cleansing effects of Jesus's death (v. 7)
   b. If we are true Christians, we confess our sins and experience the fulfillment of God's good and powerful promise to cancel our debt of sin and progressively transform us into his pure people (v. 9)

III. Sin and the Believer (2:1–6)

This section transitions from 1:1–10, concerning the message of Christ and the believers' fellowship with God, focusing now on sin in the life of the believer and living in relationship to God. The ἵνα clause (v. 1) denotes John's purpose (that they not sin). The third class cond. indicates they have an advocate in Jesus Christ who is the propitiation (ἱλασμός) concerning sins (v. 2). Verses 3–6 address what knowing God looks like in the Christian life. The protasis of the third class cond. (v. 3) introduces one of three primary realities of the Christian: obedience. The three themes of obedience, love for one another, and believing that Jesus is the Christ come in the flesh will texture the following language of the letter.

1 Τεκνία μου, ταῦτα γράφω ὑμῖν
ἵνα μὴ ἁμάρτητε.
καὶ ἐάν τις ἁμάρτῃ,
παράκλητον ἔχομεν πρὸς τὸν πατέρα = Ἰησοῦν Χριστὸν = δίκαιον·

2 καὶ αὐτὸς ἱλασμός ἐστιν
περὶ τῶν ἁμαρτιῶν ἡμῶν,
οὐ περὶ τῶν ἡμετέρων δὲ μόνον
ἀλλὰ καὶ περὶ ὅλου τοῦ κόσμου.

3 Καὶ ἐν τούτῳ
γινώσκομεν ὅτι ἐγνώκαμεν αὐτόν,
ἐὰν τὰς ἐντολὰς αὐτοῦ τηρῶμεν.

4 ὁ λέγων ὅτι ἔγνωκα αὐτὸν καὶ τὰς ἐντολὰς αὐτοῦ μὴ τηρῶν ψεύστης ἐστίν,
καὶ ἐν τούτῳ ἡ ἀλήθεια οὐκ ἔστιν·

5 ↓ὃς δ' ἂν τηρῇ αὐτοῦ τὸν λόγον,
ἀληθῶς ἐν τούτῳ ἡ ἀγάπη τοῦ θεοῦ τετελείωται·
ἐν τούτῳ γινώσκομεν ὅτι ἐν αὐτῷ ἐσμεν.

6 ὁ λέγων ἐν αὐτῷ μένειν ὀφείλει, καθὼς ἐκεῖνος περιεπάτησεν,
καὶ αὐτὸς οὕτως περιπατεῖν.

VERSE 1

Τεκνία μου
My little children,

In addressing this congregation as "my little children," John reminds them of his love and their dependence upon him (used 7× total in 1 John 2:1, 12, 28; 3:18; 4:4; 5:21). Perhaps they can trace the beginning of their Christian faith to his apostolic ministry, which would make "my little children" an especially fitting address (see Jobes 77). Τεκνία is a voc. pl. of τεκνίον, a diminutive form of τέκνον. Diminutive forms often express affection or smallness. Μου is a gen. of personal relationship. There is no voc. form of the art.

ταῦτα γράφω ὑμῖν ἵνα μὴ ἁμάρτητε.
these things I write to you so that you do not sin.

In light of John's previous insistence that the claim to be without sin is self-deception (1:8) and makes God a liar (1:10), an addressee could wrongly conclude that sin, as pervasive, can thus be excused (cf. Rom 6:1: "Shall we sin more that grace may abound? By no means!"). John says, in essence, "No, I'm not writing to you to excuse sin, but so that you will see it rightly and repent of it." Ταῦτα "these things," an independent use of the near dem. pron., is the acc. pl. neut. dir. obj. of γράφω. Note John's shift from the 1st pers. pl. used to this point in the letter (reflecting the full witness and authority of the apostolic community [see 1:1]) to the 1st sg. Ὑμῖν is the dat. indir. obj. Ἵνα introduces a purpose clause (Wallace 472). Ἁμάρτητε is a 2nd pl. aor. act. subj. of ἁμαρτάνω, "to sin" (on the term, see BDAG 49d–50a; *NIDNTTE* 1:255–63; Grundman, *TDNT* 1:267–316). Following ἵνα, the aor. form of the subj. occurs 72 percent of the time in the NT (Baugh, *Tense Form Choice*, 71), so ἁμάρτητε conforms to grammatical expectations and is fitting for the author's holistic (perfective) statement of purpose.

καὶ ἐάν τις ἁμάρτῃ,
And if anyone sins,

Note how frequently John begins clauses with καί rather than employing a particle, which reveals more explicitly the logical relationship of the subsequent clause. English translations frequently make explicit an advers. function to this clause, introducing it with "but" (most EVV; e.g., CSB, ESV, NIV), but it is debatable whether it is helpful or appropriate to speak of an "adversative καί" (cf. Yarbrough 75). Ἐάν introduces a third class cond. prot., envisioning a situation which all Christians face countless times in their lives (on third class cond., see 1:6). It is noteworthy that ἐάν overlaps in semantic range with the English words "when" or "since" (cf. BDAG 268a). Perhaps John employs the third class cond. because of the lack of specificity of the verb's subj. (τις) and the particular transgression(s). Ἁμάρτῃ is a 3rd sg. aor. act. subj. Following a cond. ἐάν, the aor. subjunc. appears 65 percent of the time in the GNT. Thus, ἁμάρτῃ is the expected form, and a fitting perfective/holistic presentation of sinning for consideration in a cond. statement.

παράκλητον ἔχομεν πρὸς τὸν πατέρα Ἰησοῦν Χριστὸν δίκαιον·
we have an advocate with the Father—Jesus Christ, the righteous one.

The clause serves as the apod. ("then" part) to the third class cond. prot. above. It is good news for the sinning Christian that we have a παράκλητον, acc. sg. masc. of παράκλητος, -ου, ὁ, "advocate" (most EVV); "legal advisor, advocate, counselor, helper" (see F. Porsch, *EDNT* 3:28c; BDAG 766c highlights the more common, general, and nontechnical sense of "mediator, intercessor, helper"; on the term, see also Behm, *TDNT* 5:800–814; MM 485b–c). The word is the acc. dir. obj. of ἔχομεν. Though παράκλητος can simply mean one who helps or assists (see Akin 79), perhaps this context favors the nuance of defender in court or legal defender (Hiebert 74; Marshall 116; cf. Brown 217 who sees both senses as likely present). This advocate intercedes on our behalf πρὸς τὸν πατέρα "with the Father." Πρός likely reflects the sense of *association or possibly location (so Culy 22, "in the presence of"). In appos. to the acc. dir. obj. παράκλητον, we find Ἰησοῦν Χριστόν, and δίκαιον appears as the final component in this appos. chain of accusatives (cf. 1:9; 3:7). Young highlights that "elements in apposition do not have to be adjoining, as illustrated by the first pair" (21). We would normally expect the subst. use of an adj. to be art. (τὸν δίκαιον). Perhaps δίκαιον lacks the art. for the sake of parallelism in the anar. chain of accusatives. Or, though an unusual cstr., perhaps δίκαιον should be taken as an attrib. adj. modifying Ἰησοῦν Χριστόν ("righteous Jesus Christ"; so Baugh 17).

VERSE 2

καὶ αὐτὸς ἱλασμός ἐστιν περὶ τῶν ἁμαρτιῶν ἡμῶν,
And he is the propitiation concerning our sins

Stott is right to point out that only Jesus's righteousness (2:1) makes him the worthy propitiation (2:2), and only the propitiatory sacrifice of himself makes him an effective advocate (2:1) (Stott 86, 88, 92). The rare word ἱλασμός, -ου, ὁ (used only here and 4:10) is correctly understood as having reference to bearing or taking away wrath on behalf of another (BDAG 474b; Hill 37–38; Morris 206; contra LN §40.12; J. Roloff, *EDNT* 2:186c, who render the term only in terms of "expiation"). Perhaps no modern English word sufficiently conveys this idea, though the older theological term "propitiation" does (so ESV, NASB, KJV; in comparison, CSB, NET, NIV render the term "atoning sacrifice"). The majority of commentaries surveyed affirm this sense in this context (not excluding the sense of "expiation," i.e., the removal of sin; e.g., Akin 85; Hiebert 75; Kruse 74; Marshall 118; Smalley 40; Stott 88–92; Yarbrough 78–79). For resources on the term, see For Further Study 14 "Ἱλασμός/Expiation/Propitiation." From the literary context, ἱλασμός is definite (John does not envision Jesus as one among many propitiations). E. C. Colwell observed that when a def. pred. nom. ("definite" as determined from contextual analysis) precedes the copulative vb. (here ἐστιν), it lacks the art. in Gk. nearly 90 percent of the time. That pattern, known as "Colwell's Rule," holds here (on the topic, see KMP 163; Moule 115–17; Young 65–66). Note the prep. phrase περὶ τῶν ἁμαρτιῶν ἡμῶν communicates reference or respect (Culy 24; cf. BDAG 798a). Jesus is not the propitiation in some abstract way. He bears the deserved wrath for sin of those who come to him in repentance and faith.

οὐ περὶ τῶν ἡμετέρων δὲ μόνον
and not concerning ours only

Both in this clause and the following clause, there is an ellipsis of the words αὐτὸς ἱλασμός ἐστιν and τῶν ἁμαρτιῶν. That is, this clause compactly asserts that *Jesus is* not *the propitiation* concerning our *sins* only (italicized words implied). Ἡμετέρων is the gen. pl. fem. pronominal adj. employed substantively, mng. "ours" (i.e., our sins). The lexical form is ἡμέτερος, -α, -ον, which occurs only seven times in its various forms in the GNT. The pronominal adj. is perhaps slightly more emphatic than the use of the nearly synonymous gen. pers. pron. It is interesting that δέ appears in the fifth position in the clause, as the postpositive particle most commonly appears second in order. Perhaps John did not want to add an implied pause (with the conj.) until he reached the end of the prep. phrase. Δέ informs the reader that additional related information is cascading from the author, but a more precise syntactical relationship among clauses must be determined by context. This is in contrast to ἀλλά (see below), which is unambiguously strongly adverse.

ἀλλὰ καὶ περὶ ὅλου τοῦ κόσμου.
but also concerning the whole world.

John asserts here that Jesus is also the propitiation ὅλου τοῦ κόσμου "concerning the whole world." The rest of John's Letter makes clear that the apostle does not affirm universalism or inclusivism. This clause must be understood in that epistolary context. Jesus's death is certainly offered to the whole world and there is no deficiency in it, but it is effective only for those who are born again, who turn to him in repentance and faith (see Akin 85; Kruse 75; Yarbrough 80; cf. Jobes 80). When functioning attrib., ὅλος, -η, -ον "whole, entire," appears in the pred. position (as here), the same as dem. prons. Κόσμος, here mng. "humanity in general," "*the world*" (BDAG 562b). Occurring twenty-three times in 1 John, the term conveys a range of meanings depending on context (on the term, see BDAG 561b–63a; Greeven, *TDNT* 3:868–96; *NIDNTTE* 2:730–36).

VERSE 3

Καὶ ἐν τούτῳ γινώσκομεν ὅτι ἐγνώκαμεν αὐτόν,
And by this we know that we have come to know him:

The dem. pron. τούτῳ is in the dat. case, as required of nouns following the prep. ἐν. The entire prep. phrase (ἐν τούτῳ) conveys an instr. idea (BW 43; see also BDF §219; Z §119). The first use of γινώσκω is cognitive ("we know" [cognitively]). The second use is relational ("we have come to know" [relationally]). Γινώσκομεν is 1st pl. pres. act. ind. Ἐγνώκαμεν is 1st pl. pf. act. ind. The pf. tense here conveys the idea of coming into relationship with the Lord and remaining in that relationship with him (stative aspect). A degree of ambiguity is present concerning the referent of αὐτόν (whether "God" or "Jesus"), a common ambiguity in the letter. Culy notes that "we may be going beyond the specificity of the text to attempt to choose a referent in every case," highlighting the trinitarian ambiguity of the letter (26).

ἐὰν τὰς ἐντολὰς αὐτοῦ τηρῶμεν.
if we keep his commandments.

Keeping the Lord's commands is evidence that we know him and provides cognitive self-assurance of that relational reality. Ἐάν introduces the prot. of a third class cond. clause (on third class cond., see 1:6). Τηρῶμεν is 1st pl. pres. act. subj. of τηρέω "keep, guard, obey." After ἐάν, an aor. vb. is more common (65 percent). In contrast, here the pres. tense is employed to convey the idea of an ongoing pattern of obedience. Τὰς ἐντολάς is the acc. pl. fem. dir. obj. of ἐντολή, -ῆς, ἡ ("command," BDAG 340b–c; "commands," CSB, NIV; "commandments," ESV, NASB, NET; on the term, see Schrenk, *TDNT* 2:545–56).

VERSE 4

ὁ λέγων ὅτι ἔγνωκα αὐτὸν καὶ τὰς ἐντολὰς αὐτοῦ μὴ τηρῶν ψεύστης ἐστίν
The person who says, "I know him" and yet does not keep his commandments is a liar,

The masc. sg. art. ὁ governs both nom. sg. masc. pres. act. ptcs., λέγων and τηρῶν. Together these ptcs. make up the compound subst.: the person who says X and does not keep Y (on ptcs. within an article-substantive–καί-substantive construction, see Wallace 274). Ὅτι introduces direct discourse (on recitative, see R 1027–28; Wallace 454–55). Ἔγνωκα is the 1st sg. pf. act. indic. of γινώσκω. The emphasis is not on the coming to know (although that is assumed), but on the ongoing claimed reality of the relationship, "I know him." Αὐτόν is the acc. dir. obj. This claim to a relationship with God is belied by a life characterized by disobedience to God's commands. Τὰς ἐντολάς is the acc. pl. fem. dir. obj. of ἐντολή, -ῆς, ἡ "mandate, ordinance, command" (see 2:3) and functions as dir. obj. of the ptc. τηρῶν. No specific commands are given, but elsewhere in his letter, John highlights love of other Christians (2:9–11; 3:10, 11, 14–16, 18, 23; 4:7, 8, 11, 12, 20, 21; 5:2) and belief in Jesus as the incarnate Christ (4:2, 9, 14–15; 5:1, 5–13, 20). The law of God as fulfilled and taught by the Lord Jesus is assumed as the content of "his commands" (for a discussion of John's contextual mng. of "commands," cf. Jobes 83; Yarbrough 82–83). Αὐτοῦ is probably best labeled a subj. gen. or gen. of source. All the words in this clause before ψεύστης ("liar"; see 1:10) function as one giant subj. in the nom. case, with ἐστίν as the copulative vb. Ψεύστης is the indef. pred. nom. Indeed, to claim to know God while living in disobedience to his commands is to reveal oneself as prevaricator, a mendacious spiritual hypocrite.

καὶ ἐν τούτῳ ἡ ἀλήθεια οὐκ ἔστιν·
and in this person, the truth is not.

Here, the dat. sg. masc. near dem. pron. τούτῳ refers back to the claimant in the previous verse (i.e., the person who says, "I know God") and thus the prep. phrase καὶ ἐν τούτῳ is rightly translated, "in this person," ("in him," CSB, NASB; "in that person," NIV) conveying a loc. metaphorical sense. The reader of this commentary is advised to keep an ongoing list of the various ways that John describes a Christian (or non-Christian). A Christian is someone in whom the truth dwells. That is, the truth has taken up residence in his or her heart, mind, and life. The truth not only indwells but directs and shapes the Christian's conduct. On the other hand, a non-Christian (whose life is ultimately characterized by a pattern of disobeying God's commands) is not indwelt by God's truth. The articular subj. ἡ ἀλήθεια is strongly supported, the UBS[5] editors giving it an "A" rating (indicating that the text is certain). Several witnesses (Ψ 436 945 1505 et al.) omit the art., reading ἀλήθεια; ℵ and a few other witnesses read ἡ ἀλήθεια τοῦ θεοῦ.

VERSE 5

ὃς δ' ἂν τηρῇ αὐτοῦ τὸν λόγον,
But whoever keeps his word

The postpositive particle δέ has elided with ἄν to become δ'. From context, the particle is translated adversatively: "but" (most EVV). The indef. rel. pron. ὃς ἄν "whoever," is followed by the 3rd sg. pres. act. subj. of τηρέω "keep, obey." The indef. rel. is followed by an aor. subj. with 80 percent frequency. Countering that pattern here is the inherent procedural nature of the activity of obeying/keeping God's word, which more naturally is expressed in the imperfective aspect of the pres. tense. The poss. pers. pron. (here αὐτοῦ) is found with much greater frequency *after* a noun it qualifies. It is likely pulled forward here for emphasis αὐτοῦ τὸν λόγον ("*his* word"). Note the variation in John's wording between vv. 4 and 5: keeping God's "commandments" (v. 4) versus keeping his "word" (v. 5). Is this an example of John's employment of near synonyms or is something more significant at stake? Does he imply that a true believer not only obeys God's commands but hold to all aspects of that word—including trusting his promises (cf. Brown 254; Hiebert 95; Stott 95)?

ἀληθῶς ἐν τούτῳ ἡ ἀγάπη τοῦ θεοῦ τετελείωται
truly in this person, the love of God has been perfected.

Students are reminded that Gk. words that end in -ῶς are frequently adverbs, often being translated with an English *-ly* ending. The prep. phrase ἐν τούτῳ is translated, "in this person," conveying a loc. metaphorical sense (BDAG 326c). Τοῦ θεοῦ is an obj. gen., "love for God" (most commentators surveyed; e.g., Culy 28; Kruse 80; Marshall 125; Smalley 46; Stott 95; also R 500 [possibly], Wallace 121; contra Yarbrough 86, who argues for subj. sense; cf. 5:3). Τετελείωται is a 3rd sg. pf. pass. indic. of τελειόω ("complete, finish, accomplish" or "make perfect," BDAG 996d; "made complete,"

NIV, CSB; "perfected," ESV, NASB; "love attains completeness and maturity," Smalley 46; on this term, see also H. Hübner, *EDNT* 3:345b). Concerning the pf. tense vb. τετελείωται, see BDF §344; Porter, *Idioms*, 41; Wallace 581 (future use); Burton §79; R 897 (gnomic). A mature Christian love for God expresses itself through keeping God's word.

ἐν τούτῳ γινώσκομεν ὅτι ἐν αὐτῷ ἐσμεν.
By this we know that we are in him:

Ἐν τούτῳ is a prep. phrase expressing means or instr. (see BDAG 328c; BDF §§195, 219). It could point backward (Kruse 81; Marshall 126; Smalley 50) or forward (Culy 29) in the text, though the sense would scarcely differ since vv. 5 and 6 make similar assertions about the evidence of true Christian experience. Perhaps the clause more likely points forward to v. 6. Γινώσκομεν is the 1st pl. pres. act. indic. of γινώσκω. Ὅτι introduces a content clause (see BDAG 731d; R 1034–35). The prep. phrase ἐν αὐτῷ is metaphorical loc./spherical (see BDAG 326c on function of prep.), describing the Christian believer in close, intimate fellowship with the Lord (in Christ, see Stott 91; in God, see Brown 259; Kruse 81; Marshall 127). Ἐσμεν is 1st pl. pres. indic. of εἰμί.

VERSE 6

ὁ λέγων ἐν αὐτῷ μένειν ὀφείλει,
the person claiming to abide in him ought,

λέγων is the nom. sg. masc. of pres. act. ptc. of λέγω. It functions substantively. Μένειν is a pres. act. inf. of μένω, expressing indir. discourse (Harris 134–36; on this topic, see KMP 375). Harris (135) helpfully notes the following relations reflected by μένω in the letter: God in believers (1 John 3:24; 4:12, 13, 15, 16), believers in God (1 John 2:6, 24; 3:24; 4:13, 15, 16), and believers in Christ (1 John 2:24, 27, 28; 3:6). The prep. phrase ἐν αὐτῷ is adv. (modifying μένειν) and expresses a metaphorical loc./spherical idea (see BDAG 326c). The syntax of this verse can be difficult for beginning students. Perhaps it can be helpful to think of ὁ λέγων ἐν αὐτῷ μένειν (the subject) as being replaced with αὐτός "he." The basic structure of the verse would then be: αὐτὸς ὀφείλει . . . περιπατεῖν. That is, he (the true Christian) ought to walk (in a pattern of life that mirrors the life of his Master).

καθὼς ἐκεῖνος περιεπάτησεν,
just as that one walked,

This brief clause reminds us that the pattern of life lived by Jesus is the template of love and sacrifice that Christians are to reflect. Ἐκεῖνος "that one," the nom. sg. masc. far dem. pron., is understood from context to refer to Jesus (consistent in letter; cf. 3:3, 5, 7, 16; 4:17). In his letters and Gospel, the apostle John demonstrates a propensity to use dem. prons. where other authors would more commonly employ pers. prons. Περιεπάτησεν is a 3rd pl. aor. act. indic. of περιπατέω. Beginning students will want to note how the augment comes after the prepositional prefix on compound vbs.

καὶ αὐτὸς οὕτως περιπατεῖν.
also he, in the same way, to walk.

Καὶ αὐτὸς οὕτως is an emphatic restatement of the idea found in the prior clause. The true Christian—*also he, in this same way* is supposed to walk. Περιπατεῖν is a complementary (Culy 31; on function, see KMP 365–66; BDF §392) pres. act. inf. of περιπατέω "walk," completing the verbal idea which has been hanging in abeyance since the reader encountered ὀφείλει "ought." Metzger (639–40) notes that the external evidence for including and excluding οὕτως is fairly evenly divided (included in ℵ C Ψ 81 et al.; omitted in A B 33 2464 et al.). The UBS[5] editors give it a "C" rating (indicating that the committee had difficulty in deciding).

FOR FURTHER STUDY

14. Ἱλασμός/Expiation/Propitiation (2:2)

Boice, J. M. "The Nature of the Atonement: Propitiation." Pages 31–47 in *Atonement*. Edited by Gabriel N. E. Fuhrer. Phillipsburg, NJ: P&R, 2010.
Büchsel, H. M. F., and J. Herrmann. *TDNT,* 3:301–23.
Dever, M. and L. Michael, eds. *It Is Well: Expositions on Substitutionary Atonement.* Wheaton, IL: Crossway, 2010.
Dodd, C. H. *The Bible and the Greeks*. London: Hodder and Stoughton, 1935 (see 82–95).
Fluhrer, G. N. E., ed. *Atonement.* Phillipsburg, NJ: P&R, 2010.
Hengel, Martin. *The Atonement: The Origins of the Doctrine in the New Testament.* Eugene, OR: Wipf & Stock, 2007.
Judisch, Douglas. "Propitiation in Old Testament Prophecy." *CTQ* 49, no. 1 (1985): 1–17.
———. "Propitiation in the Language and Typology of the Old Testament." *CTQ* 48, no. 2 (1984): 221–43.
Kruse, 75–76 (see "A Note on *Hilasmos*").
Morris, Leon. *The Apostolic Preaching of the Cross*. 3rd ed. Grand Rapids: Eerdmans. 1965 (see 144–213).
NIDNTTE 2:531–41.
Roloff, J. *EDNT,* 2:185–87.
Thornton, Timothy C. G. "Propitiation or Expiation." *ExpTim* 80, no. 2 (1968): 53–55.

15. Knowing God/Knowledge of the Believer (2:3)

Bavinck, 2:53–94.
Du Toit, B. A. "The Role and Meaning of Statements of 'Certainty' in the Structural Composition of 1 John." *Neot* 13 (1981): 84–100.
Frame, 770.
Lloyd-Jones, 73–82, 181–91.
Patzia, A. G. *DLNT,* 638–40.
Jobes, 238–40 (see "IN DEPTH: What We Know").
Packer, J. I. *Knowing God*. Downers Grove, IL: InterVarsity, 1973 (see 24–42).
Schmithals, W. *EDNT,* 1:248–51.

16. Love/Ἀγαπάω/Ἀγάπη Word Study (2:5)

BDAG 5b–7c.
Carson, D. A. *NDBT*, 646–50.
Günther, W., H. G. Link, and C. Brown. *NIDNTT,* 2:538–51.
Harrelson, Walter J. "The Idea of Agape in the New Testament." *The Journal of Religion* 31, no. 1 (1951): 169–82.
Lewis, C. S. *The Four Loves*. New York: Harcourt, 1960.
Moffat, J. *Love in the New Testament*. London: Hodder and Stoughton, 1929.
Morris, L. L. *DLNT*, 694–700.
———. *Testaments of Love: A Study of Love in the Bible.* Grand Rapids: Eerdmans, 1981.
NIDNTTE, 1:103–15.
Segovia, F. F. *Love Relationships in the Johannine Tradition: Agapē/Agapan in 1 John and the Fourth Gospel.* Chico, CA: Scholars, 1982.
Schneider, G. *EDNT,* 1:8–12.
Spicq, C. *Agape in the New Testament*. Translated by M. A. McNamara and M. H. Richter. 3 vols. Eugene, OR: Wipf & Stock, 1963–65.
Stauffer, E. and G. Quell. *TDNT,* 1:21–55.
Swinn, S. P. "Ἀγαπᾶν in the Septuagint." Pages 49–82 in *Melbourne Symposium on Septuagint Lexicography*. Edited by T. Muraoka. Atlanta: Society of Biblical Literature, 1990.
Turner, *Words*, 261–66.
Warfield B. B. "The Terminology of Love in the New Testament." *Princeton Theological Review* 16 (1918): 1–45, 153–203.

17. The Love of God (2:5)

Allred, Frank. *Rediscovering Gods Love: Are We Missing Out on the Greatest Love of All?* London: Grace Publications, 2005.
Berkhof, Hendrikus. *Christian Faith: An Introduction to the Study of the Faith*. Translated by Sierd Woudstra. Grand Rapids: Eerdmans, 1979 (see 118–32).
*Carson, D. A. *The Difficult Doctrine of the Love of God*. Wheaton, IL: Crossway, 1999.
Jobes, 197–98 (see "IN DEPTH: 'Love' in John's Letters").
Lloyd-Jones, 507–16.
Morris, L. L. *DLNT*, 694–700 (see esp. 694–95).

18. Abiding/Remaining/Μένω (2:6)

Harris, 134–36.
Hauck. *TDNT,* 4:574–76.
Jobes, 342–43 (see "Remaining in Christ").
Malesta, E. *Interiority and Covenant: A Study of* εἶναι ἐν *and* μένειν ἐν *in the First Letter of Saint John.* Analecta Biblica 69. Rome: Biblical Institute Press, 1978.
NIDNTTE 3:272–75.
Rainbow, Paul A. *Johannine Theology: The Gospel, the Epistles and the Apocalypse*. Downers Grove, IL: IVP Academic, 2014 (see 313–50).

HOMILETICAL SUGGESTIONS

Knowing God (2:1–6)

1. The reality of sin in the Christian life (vv. 1–2)
   a. Christ our advocate
   b. Christ the propitiation for our sins
2. The pattern of obedience in the Christian life (vv. 3–6)
   a. Knowing God
   b. Perfected love

IV. Old and New in the Light of the New Age (2:7–11)

This section begins with the voc. ἀγαπητοί "beloved ones," expressing John's deep love and care for the believers. Verses 7–8 introduces the command that is both old and new. It is the old command that they heard from the beginning (ἀπ' ἀρχῆς), which likely reflects the beginning of the community of faith. Πάλιν (v. 8) reflects an advers. sense. The command is also a new command in light of the new age. Verses 9–11 presents the contrast of one who remains in the light versus those who walk in darkness. Four substantival ptcs. in these two verses provide the contrasting examples. The initial phrase of v. 9 (ὁ λέγων ἐν τῷ φωτὶ εἶναι καὶ τὸν ἀδελφὸν αὐτοῦ μισῶν) functions as the subj. of the vb. The substantival ptcs. that begin v. 10 (ὁ ἀγαπῶν) and v. 11 (ὁ δέ μισῶν) reflect the contrasting examples (note postpositive δέ conveying an advers. sense) of those who walk in the light (1:5) versus darkness, respectively.

7 Ἀγαπητοί
οὐκ ἐντολὴν καινὴν γράφω ὑμῖν
ἀλλ' ἐντολὴν παλαιὰν
ἣν εἴχετε
ἀπ' ἀρχῆς
ἡ ἐντολὴ ἡ παλαιά ἐστιν ὁ λόγος
ὃν ἠκούσατε.

8 πάλιν
ἐντολὴν καινὴν γράφω ὑμῖν
ὅ ἐστιν ἀληθὲς
ἐν αὐτῷ
καὶ ἐν ὑμῖν,
ὅτι ἡ σκοτία παράγεται
καὶ τὸ φῶς τὸ ἀληθινὸν ἤδη φαίνει.

9 Ὁ λέγων ἐν τῷ φωτὶ εἶναι καὶ τὸν ἀδελφὸν αὐτοῦ μισῶν ἐν τῇ σκοτίᾳ ἐστὶν ἕως ἄρτι.

10 ὁ ἀγαπῶν τὸν ἀδελφὸν αὐτοῦ ἐν τῷ φωτὶ μένει,
καὶ σκάνδαλον ἐν αὐτῷ οὐκ ἔστιν·

11 ὁ δέ μισῶν τὸν ἀδελφὸν αὐτοῦ ἐν τῇ σκοτίᾳ ἐστὶν
καὶ ἐν τῇ σκοτίᾳ περιπατεῖ
καὶ οὐκ οἶδεν ποῦ ὑπάγει,
ὅτι ἡ σκοτία ἐτύφλωσεν τοὺς ὀφθαλμοὺς αὐτοῦ.

VERSE 7

Ἀγαπητοί, οὐκ ἐντολὴν καινὴν γράφω ὑμῖν
Beloved ones, not a new commandment I write to you all,

The form Ἀγαπητοί by itself is ambiguous. It is masc. pl., but it could be either voc. or nom. Context makes clear that John employs a voc., reassuring his readers of his pastoral love and alerting them that he is shifting to a different topic. Οὐκ is fronted for emphasis. Γράφω is 1st sg. pres. act. ind. Ὑμῖν is the dat. indir. obj. The term "new commandment" evokes Jesus's teaching from John's Gospel (John 13:34; 15:12, 17).

ἀλλ' ἐντολὴν παλαιὰν ἣν εἴχετε ἀπ' ἀρχῆς·
but an old commandment, which you all have had from the beginning.

The word παλαιός "old," only occurs nineteen times in the GNT. In alluding to Jesus's love command, John asserts that it is "old" in that the community has had the command "from the beginning." Here again, we encounter the puzzling and evocative phrase ἀπ' ἀρχῆς, which John employs to refer to several disparate situations (cf. 1:1; 2:7, 13, 14, 24; 3:8, 11). It seems likely that here John has the founding of the Christian community in view (so Kruse 82; Marshall 129; Stott 97; ZG 727; though cf. Brown 265; Culy 32; Yarbrough 97; see Hong). The command to love is old in that it was part of the initial teaching they received about what it meant to live as followers of Jesus. Εἴχετε is 2nd pl. impf. act. indic. of ἔχω "have." The spelling of the impf. form (progressive impf., so R 884; Young 115) is unusual because the actual root of ἔχω is σεχ. When the root is augmented to form the impf., the intervocalic sigma drops out and the two *epsilons* combine to become ει.

ἡ ἐντολὴ ἡ παλαιά ἐστιν ὁ λόγος ὃν ἠκούσατε.
This old commandment is the message which you all heard.

The art. preceding ἐντολή likely functions as an anaphoric art. or art. of previous reference (on this topic, see BW 74; Young 57–58), alerting the reader that "the old commandment" spoken of is the same one referred to in the immediately preceding context. This anaphoric use of the art. is brought out with the use of the near dem. pron. in English. Παλαιά "old," is acc. sg. fem. to attrib. match the noun it modifies. Ὁ λόγος is the pred. nom. The rel. pron. ὃν is both masc. and sg. to match its antecedent (ὁ λόγος). The case of ὃν (acc.) is determined by the usage in the sentence—in this case, as the dir. obj. of ἠκούσατε, the 2nd pl. aor. act. indic. of ἀκούω. The antiquity of the command is appealed to for its authority (Stott 97; see also Kruse 83; Marshall 128–29).

VERSE 8

Πάλιν ἐντολὴν καινὴν γράφω ὑμῖν
On the other hand, I am writing to you all a new commandment

Πάλιν normally means "again, once more, anew," but can also have an adversative nuance (cf. Matt 4:7; Luke 6:43; John 12:22; 1 Cor 12:2; BDAG 753a; BDF §449), as it does here ("on the other hand," NASB, NET). Γράφω is 1st sg. pres. act. ind. Ὑμῖν is the dat. pl. of the 2nd pers. pron. functioning as the indir. obj. Ἐντολὴν καινήν is the dir. obj. John alludes to the words of Jesus in his Gospel ("A new commandment I give to you: Love one another," John 13:34).

ὅ ἐστιν ἀληθὲς ἐν αὐτῷ καὶ ἐν ὑμῖν
the reality of which is true in him and in you all,

Ὅ is a nom. sg. neut. rel. pron., normally translated as "which, that." To do so here, however, would mislead the English reader into thinking that ἐντολὴν καινήν is the antecedent. Instead, the neut. rel. pron. refers to the entire prior clause (Marshall 129 n. 29; Moule 130; cf. Porter, *Idioms*, 25), as neut. rel. prons. sometimes do (Moule 130 notes Eph 5:5 as example; cf. also R 713). The somewhat paradoxical fact that John's instructions to love are "ever new" is shown to be true in the life of Christ (ἐν αὐτῷ, reference/respect, see BW 36; KMP 127–28; or metaphorical spherical, see KMP 129; Young 48) and the addressees of the letter (ἐν ὑμῖν, also reference/respect or metaphorical spherical) as they live as true Christians in a dark world. Ἀληθές is nom. sg. neut. of ἀληθής, -ές, "true," (BDAG 43b); "truly expressed," so Kruse (83).

ὅτι ἡ σκοτία παράγεται
for the darkness is passing away,

Ὅτι introduces a causal clause. Ἡ σκοτία, "darkness," is the nom. sg. fem. subj. Παράγεται is the 3rd sg. pres. mid. indic. of παράγω. Although in the act. voice παράγω means "pass by, go by a reference point," in the mid. voice, it frequently conveys the sense of "pass away" (CSB, ESV, NASB) or "disappear," as it does here (BDAG 761a; BDF §308; cf. LN §13.93).

καὶ τὸ φῶς τὸ ἀληθινὸν ἤδη φαίνει.
and the true light is already shining.

Τὸ φῶς (φῶς, φωτος, τό) is the nom. sg. neut. subj. modified by the attrib. adj. ἀληθινός, -ή, -όν, "true, genuine." The adv. ἤδη modifies φαίνει, and by including it, John challenges the recipients of the letter to reflect how the light of the new age is surprisingly already visible in some ways. Compare reading the verse with and without the adv. ἤδη. What is the difference of nuance? Φαίνει is 3rd sg. pres. act. indic. of φαίνω, "shine."

VERSE 9

Ὁ λέγων ἐν τῷ φωτὶ εἶναι καὶ τὸν ἀδελφὸν αὐτοῦ μισῶν
The person who claims to be in the light while also hating his brother

The entire Gk. phrase above functions as a large subj., with the art. ὁ governing two nom. masc. sg. subst. ptcs., λέγων and μισῶν. John speaks here of one person—the one who says X and hates Y. Εἶναι is a pres. inf. of εἰμί, communicating indir. discourse (Burton §390). The prep. phrase ἐν τῷ φωτί expresses a spherical or loc. idea (BDAG 326c). To be in the light is to be in the realm of God's people, living in the light of the new age's dawning, reflecting the God who is himself light. John asks his readers to consider a person whose behavior (hating a Christian brother) belies his verbal claims. Τὸν ἀδελφόν is the acc. dir. obj. of μισῶν. Αὐτοῦ is the gen. of personal relationship. John here, as throughout his letter (15×), employs ἀδελφός in a phenomenological way (BDAG 18c; for discussion on topic, see Brown 270–73). In other words, by stating that this person hates "his brother," John is not, by necessity, affirming that the claimant is ontologically a Christian brother.

ἐν τῇ σκοτίᾳ ἐστὶν ἕως ἄρτι.
is in the darkness until now.

The prep. phrase ἐν τῇ σκοτίᾳ communicates a loc. or spherical idea—the realm of fallen human existence apart from God's revealing and purifying light. On the term σκοτία, (here, 1:5; 2:9, 11) see BDAG 931d–32a; *NIDNTTE* 4:319–24; For Further Study 6 "Light and Darkness (Johannine Dualism)." Ἐστίν is 3rd sg. pres. indic. of εἰμί. The long Gk. phrase above (ὁ λέγων ἐν τῷ φωτὶ εἶναι καὶ τὸν ἀδελφὸν αὐτοῦ μισῶν) functions as the subj of ἐστίν. Ἐστίν is modified by the adv. phrase ἕως ἄρτι "until now." Read the verse with and without this final modifier. What different nuances are communicated? Ἕως ἄρτι perhaps speaks of the false claimant's longstanding and immediate culpability, while also holding open the possibility that he need not remain in the realm of hatred and darkness (see Hiebert 89).

VERSE 10

ὁ ἀγαπῶν τὸν ἀδελφὸν αὐτοῦ ἐν τῷ φωτὶ μένει,
Anyone who loves his brother or sister remains in the light,

As a masterful and methodological teacher, the apostle John lays out contrasting examples. Ἀγαπῶν is nom. sg. masc. of pres. act. ptc. of ἀγαπάω, functioning substantively. Τὸν ἀδελφόν is the acc. dir. obj. of ἀγαπῶν. Αὐτοῦ is a gen. of personal relationship. Μένει is 3rd sg. pres. act. indic. of μένω. The prep. phrase ἐν τῷ φωτί expresses a spherical or loc. idea (see BDAG 326c; R 585–86; see v. 9 above for more discussion of the mng. of the phrase).

καὶ σκάνδαλον ἐν αὐτῷ οὐκ ἔστιν·
and a cause for stumbling is not in him.

The person who loves his brother not only shows he is in the realm of God's revealing and purifying light; he is also positioned and dispositioned (in love) so as not to sin against others. There is no σκάνδαλον -ου, τό ("cause for stumbling," CSB, NASB, ESV; "stumbling block," Brown 274) in the person of love (on the term, see BDAG 926b–c, "temptation to sin, enticement"; LN §25.181; *NIDNTTE* 4:296). Σκάνδαλον is a nom. sg. neut. noun and functions as the subj. of ἔστιν, the 3rd sg. pres. indic. of εἰμί. The prep. phrase ἐν αὐτῷ functions in a metaphorical loc./spherical sense. Αὐτῷ should be understood as masc., referring to the believer ("in him/them," so most EVV, e.g., CSB, NASB, NIV, ESV; Culy 36; Kruse 86; Marshall 132 n. 38; contra Akin 99 and Smalley 62, who view it as referring to the light [τῷ φωτί]; so also RSV, "in it there is no cause for stumbling"). Finally, this final Gk. phrase of v. 10 (lit. "there is no stumbling in him") could be understood to convey that the *believer* does not stumble (NIV; Akin 99; Brown 275; Kruse 86; Marshall 132) or that the believer does not cause *others* to stumble (see Smalley 62, who notes potentially both views are in view).

VERSE 11

ὁ δὲ μισῶν τὸν ἀδελφὸν αὐτοῦ ἐν τῇ σκοτίᾳ ἐστὶν
But the one who hates his brother is in the darkness

The postpositive particle δέ here functions adversatively (something that can only be determined from context). Μισῶν is a nom. sg. masc. of pres. act. ptc. of μισέω, here functioning substantively. Τὸν ἀδελφόν is the acc. dir. obj of μισῶν. Αὐτοῦ is a gen. of personal relationship. Ἐστίν is 3rd sg. pres. indic. of εἰμί. The prep. phrase ἐν τῇ σκοτίᾳ, "in the darkness," is metaphorical spherical/loc. (see BDAG 326c; R 585–86). Darkness is the realm of fallen humans living apart from God's revealing and purifying light (cf. 1:6).

καὶ ἐν τῇ σκοτίᾳ περιπατεῖ
and walks around in the darkness,

John develops the metaphor to describe the person of hate not only in the realm of darkness but perambulating around in spiritual blindness. The prep. phrase ἐν τῇ σκοτίᾳ "in the darkness," is metaphorical spherical/loc. Περιπατεῖ is 3rd sg. pres. act. indic. of περιπατέω. In the Bible, "walking" often conveys the idea of a pattern or direction of life ("to conduct one's life," BDAG 803c; LN §41.11; cf. Prov 8:20 [LXX]; Eph 4:1; Col 1:10; 1 Thess 2:12).

καὶ οὐκ οἶδεν ποῦ ὑπάγει
and he does not know where he is going,

Οἶδεν is the 3rd sg. pf. act. indic. of οἶδα, an old pf. form with a pres. mng. and essentially synonymous with γινώσκω. Ποῦ "where," here functions adv. Ὑπάγει is 3rd sg. pres. act. indic. of ὑπάγω. In classical Gk., ὑπάγω had a more consistent sense of "depart, go away," but in the Koine period it frequently communicates movement without a specific directional nuance (cf. LN §15.15).

ὅτι ἡ σκοτία ἐτύφλωσεν τοὺς ὀφθαλμοὺς αὐτοῦ.
for the darkness has blinded his eyes.

῞Οτι introduces a causal clause. Σκοτία, -ας, ἡ is nom. sg. fem., functioning as the subj. of ἐτύφλωσεν, the 3rd sg. aor. act. indic. of τυφλόω ("make blind, to blind," BDAG 1020b; most EVV render the vb. as culminative aorist, so KMP 295; Young 123–24; for "has blinded," see e.g., CSB, ESV, NIV). Ὀφθαλμούς is the acc. pl. masc. of ὀφθαλμός, -οῦ, ὁ, functioning here as the dir. obj. of the vb. Αὐτοῦ is a gen. of poss. When a noun is qualified by a poss. pers. pron., the qualified noun usually is art., as here (τοὺς ὀφθαλμοὺς αὐτοῦ).

FOR FURTHER STUDY

19. Loving One Another (2:10)

Bonhoeffer, Dietrich. *Life Together: The Classic Exploration of Christian Community*. Translated by John W Doberstein. New York: HarperOne, 1954 (see 17–39, 90–122).
Furnish, V. P. *The Love Command in the New Testament*. Nashville: Abingdon, 1972.
Hellerman, Joseph H. *The Ancient Church as Family*. Minneapolis: Fortress, 2001.
Jobes, 344–45 (see "Love for God, Love for Others").
Lloyd-Jones, 191–200, 357–66.
McKnight, S. *The Jesus Creed: Loving God, Loving Others*. Brewster, MA: Paraclete, 2004.
Piper, J. *"Love Your Enemies": Jesus's Love Command in the Synoptic Gospels and the Early Christian Paranesis*. SNTSMS 38. Cambridge: Cambridge University Press, 1979.
Skinner, Christopher W. "Love One Another: The Johannine Love Command in the Farewell Discourse." Pages 25–42 in *Johannine Ethics: The Moral World of the Gospel in the Epistles of John*. Edited by Sherri Brown and Christopher W. Skinner. Minneapolis: Fortress, 2017.
Strauch, Alexander. *Love or Die: Christ's Wake-Up Call to the Church*. Littleton, CO: Lewis & Roth, 2008.

HOMILETICAL SUGGESTIONS

An Old and New Command in the Light of a New Era (2:7–11)

1. An old command from the beginning (v. 7)
2. A new command as light breaks into the darkness (v. 8)
3. Walking in the light and loving one another (vv. 9–11)

V. Encouragement to the Church (2:12–14)

In this section, John offers encouraging words to the church, twice addressing three distinct groups (children, fathers, young men). All six of the main vbs. in this section are in the 1st pers. sg. Although John writes as a representative of the apostolic community, he writes as an individual leader. Verses 12–13 reflect three vocatives (v. 12: τεκνία; v. 13: πατέρες, νεανίσκοι) followed again by three vocatives in v. 14 (παιδία, πατέρες, νεανίσκοι). The pres. tense of the main vb. used three times to address each group in vv. 12–13 shifts to the aor. tense in v. 14 to address each group. This shift in tense is likely to set off v. 14 as the second half of this poetic section of encouragement in vv. 12–14. Each main vb. is followed by a ὅτι, which conveys the reason (causal) for his writing. The subordinate phrases offer encouragement and assurance to each group addressed in the twice repeated structure.

12 Γράφω ὑμῖν, τεκνία,
    ὅτι ἀφέωνται ὑμῖν αἱ ἁμαρτίαι
        διὰ τὸ ὄνομα αὐτοῦ.

13 γράφω ὑμῖν, πατέρες,
    ὅτι ἐγνώκατε τὸν ἀπ᾽ ἀρχῆς.
γράφω ὑμῖν, νεανίσκοι,
    ὅτι νενικήκατε τὸν πονηρόν.

14 ἔγραψα ὑμῖν, παιδία,
    ὅτι ἐγνώκατε τὸν πατέρα.
ἔγραψα ὑμῖν, πατέρες,
    ὅτι ἐγνώκατε τὸν ἀπ᾽ ἀρχῆς.
ἔγραψα ὑμῖν, νεανίσκοι,
    ὅτι ἰσχυροί ἐστε
        καὶ ὁ λόγος τοῦ θεοῦ ἐν ὑμῖν μένει
        καὶ νενικήκατε τὸν πονηρόν.

VERSE 12

Γράφω ὑμῖν, τεκνία,
I write to you all, dear children,

Although John has used a 1st pl. on several occasions, here he employs the 1st sg. We are reminded that ultimately this letter comes from a singular leader, though John often speaks with the witness and authority of the entire apostolic community in view. Γράφω is 1st sg. pres. act. ind. Ὑμῖν is the dat. indir. obj. Τεκνία is the voc. of the diminutive form τεκνίον ("little child, dear child," 7× in the GNT). The diminutive ending (-ιον) can express affection or smallness. John reminds his readers of his care for them and their spiritual dependance upon him.

The voc. is the first of three (v. 12: τεκνία; v. 13: πατέρες, νεανίσκοι), which are repeated in v. 14 (παιδία, πατέρες, νεανίσκοι). Broadly, the possible interpretations concerning the twice-repeated, threefold vocs. in vv. 12–14 reflect the writer referring to either three groups, two groups, or one group:

*1. The writer is addressing three different groups in the church, using the labels metaphorically to reflect different stages of spiritual development (Stott 100; cf. Jobes 105, who seems to roughly align).
2. The writer is addressing all his readers as "children" (as he does elsewhere in the letter) and then addresses two specific groups ("young men" and "fathers") under the larger category of "children" (τεκνία, παιδία) (most commentators surveyed, e.g., Culy 38–39; Kruse 88; Smalley 67; Yarbrough 114).
3. The writer is simply using the vocs. as a "rhetorical device to indicate qualities, appropriate to the three stages of life, which ought to be true of all believers" (Marshall 138).

ὅτι ἀφέωνται ὑμῖν αἱ ἁμαρτίαι διὰ τὸ ὄνομα αὐτοῦ.
because your sins have been forgiven on account of his name.

Ὅτι can introduce communicative content ("that," NET; Kruse 88 n. 62; Z §416) or introduce a causal clause ("because," most EVV, e.g., NASB, NIV, ESV; Yarbrough 120–21). The difference in mng. is slight (Brown 301; Jobes 107; Marshall 136), but it seems the causal translation is perhaps more likely in this literary context. John has said some hard-hitting things, but here he turns to reassure his readers that their shared filial status is ultimately the reason behind his letter. Ἁμαρτίαι is nom. pl. fem. of ἁμαρτία, -ας, ἡ, "sin, wrongdoing," functioning as the subj. of ἀφέωνται, the 3rd pl. pf. pass. indic. of ἀφίημι "forgiven" (see 1:9). The vb. should be labeled a so-called divine passive, implying God as the agent of the action. The pf. vb. speaks of a completed action with an ongoing state. They stand forgiven. The text literalistically reads, "the sins have been forgiven to you." The poss. idea ("your" sins) is clearly implied by the dat. of advantage ὑμῖν. The prep. phrase διὰ τὸ ὄνομα αὐτοῦ communicates the reason for the recipients' forgiveness—"his name," most likely referring to the name of Jesus (so most commentators surveyed, e.g., Akin 104; Kruse 88–89; Marshall 138–39;

Smalley 68; Stott 101), meaning *who* Jesus is and *what* he has done is the reason that God's people are forgiven of their sins. Ὄνομα is the acc. sg. neut. obj. of the prep. Αὐτοῦ is a gen. of poss.

VERSE 13

γράφω ὑμῖν, πατέρες,
I write to you all, fathers,

Γράφω is 1st sg. pres. act. indic. of γράφω. The 1st sg. form reminds us that an *individual* apostle is ultimately the inspired author behind this letter. Ὑμῖν is the dat. indir. obj. Πατέρες is the voc. of πατήρ "father." John apparently uses the term to address the spiritually mature members of the congregation, whose constancy of relationship with the Lord reflects (in some ways) the eternal existence of the Second Person of the triune God. It is unlikely that only mature *male* members of the congregation are in view.

ὅτι ἐγνώκατε τὸν ἀπ' ἀρχῆς.
because you have known the One from the beginning.

Ὅτι most likely introduces a causal clause (see v. 12). Ἐγνώκατε is the 2nd pl. pf. act. indic. of γινώσκω. The pf. tense communicates that there was a prior point at which these "fathers in the faith" came to know the Lord, and they now remain in a relationship with him (stative aspect). The art. τόν substantivizes or nominalizes the prep. phrase ἀπ' ἀρχῆς. In other words, the art. turns the prep. phrase into a noun—"the One from the beginning" (on this function of the art., see BDF §266; Wallace 236; Hong). The text above clearly alludes to 1:1, where the reference to God the Son is clear (so most commentators surveyed, e.g., Culy 40 [views reference as to Christ's preexistence]; Kruse 90 [reference to incarnation]; contra Stott 101 [reference to God the Father]). Ἀρχῆς is anar., but definite from context. Objects of preps. frequently lack an art. even when definite (cf. 1 John 4:2; 2 John 10, 12; 3 John 15; see BDF §255; R 791–92; Wallace 247; Z §136).

γράφω ὑμῖν, νεανίσκοι,
I write to you all, young men,

Γράφω is 1st sg. pres. act. indic. of γράφω. Ὑμῖν is the dat. indir. obj. Νεανίσκοι is the voc. of νεανίσκος ("young man," 11× in GNT). As with πατέρες above, it is unlikely that only male members of the congregation are addressed here.

ὅτι νενικήκατε τὸν πονηρόν.
because you have conquered the evil one.

Ὅτι most likely introduces a causal clause (see v. 12). Νενικήκατε is the 2nd pl. pf. act. indic. of νικάω (Smalley 71 and Stott 102 see possible deliberate assonance with νεανίσκοι). The pf. tense communicates that there was a prior point at which these "young warriors in the faith" conquered the evil one (the devil), and they now stand in victory (stative aspect). They have conquered the evil one by escaping from his domain and resisting his lies and temptations. And yet, the language evokes the sense that they must stand ready for battle. Τὸν πονηρόν refers to the devil (as in vv. 2:14; 3:12; 5:18, 19) and is a subst. use of the adj. (see For Further Study 20 "Satan/Evil One").

VERSE 14

ἔγραψα ὑμῖν, παιδία,
I write to you all, dear children,

Although ἔγραψα is a 1st sg. aor. act. indic. of γράφω, most EVV render it in the present tense ("I write," ESV, NIV; cf. "I have written," CSB, NASB). Scholarship varies concerning the reason for the shift from γράφω to ἔγραψα. It appears that John's main purpose for the tense variation for the verb γράφω is to set off v. 14 as the second stanza of his poetic affirmation. Other interpretations of the shift to the aor. include the following: it refers to a previous letter (Turner, *Syntax*, 73 §3); it refers to the earlier part of the letter; it refers to the letter as a whole versus the process of writing (see Kruse 87 n. 59, 91, who adds that it functions stylistically to heighten the rhetorical effect; cf. discussion in Porter, *Idioms*, 36–37); it reflects a stylistic variant (Brown 297), or simply functions as an epistolary aor. with little interpretive significance (Stott 100; cf. ZG 728). Some scholars note the significance of the present as "more heavily marked" than the aor. (Yarbrough 121 notes the tense in this context conveys "a relatively higher degree of feeling and urgency"; cf. Culy 41; also see Porter, *Idioms*, 37). For helpful overviews of interpretations, see Brown 294–97; Smalley 72–74. Γράφω appears in many later mss., though ἔγραψα is noted as certain by the UBS[5] editors. Metzger writes, "Scribes of the later manuscripts (followed by Textus Receptus) absent-mindedly wrote γράφω in accord with the three previous instances of the present tense" (640). Ὑμῖν is the dat. indir. obj. of the 2nd pl. personal pron. Παιδία is the voc. pl. neut. of παιδίον, a diminutive form of παῖς, expressing affection or smallness (-ιον is the most common diminutive ending). There does not seem to be a significant difference between John's use of τεκνία (2:1, 12, 28; 3:18; 4:4; 5:21) and παιδία (2:14, 18; 3:7; see Kruse 88 n. 61; Smalley 65).

ὅτι ἐγνώκατε τὸν πατέρα.
because you have known the Father.

Ὅτι most likely introduces a causal clause (see v. 12). Ἐγνώκατε is 2nd pl. pf. act. indic. of γινώσκω. The pf. tense conveys a stative aspect. These "dear children" (spiritually young believers) came to know God the Father in the past and now are in relationship with him. Although all Christians know the Father, new Christians are distinctly and experientially aware that the God who was formerly their estranged and distant judge has now become their loving heavenly Father.

ἔγραψα ὑμῖν, πατέρες,
I write to you all, fathers,

Ἔγραψα is a 1st sg. aor. act. indic. of γράφω. Ὑμῖν is the dat. indir. obj. of the 2nd pl. personal pron. Πατέρες is the voc. pl. of πατήρ, πατρός, ὁ, "father."

ὅτι ἐγνώκατε τὸν ἀπ' ἀρχῆς.
because you have known the One from the beginning.

Ὅτι most likely introduces a causal clause (see v. 12). Ἐγνώκατε is the 2nd pl. pf. act. indic. of γινώσκω. The art. τόν substantivizes or nominalizes the prep. phrase ἀπ' ἀρχῆς. In other words, the art. turns the prep. phrase into a noun—"the One from the beginning" (see v. 13). On this topic, see Hong.

ἔγραψα ὑμῖν, νεανίσκοι,
I write to you all, young men,

Ἔγραψα is a 1st sg. aor. act. indic. of γράφω. Ὑμῖν is the dat. indir. obj. of the 2nd pl. personal pron. Νεανίσκοι is the voc. of νεανίσκος, -ου, ὁ ("young man," 11× in GNT; see v. 13).

ὅτι ἰσχυροί ἐστε καὶ ὁ λόγος τοῦ θεοῦ ἐν ὑμῖν μένει καὶ νενικήκατε τὸν πονηρόν.
because you are strong and the word of God remains in you all and you have conquered the evil one.

Ὅτι most likely introduces a causal clause (see v. 12). The implied subj. (ὑμεῖς) is conveyed by the vb. form, ἐστε, the 2nd pl. pres. indic. of εἰμί. Ἰσχυροί is the nom. pl. masc. of ἰσχυρός, -ά, -όν, "strong," functioning as a pred. nom. Ὁ λόγος is nom. sg. masc. functioning as the subj. of μένει, the 3rd sg. pres. act. indic. of μένω. Θεοῦ is the gen. sg. masc. of θεός, possibly best classified as a gen. of source or obj. gen. Note that both the head noun (ὁ λόγος) and the gen. that qualifies it (τοῦ θεοῦ) are articular as expected by Apollonius's Canon (see 1:1). Ἐν ὑμῖν is a prep. phrase expressing a metaphorical loc./spherical sense (see BDAG 326c; R 585–86). Νενικήκατε is the 2nd pl. pf. act. indic. of νικάω. Τὸν πονηρόν is the subst. use of the adj. πονηρός functioning as the dir. obj. of νενικήκατε (see v. 13).

FOR FURTHER STUDY

20. Satan/The Evil One (2:13)

Alexander, T. Desmond. *From Eden to the New Jerusalem: An Introduction to Biblical Theology*. Grand Rapids: Kregel, 2013 (see 98–120).
Arnold, C. E. *DLNT*, 1077–82.
———. *NBDT*, 796–801.
Bell, R. H. *DJG*, 193–202.
Böcher, O. *EDNT*, 1:297–98.
Brown, Derek R. "The Devil in the Details: A Survey of Research on Satan in Biblical Studies." *Currents in Biblical Research* 9, no. 2 (2011): 200–227.
Day, P. L. *An Adversary in Heaven: Satan in the Hebrew Bible.* Atlanta: Scholars, 1988.
Foerster, W. *TDNT*, 7:151–63.
Foerster, W., and G. von Rad. *TDNT*, 2:71–81.
Frame, 775–77.
Fuller, D. P. *ISBE*, 4:340–44.
Grudem, 412–15.

Hamilton, V. P. *ABD,* 5:985–89.
Hiers, Richard H. "Satan, Demons, and the Kingdom of God." *SJT* 27, no. 1 (1974): 35–47.
NIDNTTE 1:691–92.
*Page, Sydney H. T. *Powers of Evil: A Biblical Study of Satan and Demons*. Grand Rapids: Baker Academic, 1994.
Reid, D. G. *DPL*, 862–67.
Russell, J. B. *Satan: The Early Christian Tradition.* Ithaca: Cornell University Press, 1981.
Yates, Roy. "The Powers of Evil in the New Testament." *EvQ* 52 (1980): 97–111.

HOMILETICAL SUGGESTIONS

Encouragement and Assurance to the Church (2:12–14)

1. A word to the children
   a. Forgiven in Christ (v.12)
   b. Knowing the Father (v. 13)
2. A word to fathers: you know Christ (vv. 13–14)
3. A word to the young men
   a. You have victory over the evil one (vv. 13–14)
   b. You are strong from the word of God that abides in you (v. 14)

VI. Warning about the World (2:15–17)

Shifting from encouraging words to the church (vv. 12–14), this section begins with an impv. (v. 15), offering a warning against loving the world (with ὁ κόσμος reflecting the realm of opposition to God). The impv. is followed by a ὅτι clause (v. 16) explaining the reason for the exhortation, highlighting that everything in the world (listing three elements of the world in apposition to πᾶν τὸ ἐν τῷ κόσμῳ) is not from the Father. The two statements of v. 17 reflect a contrast between the world (which is passing away) and the one who does God's will (who remains forever).

15 Μὴ ἀγαπᾶτε τὸν κόσμον
μηδὲ τὰ ἐν τῷ κόσμῳ.
↓ἐάν τις ἀγαπᾷ τὸν κόσμον,
οὐκ ἔστιν ἡ ἀγάπη τοῦ πατρὸς ἐν αὐτῷ·

16 ὅτι πᾶν τὸ ἐν τῷ κόσμῳ, = | ἡ ἐπιθυμία τῆς σαρκὸς
καὶ ἡ ἐπιθυμία τῶν ὀφθαλμῶν
καὶ ἡ ἀλαζονεία τοῦ βίου,
οὐκ ἔστιν ἐκ τοῦ πατρὸς
ἀλλ' ἐκ τοῦ κόσμου ἐστίν.

17 καὶ ὁ κόσμος παράγεται
καὶ ἡ ἐπιθυμία αὐτοῦ [*παράγεται*],
ὁ δὲ ποιῶν τὸ θέλημα τοῦ θεοῦ μένει εἰς τὸν αἰῶνα.

VERSE 15

Μὴ ἀγαπᾶτε τὸν κόσμον μηδὲ τὰ ἐν τῷ κόσμῳ.
Do not love the world nor the things in the world.

Μή negates the 2nd pl. pres. act. impv. of ἀγαπάω. The pres. impv. (the first of ten in the letter; cf. 2:24, 27, 28; 3:1, 7, 13; 4:1 [2×]; 5:21) is used to forbid the activity in a general sense. Also, the pres. tense (as opposed to aor.) is expected because the procedural nature of the vb. is more naturally described with imperfective aspect. Κόσμον is acc.

sg. masc. of *κόσμος, -ου, ὁ*, functioning as a dir. obj. *Κόσμος* occurs twenty-three times in 1 John and reflects a range of meanings depending on context. Marshall notes that here, John "is thinking of the source of opposition to God and temptation to sin" (142; see also Jobes 114–15; Stott 105–7). *Μηδέ* continues the negation with an ellipsis of *ἀγαπᾶτε*. The dir. obj. of the implied impv. is *τὰ ἐν τῷ κόσμῳ*. Here *τά* nominalizes or substantivizes the prep. phrase *ἐν τῷ κόσμῳ* (BW 79; KMP 426; Young 60). The prep. phrase functions in a metaphorical loc./spatial sense (see BDAG 326c; R 585–86).

ἐάν τις ἀγαπᾷ τὸν κόσμον,
If anyone loves the world,

Ἐάν introduces a third class cond. clause and by necessity will be followed by a subjunc. vb. The prot. presents a topic for consideration (on third class cond., see 1:6). *Τις* is the nom. sg. masc. indef. pron. *Ἀγαπᾷ* is 3rd sg. pres. act. subj. of *ἀγαπάω*. *Κόσμον* is acc. sg. masc. of *κόσμος*, functioning as a dir. obj. of *ἀγαπᾷ*.

οὐκ ἔστιν ἡ ἀγάπη τοῦ πατρὸς ἐν αὐτῷ·
the love of the Father is not in him,

Ἀγάπη is nom. sg. fem. functioning as subj. of *ἔστιν*, the 3rd sg. pres. indic. of *εἰμί*. *Πατρός* is the gen. sg. masc. of *πατήρ*, serving as the obj. gen. (Young 31; Jobes 111; Kruse 95; Yarbrough 130) of the head noun *ἀγάπη*. Love for God the Father and for the world are mutually exclusive (Stott 103; also Marshall 143; cf. Jas 4:4). The prep. phrase *ἐν αὐτῷ* functions in a metaphorical loc./spatial sense.

VERSE 16

ὅτι πᾶν τὸ ἐν τῷ κόσμῳ,
because everything in the world,

Ὅτι is causal and introduces an explanation as to why one cannot love both the Father and the world. *Τό* substantivizes/nominalizes the prep. phrase *ἐν τῷ κόσμῳ*, "the thing in the world," which is then modified by *πᾶν*, resulting in "everything in the world." *Κόσμῳ* is dat. sg. masc. of *κόσμος* (see 1:5). The noun is dat., as required of all objects of *ἐν*.

ἡ ἐπιθυμία τῆς σαρκὸς καὶ ἡ ἐπιθυμία τῶν ὀφθαλμῶν καὶ ἡ ἀλαζονεία τοῦ βίου,
the evil desire of the flesh and the evil desire of the eyes and the boasting in one's possessions,

Ἐπιθυμία can refer to both positive or negative desires, but the context here is clearly negative ("lust," CSB, NASB, NIV; BDAG 372b–c). These three nominatives (*ἡ ἐπιθυμία . . . καὶ ἡ ἐπιθυμία . . . καὶ ἡ ἀλαζονεία*) are in appos. to *πᾶν τὸ ἐν τῷ κόσμῳ* above. *Σαρκός* (from *σάρξ, ἡ*), is a subj. gen. (Moule 40; Jobes 112; Smalley 79; ZG 728; contra Yarbrough 132, who views it as obj. gen.; cf. Turner, *Style*, 135). Here "the flesh" refers to human nature in its fallen and debased state. The "worldliness" that John hones in on is the sinful cravings and vauntings of fallen humans. Apollonius's Canon (see 1:1) is represented three times in this clause with each articular head noun being qualified by an articular gen. Ὀφθαλμῶν is the gen. pl. masc. of ὀφθαλμός, -οῦ, ὁ, "eye," and functions as a subj. gen. (Smalley 80). Ἀλαζονεία ("pride, boasting"or "arrogant boasting," A. Sand, *EDNT* 1:56d; on the term also see *NIDNTTE* 1:213–15; Delling, *TDNT* 1:226–27) is nom. sg. fem. Βίου is the gen. sg. masc. of βίος, -ου, ὁ, "life, sustenance of life, belongings," and functions here as an obj. gen. ("pride in one's possessions," BDAG 41d; CSB; "the pride in worldly possessions," LN §57.18; "boasting of what he has and does," Stott 103); contra NET, which views it as subj. gen. (i.e., "arrogance produced by material possessions"). Βίος has an almost identical semantic nuance in its only other appearance in 1 John (3:17).

οὐκ ἔστιν ἐκ τοῦ πατρὸς ἀλλ' ἐκ τοῦ κόσμου ἐστίν.
is not from the Father but is from the world.

At first glance, the completion of the sentence in v. 16 seems puzzling: "because everything in the world . . . is from the world." Through pleonastic, overlapping categories, John makes unmistakable that the fallen world system, with fist raised towards God, cannot be integrated in any way into a true Christian's priorities. Ἔστιν (2×) is 3rd sg. pres. indic. of εἰμί. The prep. phrase ἐκ τοῦ πατρός conveys an idea of source (BDAG 296c) and fills the grammatical slot of a pred. nom. Likewise, the prep. phrase ἐκ τοῦ κόσμου communicates source/origin (cf. 4:5; on prep., see BDAG 296d) and functions in the same way a pred. nom. would.

VERSE 17

καὶ ὁ κόσμος παράγεται καὶ ἡ ἐπιθυμία αὐτοῦ,
And the world and its evil desire are passing away,

The sinful world system gives an illusion of stability, but it is a mirage. Παράγεται is the 3rd sg. pres. mid. indic. of παράγω. Although in the act. voice παράγω means "pass by, go by a reference point," in the mid. voice it frequently conveys the sense of "pass away" (CSB, ESV, NASB) or "disappear," as it does here (BDAG 761a; BDF §308). See John's similar use of it in 2:8. The nom. sg. subj. ὁ κόσμος is initially followed by the vb. παράγεται and then the subj. is expanded to include ἡ ἐπιθυμία αὐτοῦ (a Pindaric constr.; see KMP 46; R 404–5). Alternately, one could postulate an ellipsis of a second παράγεται in the latter half of the clause. Αὐτοῦ is a subj. gen.

ὁ δὲ ποιῶν τὸ θέλημα τοῦ θεοῦ μένει εἰς τὸν αἰῶνα.
but the person doing the will of God remains forever.

True, eternal stability is found in relationship to God, as expressed by submission to his Word. The postpositive particle δέ carries the conversation forward, but it is only the context that indicates an advers. sense "but." Ὁ ποιῶν, functioning as the subj. of μένει, is the subst. use of the ptc. (nom. sg. masc. of pres. act. ptc. of ποιέω). Τὸ θέλημα "will," is the acc. sg. neut. dir. obj. of the ptc. ποιῶν. Θεοῦ is a subj. gen. (Culy 46). The prep. phrase εἰς τὸν αἰῶνα ("forever," most EVV, e.g., CSB, NET, NIV; "eternity," BDAG 32b–c; 289d) is rendered literalistically "into the age." Some interpreters question if we miss the biblical expectation of a coming everlasting age by employing the gloss of "forever." Others question if the phrase εἰς τὸν αἰῶνα carries such weight and suggest, rather, that idiomatically the Greek phrase had come to be synonymous with the English adverb "forever" (on the phrase, see Harris 94; *NIDNTTE* 1:196).

FOR FURTHER STUDY

21. World/Κόσμος in John's Letters and the New Testament (2:15–17)

Balz, H. *EDNT,* 2:309–13.
BDAG 561b–63a.
Bratcher, Robert Galveston. "The Meaning of Kosmos, 'World', in the New Testament." *BT* 31, no. 4 (1980): 430–34.
Cassem, N H. "Grammatical and Contextual Inventory of the Use of Κόσμος in the Johannine Corpus with Some Implications for a Johannine Cosmic Theology." *NTS* 19, no. 1 (1972): 81–91.
Dodd, B. J. *DLNT*, 1222–24.
Jobes, 114–15 (see "IN DEPTH: The 'World' in John's Letters").
Muller, R. A. *ISBE,* 4:1112–16.
NIDNTTE 2:730–36.
Renz, T. *NDBT,* 853–55.
Sasse, H. *TDNT,* 3:867–98.
See also For Further Study 7 "Obedience/Christian Growth"

HOMILETICAL SUGGESTIONS

A Warning about the World (2:15–17)

1. The love of the world vs. the love of the Father (v. 15)
   a. A clear warning
   b. No middle ground
2. Enticement of the world (v. 16)
   a. Desires of the flesh
   b. Desires of the eyes
   c. Boasting in one's possessions
3. A dying world and eternal life (v. 17)

Either/Or (2:15–17)

1. Do not love the world.
   a. "The world" as used by John here: system of defiant rebellion against the nature and will of God.
   b. The things in the world are of the world (v. 16)
      (1) Desires of the flesh
      (2) Desires of the eyes
      (3) Boasting in one's possessions

  c. The world is passing away as the reign of God breaks in upon this present world (v. 17)
    (1) Inaugurated with the coming of Christ
    (2) Completed at his return
2. Either love for God or love for the world; we cannot love both (v. 15)
  a. What this doesn't mean: Not "loving the world" in the sense of John 3:16. We are called to reflect the love of Christ.
  b. What this does mean: devotion, worship, allegiance, service, commitment, etc. is to God alone.

VII. Warning against the Antichrist (2:18–27)

This section offers a warning against the antichrists and offers encouragement to the readers. Verse 18 opens with another voc. ("children") and describes the arrival of many antichrists (ἀντίχριστοι πολλοί). These antichrists are the false teachers who have seceded from the community. The ἵνα (v. 19) provides the reason why they departed. John's paratactic style continues as he encourages the faithful concerning these antichrists in vv. 20–21. They have τὸ χρῖσμα that will guard them against ὁ ἀντίχριστος. The three ὅτι conjunctions likely all function causally in v. 21, conveying that the author writes *because* they do know the truth. Verse 22 begins with a question, and (along with v. 23) further highlights the nature of the antichrist as the one who denies that Jesus is the Christ. Verse 24 begins with a pendent nominative, reflecting the contrast of the believers with those who have departed. The believers remain in the Father and the Son. The third class cond. in v. 24 highlights a condition: "if" they hold on to the gospel message they received in the beginning. Verse 27 returns to the topic of their anointing, which provides the foundational truth they need in confronting the false teachers. The impv. μένετε concludes the section. The believers are to hold fast to the teaching and remain in Christ. The dative sg. pron. αὐτῷ could refer to the teaching, but v. 28 of the next section clarifies it refers to Christ.

18 Παιδία, ἐσχάτη ὥρα ἐστίν,
καὶ ↓καθὼς ἠκούσατε ὅτι ἀντίχριστος ἔρχεται,
↓καὶ νῦν
ἀντίχριστοι πολλοὶ γεγόνασιν,
ὅθεν γινώσκομεν ὅτι ἐσχάτη ὥρα ἐστίν.

19 ἐξ ἡμῶν ἐξῆλθαν
ἀλλ' οὐκ ἦσαν ἐξ ἡμῶν,
↓εἰ γὰρ ἐξ ἡμῶν ἦσαν,
μεμενήκεισαν ἂν μεθ' ἡμῶν—
ἀλλ' [*ἐξῆλθαν*]
ἵνα φανερωθῶσιν ὅτι οὐκ εἰσὶν πάντες ἐξ ἡμῶν.

20 καὶ ὑμεῖς χρῖσμα ἔχετε
ἀπὸ τοῦ ἁγίου
καὶ οἴδατε πάντες.

21 οὐκ ἔγραψα ὑμῖν
ὅτι οὐκ οἴδατε τὴν ἀλήθειαν
ἀλλ' [*ἔγραψα*]
ὅτι οἴδατε αὐτὴν
καὶ ὅτι πᾶν ψεῦδος ἐκ τῆς ἀληθείας οὐκ ἔστιν.

22 Τίς ἐστιν ὁ ψεύστης
εἰ μὴ ὁ ἀρνούμενος ὅτι Ἰησοῦς οὐκ ἔστιν ὁ Χριστός;
οὗτός ἐστιν ὁ ἀντίχριστος = ὁ ἀρνούμενος τὸν πατέρα
καὶ τὸν υἱόν.

23 πᾶς ὁ ἀρνούμενος τὸν υἱὸν οὐδὲ τὸν πατέρα ἔχει,
ὁ ὁμολογῶν τὸν υἱὸν καὶ τὸν πατέρα ἔχει.

24 ὑμεῖς
ὃ ἠκούσατε
ἀπ' ἀρχῆς,
ἐν ὑμῖν μενέτω.
ἐὰν ἐν ὑμῖν μείνῃ
ὃ ἀπ' ἀρχῆς ἠκούσατε,
καὶ ὑμεῖς ἐν τῷ υἱῷ καὶ ἐν τῷ πατρὶ μενεῖτε.

25 καὶ αὕτη ἐστὶν ἡ ἐπαγγελία
ἣν αὐτὸς ἐπηγγείλατο ἡμῖν = τὴν ζωὴν τὴν αἰώνιον.

26 Ταῦτα ἔγραψα ὑμῖν
περὶ τῶν πλανώντων ὑμᾶς.

27 καὶ ὑμεῖς
τὸ χρῖσμα
ὃ ἐλάβετε
ἀπ' αὐτοῦ
μένει ἐν ὑμῖν
καὶ οὐ χρείαν ἔχετε
ἵνα τις διδάσκῃ ὑμᾶς,
ἀλλ'
ὡς τὸ αὐτοῦ χρῖσμα διδάσκει ὑμᾶς
περὶ πάντων,
καὶ ἀληθές ἐστιν
καὶ οὐκ ἔστιν ψεῦδος,
καὶ καθὼς ἐδίδαξεν ὑμᾶς
μένετε ἐν αὐτῷ

VERSE 18

Παιδία, ἐσχάτη ὥρα ἐστίν,
Dear children, it is the last hour,

Παιδία is the voc. pl. neut. of παιδίον, -ου, τό, a diminutive form of παῖς, expressing affection or smallness (-ιον is the most common diminutive ending). Ἐστίν is 3rd sg. pres. indic. of εἰμί, with an implied impersonal subj. "it." Ὥρα, "hour," nom. sg. fem., functions as the pred. nom. and is modified attrib. by ἐσχάτη "last." From context, the time spoken of is specific, so a def. art. is provided in English translation ("*the* last hour"; on the phrase, see Smalley 90–93; Stott 111–13; For Further Study 23 "Eschatology/Last Hour"). A def. pred. nom. that precedes the copulative vb. is expected to be anar. nearly 90 percent of the time (Colwell's Rule; see 1:2). John reminds his readers (and us) that we live in the final stage of world history (see Marshall 148). We no longer await the revelation of the Messiah or the completion of his saving work. We only await his return, living in a sinful world that is in its final throes of rebellion.

καὶ καθὼς ἠκούσατε ὅτι ἀντίχριστος ἔρχεται,
and just as you heard that Antichrist is coming,

Ἠκούσατε is 2nd pl. aor. act. indic. of ἀκούω. Ὅτι introduces indir. discourse (most EVV) or perhaps dir. discourse, "Antichrist is coming!" Though lacking in some mss., ὅτι is strongly supported by א* B C Ψ 5 1739 et al., receiving a "B" rating (almost certain) from the UBS[5] editors. The conj. is followed by the masc. art. in some mss. (א[2] A L 1881 et al.), likely introduced by scribes to emphasize the anar. noun ἀντίχριστος, -ου, ὁ, "one who is opposed to Christ, in the sense of usurping the role of Christ" (LN §53.83; on this term, see also BDAG 90a; MM 49b–c; For Further Study 22 "Antichrist"). Only in John's Letters does the term ἀντίχριστος "antichrist," appear (2:18, 22; 4:3; 2 John 7), though the idea of an eschatological arch-opponent of Christ and his people is testified to elsewhere in Scripture (2 Thess 2:1–10 and the man of lawlessness; cf. Matt 24:24; Mark 13:22; Rev 12–13). Ἔρχεται is 3rd sg. pres. mid. indic. of ἔρχομαι. As in English, Gk. verbs of motion in the pres. tense can express an imminent future idea.

καὶ νῦν ἀντίχριστοι πολλοὶ γεγόνασιν,
even now many antichrists have arisen,

Καί is ascensive ("even"; e.g., CSB, NASB). Ἀντίχριστοι is nom. pl. masc. of ἀντίχριστος, -ου, ὁ, "antichrist," modified by πολλοί (πολύς, "many"). Γεγόνασιν is 3rd pl. pf. act. indic. of γίνομαι. "The many antichrists are forerunners of the one still to come" (Stott 108).

ὅθεν γινώσκομεν ὅτι ἐσχάτη ὥρα ἐστίν.
by which we know that it is the last hour.

Students looking for a one-word English equivalent of ὅθεν ("by which"; "by this," CSB; "from this," NASB, NET) must fall back on the antiquated "whence" (see BDAG 692d–93a). John asserts that the multiplicity of opposers and distorters of the gospel are another indication that Christians are living in the final era of world history. Γινώσκομεν is 1st pl. pres. act. indic. of γινώσκω, an inclusive use of the 1st pl. Ὅτι introduces indir. discourse/content clause, "that" (see BDAG 731d; R 1034–35; Wallace 456–58). See above for a discussion of the phrase ἐσχάτη ὥρα ἐστίν.

VERSE 19

ἐξ ἡμῶν ἐξῆλθαν ἀλλ' οὐκ ἦσαν ἐξ ἡμῶν,
They went out from us, but they were not of us,

It is common in Koine Gk. for the prep. prefix of a compound vb. to be repeated in a prep. phrase next to the vb., as here (ἐξ ἡμῶν ἐξῆλθαν). Such a cstr. is not emphatic. Ἐξῆλθαν is an irregular (second) aorist 3rd pl. aor. act. indic. of ἐξέρχομαι. Note how the *alpha* endings of the 1st aor. forms (-αν) encroach on 2nd aor. stems in Koine Gk. Ἦσαν is impf. indic. of εἰμί. John uses the same phrase with subtly different meanings. He says that the schismatic group went out "from us" (ἐξ ἡμῶν, directional/source), but they were not really "of us" (ἐξ ἡμῶν, belonging, e.g., CSB, NIV; see BDAG 296c).

εἰ γὰρ ἐξ ἡμῶν ἦσαν, μεμενήκεισαν ἂν μεθ' ἡμῶν—
for if they had been of us, they would have remained with us,

A second class (contrary-to-fact) cond. sentence (BDF §360; see also Young 225–27; Wallace 694–96; Z §313) usually has an εἰ in the prot. and an ἄν in the apod., as here, although sometimes the ἄν is missing (e.g., John 15:22, 24). When translating a contrary-to-fact Gk. sentence into English, it is best to let English idiom be the guide: "If they had . . . , they would have . . . ." The postpositive particle γάρ introduces this sentence as explanatory (i.e., "for"). John continues his rhetorically masterful usage of the prep. phrase ἐξ ἡμῶν, here conveying the sense of belonging again. Ἦσαν is impf. indic. of εἰμί. Μεμενήκεισαν is 3rd pl. pluperf. act. indic. of μένω. When parsing a pluperf. vb., students should look for reduplication and a *kappa* tense formative followed by the diphthong ει. Sometimes a pluperf. vb. has an additional augment before the reduplication (e.g., ἐμεμενήκεισαν). The prep. phrase μεθ' ἡμῶν communicates association (see BDAG 636b–37a).

ἀλλ' ἵνα φανερωθῶσιν ὅτι οὐκ εἰσὶν πάντες ἐξ ἡμῶν.
but they departed so that they would be revealed—they all are not of us.

After the advers. ἀλλά there is an ellipsis of the idea "they departed" (which is provided in the English translation above; so also most EVV). Ἵνα introduces a purpose clause (Robertson, *Pictures* 6:216; Rogers and Rogers 594). God's divine purpose should be seen in unveiling the true nature of the schismatics through their departure.

Φανερωθῶσιν, 3rd pl. aor. pass. subj. of φανερόω, is a divine pass. (revealed *by God*). Ὅτι is epex. (on this topic, see Wallace 459–60), explaining what the schismatics' unveiling revealed. Εἰσίν is pres. indic. of εἰμί, with πάντες as the nom. pl. masc. subj. John ends with the repeated prep. phrase ἐξ ἡμῶν, again conveying the nuance of belonging.

VERSE 20

καὶ ὑμεῖς χρῖσμα ἔχετε ἀπὸ τοῦ ἁγίου
And you all have an anointing from the Holy One

Καί is emphasized as advers. "but," by some (most EVV; Yarbrough 148–49; cf. "more over," in Smalley 99). Yet, see Culy, who rightly highlights thematic continuity with the preceding verse (50–51). John reassures his readers that their χρῖσμα, -ατος, τό, "anointing," (BDAG 1090c; so most EVV; on term, see H. Balz, *EDNT* 3:477b–d) will protect them from the ἀντίχριστοι, "antichrists." Note the repetition of similar sounds. The χρῖσμα (acc. sg. neut., dir. obj. of ἔχετε, 2nd pl. pres. act. indic.) here likely points to the indwelling presence of the Holy Spirit (Grundmann, *TDNT* 9:572; ZG 728; Akin 118; Culy 51–52; Kruse 103; Stott 110; cf. Marshall 155, who identifies the term with both the Spirit and the word of God) but could also refer to any number of conceptually overlapping and divinely orchestrated works in the lives of believers (e.g., regeneration, the indwelling word, the indwelling truth, etc.). The presence of the nom. 2nd pl. pers. pron. (ὑμεῖς) is emphatic: "*you all*," as opposed to the schismatic deceivers. The prep. phrase ἀπὸ τοῦ ἁγίου communicates source/origin. Τοῦ ἁγίου is the gen. sg. masc. of ἅγιος, -ία, -ον, functioning substantively ("the Holy One," most EVV) to refer to God. (Cf. Akin 119; Culy 52; Kruse 103; Marshall 155 who all suggest the reference is to Christ specifically. Smalley 102 notes "John is possibly being deliberately ambivalent at this point.")

καὶ οἴδατε πάντες.
And all of you have knowledge.

Οἴδατε is 2nd pl. pf. act. indic. of οἶδα, "know," a pf. form with a pres. meaning. John uses the vb. interchangeably with γινώσκω. Πάντες "all," modifies the implied subj. of the vb., ὑμεῖς, the 2nd pl. pers. pron. "*All of you*" have knowledge (you are *not* like the schismatics, who claim the necessity of some special guru or additional secret knowledge). Some mss. (including *Byz*) read πάντα here, with the acc. pl. neut. form as the object of the vb., "And you [pl.] know all things." John makes essentially this same affirmation later in the letter (cf. 2:27); if original (unlikely), the variant reading should not be taken as an affirmation of the congregation's omniscience, but the reassurance that they possess all of the spiritual insight they need. Most commentaries surveyed (e.g., Akin 119 n. 283; Marshall 156; Smalley 103; contra Kruse 103) and most EVV follow πάντες, the nominative reading.

VERSE 21

οὐκ ἔγραψα ὑμῖν ὅτι οὐκ οἴδατε τὴν ἀλήθειαν ἀλλ' ὅτι οἴδατε αὐτὴν
I do not write to you all because you don't know the truth, but because you know it,

Ἔγραψα is 1st sg. aor. act. indic. of γράφω, translated above as an epistolary aor. (KMP 297; Marshall 156 n. 27). Ὑμῖν is dat. pl. of ὑμεῖς, functioning as an indir. obj. All three instances of ὅτι in this verse are likely causal. Possible ways to understand the three uses of ὅτι include the following:

*1. All three are causal (CSB, ESV, NASB, NIV).
2. The first two are causal and the third indicates content (i.e., "that") and they are subordinate to:
   a. ἔγραψα (Schnackenburg; KJV).
   b. the preceding οἴδατε (Culy 53–54; Marshall 156 n. 30; Smalley 104; Culy refers to the third as introducing a "clausal complement," whereas Marshall and Smalley label it "recitative").
3. All three indicate content (i.e., "that") and are subordinate to ἔγραψα (NET; Brown 350).

John reassures his readers that he is confirming them in the truth and not trying to persuade them to leave error. Οἴδατε is 2nd pl. pf. act. indic. of οἶδα, "know," a pf. form with a pres. mng. Ἀλήθειαν is the acc. sg. fem. of ἀλήθεια, -ας, ἡ, here serving as the dir. obj. of οἴδατε. Αὐτήν ("it," antecedent: ἀλήθειαν) serves as the dir. obj. of the second occurrence of οἴδατε.

καὶ ὅτι πᾶν ψεῦδος ἐκ τῆς ἀληθείας οὐκ ἔστιν.
and because you know that no lie is from the truth.

If we provide no implied words and translate the above clause literalistically, it is rendered: "and because every lie is not from the truth." Most likely we should understand an ellipsis of the verb οἴδατε, as well as conforming the translation to normal English usage ("no lie is from the truth" rather than "every lie is not from the truth"). Young refers to this cstr. (πᾶς modifying the subj. with a negated vb.) as a "universal negative" (203–4; cf. 1 John 3:15; 4:3; 5:18; 2 John 9; as well as Gal 2:16; Matt 24:22; Eph 4:29). Moule notes that πᾶς . . . οὐ, instead of οὐδέις, is a frequent idiom in 1 John and reflects a "normal and idiomatic construction in Hebrew," but he also adds that "it is by no means un-Greek" (182; see also Z §446). Ψεῦδος ("lie, falsehood," BDAG 1097c) is nom. sg. neut., from ψεῦδος, -ους, τό, functioning as the subj. of ἔστιν (3rd sg. pres. indic. of εἰμί) and modified by πᾶν, "every." Ἀληθείας is gen. as required of objects of the prep. ἐκ. The prep. phrase ἐκ τῆς ἀληθείας fills the slot of a pred. nom. and communicates source or origin.

VERSE 22

Τίς ἐστιν ὁ ψεύστης
Who is the liar

Τίς is the nom. sg. masc. interrog. pron. functioning as the pred. nom. Ἐστιν is the 3rd sg. pres. indic. of εἰμί. Ψεύστης, "liar" (see 1:10), a nom. sg. masc., is the subj. Note that ψεύστης is articular, perhaps because the person denying the true identity of Jesus is the preeminent liar (on the "par excellence" article, see BDF §263; Wallace 222–23; KMP 158).

εἰ μὴ ὁ ἀρνούμενος ὅτι Ἰησοῦς οὐκ ἔστιν ὁ Χριστός;
if not the person making the denial, "Jesus is not the Christ"?

Ἀρνούμενος is the nom. sg. masc. of pres. mid. ptc. of ἀρνέομαι, "deny" (BDAG 132c; LN §31.25). Here the subst. use of the ptc. has been translated as "the person making the denial." This translation is to avoid the confusing literalism of "the person denying that Jesus is not the Christ." (To *deny* that someone is *not* something is to affirm it, which the apostle John is not saying here.) Ὅτι could introduce direct (Jobes 129; Yarbrough 156) or indir. discourse (most EVV, e.g., CSB, NIV, NLT); it has been rendered as marking direct discourse above. It is grammatically possible that Χριστός functions as the subject (e.g., Carson, "Syntactical and Text-Critical Observations"; Carson follows Goetchius, who argues McGaughy's rule 3c from *Toward a Descriptive Analysis of* Εἶναι should be followed, noting no syntactical or contextual reason exists for not viewing the articular Χριστός as the subject). If so, the author would be reasoning from a (partially) shared understanding that the exalted Christ figure the schismatics were denying was the same person as the historical Jesus. Even though ὁ Χριστός is articular (sometimes a sign of the subject in an equative clause as noted by McGaughy), the personal name Ἰησοῦς more likely is the subject (most EVV). McGaughy himself viewed the cstr. in this verse (along with 1 John 4:15; 5:1, 5; John 20:31) as an exception, viewing "Jesus" as the subject (see also the discussion in Jobes 129 concerning the early church's understanding of "Christ" as a title in contrast to the broad sense of the term in Second Temple Judaism).

οὗτός ἐστιν ὁ ἀντίχριστος,
This is the Antichrist,

John moves rapidly from labeling this Christ-denier as "the liar" to "the Antichrist"! In fact, to embrace and spread erroneous views of Jesus's identity and person is to be a mouthpiece of the arch-opponent of Christ. The nom. sg. masc. dem. pron. οὗτός serves as the subj. even though the other noun in his equative clause is art. (as noted by McGaughy's rules). Ὁ ἀντίχριστος, "the Antichrist," nom. sg. masc., is the pred. nom.

ὁ ἀρνούμενος τὸν πατέρα καὶ τὸν υἱόν.
the one denying the Father and the Son.

Ἀρνούμενος is the nom. sg. masc. of pres. mid. ptc. of ἀρνέομαι, "deny." Here the subst. ptc. is in appos. to ὁ ἀντίχριστος. The ptc. has a compound dir. obj.: τὸν πατέρα and τὸν υἱόν, both acc. sg. masc. To embrace an untruth about God the Son is to oppose God the Father as well.

VERSE 23

πᾶς ὁ ἀρνούμενος τὸν υἱὸν οὐδὲ τὸν πατέρα ἔχει,
Everyone who denies the Son neither has the Father.

Ἀρνούμενος is the nom. sg. masc. of pres. mid. ptc. of ἀρνέομαι, "deny" (see v. 22). The subst. ptc. is modified by πᾶς, "every," and has the acc. sg. masc. τὸν υἱόν as its object. Πᾶς ὁ ἀρνούμενος τὸν υἱόν functions as the subj. of ἔχει, the 3rd sg. pres. act. indic. of ἔχω (a gnomic present; so KMP 260–61; Wallace 524). The dir. obj. of ἔχει is τὸν πατέρα, the acc. sg. masc. of πατήρ, πατρός, ὁ. The teaching here accords with the words of Jesus in the Gospel of John: "I am the way, the truth, and the life. No one comes to the Father except through me" (John 14:6 CSB).

ὁ ὁμολογῶν τὸν υἱὸν καὶ τὸν πατέρα ἔχει.
The person confessing the Son also has the Father.

Ὁμολογῶν is the nom. sg. masc. of pres. act. ptc. of ὁμολογέω ("confess, publicly profess allegiance to," see BDAG 708c–d; LN §33.274). Τὸν υἱόν is the acc. masc. sg. dir. obj. of ὁμολογῶν. Ὁ ὁμολογῶν τὸν υἱόν serves as the subj. of ἔχει, the 3rd sg. pres. act. indic. of ἔχω. The dir. obj. of ἔχει is τὸν πατέρα, the acc. sg. masc. of πατήρ. The context here favors understanding καί as an adv. mng. "also" or "likewise" (most EVV).

VERSE 24

ὑμεῖς ὃ ἠκούσατε ἀπ' ἀρχῆς, ἐν ὑμῖν μενέτω.
But you all, what you heard from the beginning—make sure it remains in you.

Ὑμεῖς (pendent nominative, so Culy 57; KMP 61–62; Young 15; "as for you," NASB, NET, NIV) is drawn forward to contrast the recipients of the letter with those who do not rightly confess the Son (vv. 22–23)—*but you all* (as opposed to the false believers). Even though John can affirm many wonderful things about his recipients, they still must be commanded to strive for the gospel message to remain within them. Ὅ, "what," is the acc. sg. neut. rel. pron. Ὅ begins a headless rel. clause and serves as the dir. obj. of ἠκούσατε. Ἠκούσατε is 2nd pl. aor. act. indic. of ἀκούω. The prep. phrase ἀπ' ἀρχῆς, "from the beginning" (see 1:1), functions in an adv. temp. fashion, referencing the gospel message (Kruse 57; cf. Jobes 130; Smalley 112) that has been part of this believing community since its beginning (founding). Def. dir. objects of preps. frequently are anar., as here (ἀρχῆς). Ἐν ὑμῖν is a prep. phrase communicating a metaphorical loc./spatial sense (see BDAG 326c; R 585–86). Μενέτω is 3rd sg. pres.

act. impv., "let it remain, it must remain, make sure it remains." The prior rel. clause (ὃ ἠκούσατε ἀπ' ἀρχῆς) functions as the subj. of the impv.

ἐὰν ἐν ὑμῖν μείνῃ ὃ ἀπ' ἀρχῆς ἠκούσατε,
If what you heard from the beginning remains in you all,

'Εάν introduces the prot. of the third class cond. clause (on third class cond., see 1:6). 'Εν ὑμῖν is a prep. phrase communicating a metaphorical loc./spatial sense. Μείνῃ is 3rd sg. aor. act. subjunc. of μένω. As a liquid vb., μένω rejects a sigma after its liquid consonant (ν) and the stem vowel lengthens in compensation (ει). The entire rel. clause ὃ ἀπ' ἀρχῆς ἠκούσατε functions as the subj. of μείνῃ. See immediately above for a discussion of this headless rel. clause.

καὶ ὑμεῖς ἐν τῷ υἱῷ καὶ ἐν τῷ πατρὶ μενεῖτε.
you also will remain in the Son and in the Father.

This apod. (i.e., "then" clause in an "if-then" cond. sentence) serves as an implied warning: to abandon the gospel message is to abandon the Father and the Son. Καί is likely adv. here meaning "also." Μενεῖτε is 2nd pl. fut. act. indic. of μένω. The lack of a sigma and spelling variation in the ending is because μένω is a liquid vb. The compound prep. phrase ἐν τῷ υἱῷ καὶ ἐν τῷ πατρί, "in the Son and in the Father," is adv., functioning in a metaphorical loc./spatial sense. Υἱῷ is dat. sg. masc. of υἱός. Πατρί is dat. sg. masc. of πατήρ, πατρός, ὁ.

VERSE 25

καὶ αὕτη ἐστὶν ἡ ἐπαγγελία ἣν αὐτὸς ἐπηγγείλατο ἡμῖν,
And this is the promise which he promised to us,

Relationship with the Father and the Son is not for this life only; it is a proleptic experience of the eternal relationship of joy that has been promised to us. Αὕτη is nom. sg. fem. near dem. pron., serving here as the subj. of ἐστίν, the 3rd sg. pres. indic. of εἰμί. 'Επαγγελία, "promise," the nom. sg. fem. noun, serves as the pred. nom. Ἥν, an acc. sg. fem. rel. pron., refers back to the antecedent ἐπαγγελία and serves as the dir. obj. of ἐπηγγείλατο. Αὐτός is the nom. masc. sg. subj. ("he himself," CSB, NASB, NET) of ἐπηγγείλατο, the 3rd sg. aor. mid. indic. of ἐπαγγέλλομαι. Verbs of reciprocity often occur in the middle voice. A vb. of reciprocity is one in which two parties are needed, and if one is removed, the action cannot happen. Ἡμῖν is dat. pl. of ἡμεῖς (ἐγώ), serving as the indir. obj.

τὴν ζωὴν τὴν αἰώνιον.
eternal life.

This phrase functions as an appositional acc. for the rel. pron. ἥν above (NET Translation Notes; see also Marshall 161 n. 43; BDF §295; cf. Culy 58, who views the acc. case as likely due to ellipsis though no significant difference in mng.). The promise that he promised to us is eternal life. Ζωήν is acc. sg. fem. of ζωή, -ῆς, ἡ, modified by the acc.

sg. fem. adj. αἰώνιον, "eternal, everlasting, characteristic of the age to come" (cf. 1:2; 2:25; 3:15; 5:11, 13, 20). Αἰώνιος is a two-termination adj., which usually follows only 2nd decl. endings, with the endings for λόγος functioning to modify both masc. and fem. nouns (see BDF §59[1]; Decker 95; R 272–73; see 1:2). Occasionally, however, αἰώνιος is found with 1st decl. (καρδία) endings. On the topic "eternal life," see For Further Study 26 "Eternal Life."

VERSE 26

Ταῦτα ἔγραψα ὑμῖν περὶ τῶν πλανώντων ὑμᾶς.
I write these things to you concerning those seeking to deceive you.

Ταῦτα, "these things," apparently a reference to John's entire letter (cf. Culy 59; Hiebert 121; and Smalley 116, who all see the referent as the letter or possibly the immediate context), is the acc. pl. neut. dem. pron. Ταῦτα serves as the dir. obj. of ἔγραψα. Ἔγραψα, translated as an epistolary aor. above, is 1st sg. aor. act. indic. of γράφω. Ὑμῖν is dat. pl. of the 2nd pers. personal pron. ὑμεῖς (σύ), serving as the indir. obj. of ἔγραψα. The prep. phrase περὶ τῶν πλανώντων ὑμᾶς functions adv., modifying ἔγραψα, and communicates reference. Τῶν πλανώντων, "those seeking to deceive," is translated as a conative present above (most EVV, e.g., CSB "those who are trying to deceive you"; ZG 729; Smalley 117; Stott 116–17; Yarbrough 162). Context favors this nuance, as John does not believe the recipients of his letter have been deceived; they must, however, be warned against the deceivers and schismatics. Τῶν πλανώντων is the gen. pl. masc. of pres. act. ptc. of πλανάω, "deceive, lead astray." The ptc. functions substantivally as the obj. of the prep. περί. Thus, τῶν πλανώντων is in the gen. case to narrow the semantic range of the prep. to "concerning/about." Ὑμᾶς is the acc. pl. of ὑμεῖς (σύ) and functions as the dir. obj. of the ptc.

VERSE 27

καὶ ὑμεῖς τὸ χρῖσμα ὃ ἐλάβετε ἀπ' αὐτοῦ μένει ἐν ὑμῖν,
But you all, the anointing which you received from him remains in you,

Although it is not linguistically correct to label the initial conj. as an "adversative καί," v. 27 presents a clear contrast between ὑμεῖς (the recipients of the letter) and τῶν πλανώντων ὑμᾶς (v. 26, the schismatic deceivers). The EVV are warranted from literary context to begin v. 27 with an advers. conj. ("as for you," CSB, NASB, NET; cf. Smalley 162 n. 48; see BDF §466[1] on the unexpected grammatical cstr. [i.e., anacoluthon] with καὶ ὑμεῖς reflecting emphasis). Τὸ χρῖσμα, "the anointing" (see 2:20) is nom. sg. neut. and functions as the subj. of μένει. Τὸ χρῖσμα likely refers to the Holy Spirit (Brown 347; Kruse 109; cf. commentators who suggest a reference to the Spirit and the Divine Word; Akin 125; Jobes 128, 132; Marshall 154–55; Smalley 117). This unusual Gk. word was chosen because of its similar sound to ἀντίχριστος. The χρῖσμα protects believers from ἀντίχριστος. Ὅ (acc. sg. neut. rel. pron.) refers back to the antecedent χρῖσμα and serves as the dir. obj. of ἐλάβετε, the irreg. 2nd pl. aor.

act. indic. of λαμβάνω. The prep. phrase ἀπ' αὐτοῦ indicates the source/origin of the anointing (on prep., see BDAG 106d). Μένει is 3rd sg. pres. act. indic. of μένω. The prep. phrase ἐν ὑμῖν functions in a metaphorical loc./spherical sense.

καὶ οὐ χρείαν ἔχετε ἵνα τις διδάσκῃ ὑμᾶς,
and you don't have need that anyone teach you,

Χρείαν, "need, necessity," is acc. sg. fem. of χρεία, -ας, ἡ, here acting as the dir. obj. of ἔχετε, the 2nd pl. pres. act. indic. of ἔχω. Ἵνα introduces a content or epex. clause (cf. Burton §216 [complementary]; Wallace 473 [result]), clarifying what the need is (i.e., that anyone teach you). Τις is the nom. sg. masc. indef. pron. and subj. of διδάσκῃ, the 3rd sg. pres. act. subj. of διδάσκω.

ἀλλ' ὡς τὸ αὐτοῦ χρῖσμα διδάσκει ὑμᾶς περὶ πάντων, καὶ ἀληθές ἐστιν καὶ οὐκ ἔστιν ψεῦδος,
but as his anointing teaches you concerning all things, and is true and is not a lie,

Αὐτοῦ divides the noun and its art. (τὸ . . . χρῖσμα). It is drawn forward for emphasis (*his* anointing). Χρῖσμα, "anointing," is nom. sg. neut. and subj. of διδάσκει, the 3rd sg. pres. act. indic. of διδάσκω. Ὑμᾶς is the acc. pl. of the 2nd pers. personal pron. and dir. obj. of διδάσκει. The prep. phrase περὶ πάντων, "concerning all things," communicates reference/respect hyperbolically (i.e., *all things* necessary for salvation and spiritual health; on the phrase, see Harris 181–82). Τὸ αὐτοῦ χρῖσμα continues as the subj. of both instances of ἐστιν, the 3rd sg. pres. indic. of εἰμί. The first instance of ἐστιν takes a pred. adj., ἀληθές, "true, genuine," the nom. sg. neut. of ἀληθής, -ές (a third decl. adj., thus unfamiliar in form to many students). The second (negated) instance of ἔστιν takes a pred. nom., ψεῦδος, "lie, falsehood," a nom. sg. neut. noun.

καὶ καθὼς ἐδίδαξεν ὑμᾶς, μένετε ἐν αὐτῷ.
and just as he taught you: remain in him.

Ἐδίδαξεν is 3rd sg. aor. act. indic. of διδάσκω, with ὑμᾶς, the acc. pl. of the 2nd pers. personal pron., as the dir. obj. The grammatical form μένετε could be indic. or impv., with most EVV favoring the impv. translation from the literary context (e.g., CSB, ESV, NIV; contra NET). If impv., it is 2nd pl. pres. act. impv. of μένω. Ἐν αὐτῷ is a prep. phrase communicating a metaphorical loc./spherical sense.

FOR FURTHER STUDY

22. Antichrist (2:18)

Koester, Craig R. "The Antichrist Theme in the Johannine Epistles and Its Role in Christian Tradition." Pages 187–96 in *Communities in Dispute: Current Scholarship on the Johannine Epistles*. Edited by R. Alan Culpepper and Paul N. Anderson. Atlanta: SBL, 2014.

———. "Antichrist Then and Now: The Johannine Epistles and Antichrist in Popular Culture." *WW* 41, no. 1 (2021): 3–10.

Kruse, 99–102 (see "A Note on Antichrist").

Lietaert Peerbolte, L. J. *The Antecedents of Antichrist: A Traditio-Historical Study of the Earliest Christian Views on Eschatological Opponents*. Leiden: Brill, 1996.
Lorein, Geert Wouter. *The Antichrist Theme in the Intertestamental Period*. London: T&T Clark, 2003.
McGinn, Bernard. *Antichrist: Two Thousand Years of the Human Fascination with Evil*. New York: Columbia University Press, 2000.
Sloyan, Gerard S. *Walking in the Truth: Perseverers and Deserters: The First, Second, and Third Letters of John*. Valley Forge, PA: Trinity Press International, 1995 (see esp. 28–29).
Thomson, J. E. H. *ISBE*, 1:139–40.
Watson, D. F. *DLNT*, 50–53.

23. Eschatology/Last Hour (2:18)

Bavinck, 4:691–714.
*Beale, G. K. *DLNT*, 330–45 (see esp. 335–37).
———. "The Old Testament Background of the 'Last Hour' in 1 John 2,18." *Biblica* 92, no. 2 (2011): 231–54.
Carson, D. A. "The Three Witnesses and the Eschatology of 1 John." Pages 216–32 in *To Tell the Mystery: Essays on New Testament Eschatology in Honour of Robert H. Gundry*. Edited by Thomas E. Schmidt and Moisés Silva. JSNTSup 100. Sheffield: JSOT, 1994.
Daley, Brian E. *Hope of the Early Church: A Handbook of Patristic Eschatology*. Grand Rapids: Baker Academic, 2002.
Doyle, Robert C. *Eschatology and the Shape of Christian Belief*. Carlisle, PA: Paternoster, 1999.
Harris, W. H. "Eschatology in the Johannine Writings." Pages 233–42 in *A Biblical Theology of the New Testament*. Edited by R. B. Zuck and D. L. Bock. Chicago: Moody, 1994.
Hill, Craig C. *In God's Time: The Bible and the Future*. Grand Rapids: Eerdmans, 2002.
Ladd, G. E. *ISBE*, 2:130–43.
Marshall, 148–50.
Mihalios, Stefanos. *The Danielic Eschatological Hour in the Johannine Literature*. LNTS 436. London: T&T Clark, 2011.

24. Anointing (2:20)

Davids, P. H. *DLNT*, 48–50.
Kruse, 109–10 (see "A Note on *Chrisma*, Spirit or Word?").
NIDNTTE 4:697–701.

25. Holy Spirit (2:20)

Allison, Gregg, and Andreas J. Köstenberger. *The Holy Spirit*. Edited by David S. Dockery, Nathan A. Finn, and Christopher W. Morgan. Nashville: B&H Academic, 2020.
Bloesch, Donald G. *The Holy Spirit: Works and Gifts*. Downers Grove, IL: IVP Academic, 2005.
Bromiley, G. W. *ISBE*, 2:730–46.

Burge, Gary M. *The Anointed Community: The Holy Spirit in the Johannine Tradition*. Grand Rapids: Eerdmans, 1987.
———. "Spirit-Inspired Theology and Ecclesial Correction: Charting One Shift in the Development of Johannine Ecclesiology and Pneumatology." Pages 179–86 in *Communities in Dispute: Current Scholarship on the Johannine Epistles*. Edited by R. Alan Culpepper and Paul N. Anderson. Atlanta: SBL, 2014.
Ferguson, Sinclair B. *The Holy Spirit*. Downers Grove, IL: IVP Academic, 1997.
Frame, 923–33.
Green, M. B. *I Believe in the Holy Spirit*. Grand Rapids: Eerdmans, 1989.
Grudem, 634–53.
Harvey, J. D. *Anointed with the Spirit and Power: The Holy Spirit's Empowering Presence*. Phillipsburg, NJ: P&R, 2008.
Hawthorne, G. F. *DLNT*, 489–99.
Horne, F. W. *ABD*, 3:260–80.
Köstenberger, *Theology*, 400–409.
Kruse, 151–55 (see "A Note on the Role of the Spirit").
Schweizer, E. *TDNT*, 6:396–453.

26. Eternal Life (2:25)

Berkhof, Hendrikus. *Christian Faith: An Introduction to the Study of the Faith*. Translated by Sierd Woudstra. Grand Rapids: Eerdmans, 1979 (see 533–41).
Blanton, Ward. "Resurrection, Immortality, and Eternal Life in Intertestamental Judaism and Early Christianity." *JSNT* 30, no. 5 (2008): 23–24.
Davis, J. C. "The Johannine Concept of Eternal Life as a Present Possession." *ResQ* 27, no. 3 (1984): 161–69.
Jobes, 340.
Kruse, 184.
Osborne, G. R. *DJG*, 518–22.
Porter, S. E. *DLNT*, 345–47.

HOMILETICAL SUGGESTIONS

Warning about the Antichrists (2:18–27)

1. False teachers in the world (vv. 18–19)
2. Knowledge of the truth: the message of Jesus Christ (vv. 20–23)
   a. Doctrinal foundation: belief in Jesus
   b. Internalizing and living out the truth of the gospel
3. The promise of God—eternal life (v. 25)
4. Abide in God (v. 27)

Those Who Stay and Those Who Go (2:18–27)

1. Those who depart:
   a. Show by their actions that they were not truly among the community of faith (v. 18)

   b. Speak the message of the Antichrist (v. 18)
   c. Deny Jesus as the Christ (v. 22)
   d. Seek to deceive believers (v. 26)
2. Those who remain:
   a. Have an anointing (v. 20)
      (1) This likely refers to the gift of the Holy Spirit
      (2) Yet, it may also include a panorama of ideas (e.g., regeneration, the apostolic teaching)
   b. Know the truth (v. 20)
      (1) Their knowledge is not exhaustive. The believer is always to be learning and growing in the word of God and his or her knowledge of God
      (2) Yet, their knowledge is sufficient for the challenge of the false teachers. Do you have a sufficient understanding of your faith? Do you continue to grow in your understanding of the gospel?
   c. Persevere by remaining in Christ (v. 27)
      (1) They hold fast to the cross. Christ died for sinners
      (2) They hold fast to biblical teaching
      (3) They hold fast to Christ. He is faithful

VIII. The Children of God and the Children of the Devil (2:28–3:10)

The section begins with the voc. τεκνία. The first of three impvs. in this section (μένετε) is followed by the ἵνα, which provides the reason to "remain in him": that believers will have confidence at his coming. Verse 1 of chapter 3 begins with the second impv. (ἴδετε), highlighting what great love the Father has given. The ἵνα which follows is epex., explaining this love: "that we are called children of God." Verses 2–3 introduce aspects of the hope of Christ's coming and the implications of this hope on the life of the believer. Verses 4–10 shift more specifically to the topic of sin and the Christian. The Christian does not practice sin. The ἵνα of v. 5 gives the reason that Christ was revealed: that he may take away sin. Following another voc., the third impv. of the section exhorts the believers to not be led astray. It is ὁ ποιῶν τὴν δικαιοσύνην that is righteous (v. 7b). In contrast, ὁ ποιῶν τὴν ἁμαρτίαν is of the devil (v. 8). Verse 9 affirms that those born of God do not sin (v. 9), with the ὅτι introducing a causal clause (i.e., "because his seed remains in him"). Verse 10 provides a summary of vv. 4–10 and offers an echo of the theme that will follow. Two criteria of the children of God are noted in negative terms (μή) with two substantival ptcs: πᾶς ὁ μὴ ποιῶν δικαιοσύνην and ὁ μὴ ἀγαπῶν τὸν ἀδελφὸν αὐτοῦ. This theme of loving one another will be picked up in the next section.

28 Καὶ νῦν, τεκνία,
μένετε ἐν αὐτῷ,
ἵνα ↓ἐὰν φανερωθῇ,
σχῶμεν παρρησίαν
καὶ μὴ αἰσχυνθῶμεν
ἀπ' αὐτοῦ
ἐν τῇ παρουσίᾳ αὐτοῦ.

29 ἐὰν εἰδῆτε ὅτι δίκαιός ἐστιν,
γινώσκετε ὅτι καὶ πᾶς ὁ ποιῶν τὴν δικαιοσύνην ἐξ αὐτοῦ γεγέννηται.

3:1 Ἴδετε ποταπὴν ἀγάπην δέδωκεν ἡμῖν ὁ πατήρ,
ἵνα τέκνα θεοῦ κληθῶμεν,
καὶ ἐσμέν.
↓διὰ τοῦτο
ὁ κόσμος οὐ γινώσκει ἡμᾶς,
ὅτι οὐκ ἔγνω αὐτόν.

2 ἀγαπητοί,
νῦν
τέκνα θεοῦ ἐσμεν,
καὶ οὔπω ἐφανερώθη
τί ἐσόμεθα.
οἴδαμεν ὅτι ↓ἐὰν φανερωθῇ,
ὅμοιοι αὐτῷ ἐσόμεθα,
ὅτι ὀψόμεθα αὐτόν,
καθώς ἐστιν.

3 καὶ πᾶς ὁ ἔχων τὴν ἐλπίδα ταύτην ἐπ᾽ αὐτῷ ἁγνίζει ἑαυτόν,
καθὼς ἐκεῖνος ἁγνός ἐστιν.

4 Πᾶς ὁ ποιῶν τὴν ἁμαρτίαν
καὶ τὴν ἀνομίαν ποιεῖ,
καὶ ἡ ἁμαρτία ἐστὶν ἡ ἀνομία.

5 καὶ οἴδατε ὅτι ἐκεῖνος ἐφανερώθη,
ἵνα τὰς ἁμαρτίας ἄρῃ,
καὶ ἁμαρτία ἐν αὐτῷ οὐκ ἔστιν.

6 πᾶς ὁ ἐν αὐτῷ μένων οὐχ ἁμαρτάνει·
πᾶς ὁ ἁμαρτάνων οὐχ ἑώρακεν αὐτὸν
οὐδὲ ἔγνωκεν αὐτόν.

7 Παιδία, μηδεὶς πλανάτω ὑμᾶς·
ὁ ποιῶν τὴν δικαιοσύνην δίκαιός ἐστιν,
καθὼς ἐκεῖνος δίκαιός ἐστιν·

8 ὁ ποιῶν τὴν ἁμαρτίαν ἐκ τοῦ διαβόλου ἐστίν,
ὅτι ἀπ᾽ ἀρχῆς ὁ διάβολος ἁμαρτάνει.
εἰς τοῦτο ἐφανερώθη ὁ υἱὸς τοῦ θεοῦ,
ἵνα λύσῃ τὰ ἔργα τοῦ διαβόλου.

9 Πᾶς ὁ γεγεννημένος ἐκ τοῦ θεοῦ ἁμαρτίαν οὐ ποιεῖ,
ὅτι σπέρμα αὐτοῦ ἐν αὐτῷ μένει,
καὶ οὐ δύναται ἁμαρτάνειν,
ὅτι ἐκ τοῦ θεοῦ γεγέννηται.

10 ἐν τούτῳ
φανερά ἐστιν τὰ τέκνα τοῦ θεοῦ
καὶ τὰ τέκνα τοῦ διαβόλου·
πᾶς ὁ μὴ ποιῶν δικαιοσύνην οὐκ ἔστιν ἐκ τοῦ θεοῦ
καὶ ὁ μὴ ἀγαπῶν τὸν ἀδελφὸν αὐτοῦ.

VERSE 28

Καὶ νῦν, τεκνία, μένετε ἐν αὐτῷ,
And now, dear children, remain in him,

Τεκνία is a voc. pl. of *τεκνίον*, a diminutive form of *τέκνον*. Diminutive forms often express affection or smallness (see 2:1). *Μένετε* is 2nd pl. pres. act. impv. of *μένω*. *Ἐν αὐτῷ* is a prep. phrase communicating a metaphorical loc./spherical sense. Regardless of whether *μένετε* in v. 27 is understood as an impv., the context in v. 28 makes clear that the form here is impv.

ἵνα ἐὰν φανερωθῇ, σχῶμεν παρρησίαν καὶ μὴ αἰσχυνθῶμεν ἀπ' αὐτοῦ ἐν τῇ παρουσίᾳ αὐτοῦ.
so that when he is revealed, we will have confidence and not shrink in shame from him at his appearing.

Ἵνα introduces a purpose clause (Robertson, *Pictures* 6:219). Believers are given an incentive for remaining in Christ (i.e., that on the last day, they might hear the words from him, "Well done, good and faithful servant," Matt 25:23). Note the *ἵνα* clause (which will be followed by two subjunc. vbs.) is "interrupted" at this point by *ἐάν*, followed by its own subjunc. vb. *φανερωθῇ*. The clause is subordinate to the *ἵνα* clause (see phrase diagram above). *Ἐάν* is sometimes translated as "since" or "when" (most EVV), and those nuances are arguably in the word's broad semantic range (BDAG 267a: "at times the mng. of *ἐάν* approaches closely that of *ὅταν*"; see also Young 184). Regardless, the translator is warranted to translate *ἐάν* as "when" to avoid giving modern readers the impression that John thinks that Jesus might not return (unthinkable in light of the rest of the letter, not to mention the rest of the NT). The *ἐάν*, however, may also function rhetorically to invite the reader to consider a train of events (Culy 62–63). *Φανερωθῇ* is 3rd sg. aor. pass. subjunc. of *φανερόω*. Though many EVV favor the middle sense here ("appears," e.g., CSB, NASB, NIV), the passive form likely is employed to imply divine paternal agency (i.e., the Son is revealed by the Father). *Σχῶμεν* is 1st pl. aor. act. subjunc. of *ἔχω*, the odd spelling of the aor. form is because the true root of *ἔχω* is *σεχ*. *Παρρησίαν*, "boldness, confidence" (BDAG 781d–82a; on term, see also LN §25.158; MM 497c; H. Balz, *EDNT* 3:45a; For Further Study 28 "*Παρρησία*/Boldness Word Study"), acting here as the dir. obj., is the acc. sg. fem. of *παρρησία, -ας, ἡ*. The negated *αἰσχυνθῶμεν* is 1st pl. aor. pass. subjunc. of *αἰσχύνω*. The passive form here likely conveys a middle sense of "shrink away in shame" (NASB, NET; "to be put to shame, be disgraced," BDAG 30b; on the term, see also A. Horstmann, *EDNT* 1:42a–43a) with the following prep. phrase *ἀπ' αὐτοῦ* (expressing disassociation) making this nuance more likely (cf. Smalley 154). The prep. phrase ἐν τῇ παρουσίᾳ αὐτοῦ expresses a point in time (i.e., at the time of his appearing). Παρουσίᾳ "appearing, appearance, coming" (BDAG 780d–81a; on term, see *NIDNTTE* 3:647–57; MM 497a–c; Oepke, *TDNT* 5:858–71), is dat. sg. fem. of παρουσία, -ας, ἡ. (Note the play on words—παρρησία at the παρουσία.) Αὐτοῦ, the gen. sg. masc. of the 3rd pers. personal pron., functions as an subj. gen.

VERSE 29

ἐὰν εἰδῆτε ὅτι δίκαιός ἐστιν,
If you know that he is righteous,

'Εάν is sometimes translated as "since," and such a nuance is arguably in the word's broad semantic range (BDAG 268a). See v. 28 for more discussion of John's usage of ἐάν as a rhetorical device. Εἰδῆτε is the 2nd pl. pf. act. subjunc. of οἶδα (see Campbell 60–65 for discussion on pf. subjunc.). The vb. οἶδα derives its forms from two roots, one beginning with the antiquated Gk. letter digamma (*οιδ *ϝιδ). Thus, Gk. resources will sometimes disagree in how to list the lexical form of εἰδῆτε (MBG 263). It is unusual to find a subjunc. vb. form in the pf. tense (10× in GNT); almost all subjuncs. in the GNT are pres. or aor. To convey a stative sense, a NT author would more commonly employ a form of εἰμί + the pf. ptc. (see 1:4). Ὅτι introduces a content clause. 'Εστιν is 3rd sg. pres. indic. of εἰμί, with the implied subject αὐτός or ἐκεῖνος. Δίκαιός is nom. sg. masc. and functions as the pred. adj.

γινώσκετε ὅτι καὶ πᾶς ὁ ποιῶν τὴν δικαιοσύνην ἐξ αὐτοῦ γεγέννηται.
you also know that everyone who practices righteousness has been born from him.

John invites the reader to consider that the spiritual offspring of God will certainly resemble him in righteousness. Γινώσκετε is 2nd pl. pres. act. indic. of γινώσκω. Note how John's idiolect favors the interchangeable use of near synonyms (οἶδα, γινώσκω). Ὁ ποιῶν is the nom. sg. masc. of pres. act. ptc. of ποιέω, functioning as a subst. modified by πᾶς (i.e., "everyone who practices"). Δικαιοσύνην is the acc. sg. fem. of δικαιοσύνη, -ης, ἡ, serving as the dir. obj. of the ptc. ποιῶν. Πᾶς ὁ ποιῶν τὴν δικαιοσύνην serves as the subj. of γεγέννηται, "has been born" (CSB, ESV, NIV), the 3rd sg. pf. pass. indic. of γεννάω. The vb. γεννάω is most frequently employed with a male subj., emphasizing the male role in reproduction (see Matt 1:1–16). Here, of course, the word is used metaphorically to speak of the spiritual life that God the Father gives to his children (cf. 3:9; 4:7; 5:1, 4, 18). Jobes notes that "there is perhaps no more sweeping an expression of the newness of a life redeemed by Christ than that of the birth metaphor" (140). On the concept of "new birth," see For Further Study 30 "Born of God/New Birth/Children of God." The prep. phrase ἐξ αὐτοῦ communicates source or origin (see Harris 105). Αὐτοῦ is the gen. sg. masc. of the 3rd pers. personal pron., the gen. case here being required of the obj. of the prep. ἐκ.

CHAPTER 3, VERSE 1

Ἴδετε ποταπὴν ἀγάπην δέδωκεν ἡμῖν ὁ πατήρ, ἵνα τέκνα θεοῦ κληθῶμεν, καὶ ἐσμέν.
See what sort of love the Father has given to us—that we are called children of God. And we are!

Ἴδετε is 2nd pl. aor. act. impv. of ὁράω (the inflected form here builds off the second aor. root of εἶδον, which has lost its augment in the impv. mood.). This impv. form is akin to a modern preacher beginning a new section of his message with "Hey, listen up!" Ἀγάπην is acc. sg. fem. of ἀγάπη, -ης, ἡ, serving as the dir. obj. of δέδωκεν. Ἀγάπην is modified by the interrog. adj. ποταπήν from ποταπός, -ή, -όν, "what sort or kind" (BDAG 856b), which only occurs seven times in the GNT. Here the sense seems to be of "what *wonderful* sort" (e.g., "what great love," CSB). Δέδωκεν is 3rd sg. pf. act. indic. of δίδωμι, with ὁ πατήρ as subj. of the vb. and ἡμῖν as its indir. obj. Ἵνα introduces a content or epex. clause (NET Translation Notes; Culy 66), functioning like a colon, dash, or "i.e., *id est*." What is this amazing sort of love? None other than that God has called us his children (cf. 3:2, 10; 5:2). (On similar use of ἵνα, see 3:8, 11, 23; 4:21; 5:3; 2 John 6; 3 John 4; on τηισ topic, see BW 180; R 991–92; Wallace 471–77, 678, 762; Young 187; Z §410.) And this is not some sort of delusion. We *actually* have been spiritually reborn and adopted into God's family. As demanded by a verbal form in a clause immediately following ἵνα, κληθῶμεν is in the subjunc. mood, the 1st pl. aor. pass. subjunc. of καλέω. The vb. καλέω frequently appears with zero vowel gradation (dropping the vowel in its stem). Some grammarians classify τέκνα as a nom. of appellation (KMP 60). Culy labels the nom. pl. neut. noun as a "nominative complement in a subject-complement double nominative construction" (67). He helpfully notes, "When a double accusative construction is passivized, the result is a double nominative construction" (67). Θεοῦ, the gen. sg. masc. of θεός, is a gen. of poss. or relationship. Ἐσμέν is 1st pl. pres. indic. of εἰμί.

διὰ τοῦτο ὁ κόσμος οὐ γινώσκει ἡμᾶς, ὅτι οὐκ ἔγνω αὐτόν.
Because of this, the world does not know us—because it knew not him.

Τοῦτο is the acc. sg. neut. of the near dem. pron., serving as the object of the prep. διά here. The prep. phrase διὰ τοῦτο points forward (most EVV, e.g., CSB, NET, NIV; contra Marshall 171 n. 25, Yarbrough 176) to the ὅτι clause (ὅτι οὐκ ἔγνω αὐτόν). It is because the rebellious world did not recognize the true identity of the Savior that it also cannot recognize his followers for who they are. Ὁ κόσμος is the nom. subj. of γινώσκει. The negated vb. γινώσκει is parsed as 3rd sg. pres. act. indic. of γινώσκω. Ἡμᾶς is the 1st pers. personal pron. functioning as the acc. dir. obj. of γινώσκει. Ὅτι introduces a causal clause. The negated vb. ἔγνω is a 3rd sg. aor. act. indic. of γινώσκω. Students frequently stumble over this form, so the entire 2nd aor. paradigm is listed here for review: ἔγνων, ἔγνως, ἔγνω, ἔγνωμεν, ἔγνωτε, ἔγνωσαν. Αὐτόν is the acc. sg. masc. of the 3rd pers. personal pron., functioning here as a dir. obj. of ἔγνω.

VERSE 2

ἀγαπητοὶ νῦν τέκνα θεοῦ ἐσμεν, καὶ οὔπω ἐφανερώθη τί ἐσόμεθα.
Beloved, we are now children of God, but not yet is revealed what we will be.

Ἀγαπητοί is the voc. pl. masc. of ἀγαπητός, -ή, -όν. Ἐσμεν is the 1st pl. pres. indic. of εἰμί, with the implied subj. ἡμεῖς. Τέκνα is nom. pl. neut. of τέκνον, -ου, τό, here functioning as the pred. nom. Θεοῦ, the gen. sg. masc. of θεός, is a gen. of poss. or relationship. Οὔπω, "not yet," is an adv. that occurs twenty-six times in the GNT.

Ἐφανερώθη is 3rd sg. aor. pass. indic. of φανερόω, with the phrase τί ἐσόμεθα "what we will be," functioning as the subj. of the vb. Τί "what," is the nom. sg. neut. interrog. pron. Ἐσόμεθα is 1st pl. fut. indic. of εἰμί.

οἴδαμεν ὅτι ἐὰν φανερωθῇ, ὅμοιοι αὐτῷ ἐσόμεθα,
We know that when he is revealed, we will be like him,

Οἴδαμεν is 1st pl. pf. act. indic. of οἶδα, an old pf. with a pres. mng. (used by John as interchangeable with γινώσκω). Ὅτι introduces indir. discourse (see BDAG 731d; R 1034–35; Wallace 456–58). Ἐάν (here rendered "when"; see 2:28 on semantic sense) begins a third class cond. prot. (ἐὰν φανερωθῇ), requiring a vb. in the subjunc. mood. Φανερωθῇ is 3rd sg. aor. pass. subjunc. of φανερόω. The understood subj. is Jesus (most EVV; also, Marshall 172 n. 29; Smalley 138; cf. NET which renders implied subj. as "it," referring back to τί ἐσόμεθα). Ἐσόμεθα is 1st pl. fut. indic. of εἰμί, with ὅμοιοι (nom. pl. masc. of ὅμοιος, -οία, -οιον) functioning as the pred. adj. Αὐτῷ, the dat. sg. masc. of the 3rd pers. personal pron., serves as the dat. complement of ὅμοιοι, which could perhaps also be classified as a dat. of respect/reference "likeness with respect to him."

ὅτι ὀψόμεθα αὐτόν, καθώς ἐστιν.
because we will see him just as he is.

Ὅτι is causal (so most EVV). Ὀψόμεθα is 1st pl. fut. mid. indic. of ὁράω, with αὐτόν as the dir. obj. of the vb. Αὐτόν is acc. sg. masc. of the 3rd pers. personal pron. Καθώς, "just as," introduces a comparison. Ἐστιν is 3rd sg. pres. indic. of εἰμί, with an implied subj. of αὐτός or ἐκεῖνος. Law describes the theological point here as "Vision becomes assimilation" (334). Although the full reality of the theological truth in 1 John 3:2 is too much for the fallen human mind to comprehend, the reader is encouraged to pause and prayerfully ponder this text (cf. 1 Cor 15:35–58).

VERSE 3

καὶ πᾶς ὁ ἔχων τὴν ἐλπίδα ταύτην ἐπ᾽ αὐτῷ ἁγνίζει ἑαυτόν,
And everyone who has this hope in him purifies himself,

Ἔχων is a nom. sg. masc. of pres. act. ptc. of ἔχω, here functioning as a subst. modified by πᾶς. Ἐλπίδα, "hope," is the acc. sg. fem. of ἐλπίς, -ίδος, ἡ, the dir. obj. of ἔχων. Ταύτην is an acc. sg. fem. dem. adj., here functioning attrib. to modify ἐλπίδα. As Jobes notes concerning this hope, "it is a certain hope that is merely awaited" (142). Note that dem. prons. occur in the predicate position when they function attrib. The prep. phrase ἐπ᾽ αὐτῷ functions adv. to modify ἔχων. John speaks of the believer as having his hope set *on Christ* (ἐπ᾽ αὐτῷ) and the transforming power to be displayed at his return (see Culy 70; Marshall 173 n. 31; Yarbrough 180; on this mng. of ἐπί + dat., see BDF §235[2]). Paradoxically perhaps, this hope in the eschatological sanctifying power of Christ draws one to live a holy life now. The phrase πᾶς ὁ ἔχων τὴν ἐλπίδα ταύτην ἐπ᾽ αὐτῷ functions as the subj. of the vb. ἁγνίζει, "to purify" (LN §88.30; see also BDAG 12c) parsed as a 3rd sg. pres. act. indic. with the acc. sg. masc. ἑαυτόν, "himself" (a form of the reflexive pron.), as the dir. object. KMP (260–61) and Wallace (524) view the vb. ἁγνίζει as a gnomic pres. Also, see Culy, who suggests the semantics of the verse reflect a "mitigated command" (70; see 1:6). Undoubtedly, John is seeking to inspire and motivate his readers to holiness, not just to instruct their noetic faculties.

καθὼς ἐκεῖνος ἁγνός ἐστιν.
just as that one is pure.

The holiness of a Christian believer's life is reflective of Christ's holiness, as this brief comparative clause makes clear. Ἐκεῖνος, "that one," is the nom. sg. masc. of the far dem. pron., one of John's favorite forms to refer to Christ throughout this letter (cf. 2:6; 3:3, 5, 7, 16; 4:17). Ἐστιν is the 3rd sg. pres. indic. of εἰμί, with the nom. sg. masc. adj. ἁγνός, -ή, -όν, "pure, holy" (BDAG 13c), functioning as the pred. adj.

VERSE 4

Πᾶς ὁ ποιῶν τὴν ἁμαρτίαν καὶ τὴν ἀνομίαν ποιεῖ,
Everyone who practices sin also practices lawlessness,

Ποιῶν is a nom. sg. masc. of pres. act. ptc. of ποιέω, here functioning as a subst. modified by πᾶς. Ἁμαρτίαν "sin," is the acc. sg. fem. of ἁμαρτία, the dir. obj. of ποιῶν. Καί is functioning adv. with the sense "also" (see BDAG 495d). Ποιεῖ is the 3rd sg. pres. act. indic. of ποιέω, with the acc. sg. fem. ἀνομίαν, "lawlessness" (BDAG 85b; only here in 1 John, though 15× in GNT), from ἀνομία, -ας, ἡ, serving as the dir. obj. Contextually, the term goes beyond the traditional understanding of "breaking the law of God" (see Smalley 147). It appears that John has chosen the term ἀνομία to convey a sense of opposition to God in the final days (cf. 2 Thess 2:1–12). John instructs his readers on the true nature of sin; it is cut from the cloth of eschatological hostility toward God. Marshall notes the term was "associated with the final outbreak of evil against Christ and that it signifies rebellion against the will of God. To commit sin is thus to place oneself on the side of the devil and the Antichrist and to stand in opposition to Christ" (176).

καὶ ἡ ἁμαρτία ἐστὶν ἡ ἀνομία.
and sin is lawlessness.

Fond of circling back to the same truth in nearly identical ways, John makes the provocative statement that sin is lawlessness. That is, sin is none other than rebels shaking their fists at God in the last days (Marshall 176–77; Smalley 147; cf. Kruse 118). Ἁμαρτία is nom. sg. fem. and serves as the subj. of ἐστίν, the 3rd sg. pres. indic. of εἰμί. Ἀνομία, rendered as "lawlessness" (BDAG 85b–c) or "breaking of the law" (M. Limbeck, *EDNT* 1:106b; see Kruse 118, who equates [following de la Potterie] the term ἡ ἀνομία with the state of being "children of the devil" [vv. 8, 10]) is nom. sg. fem. and functions as the pred. nom. Note that both the subj. and pred. nom are articular. In such cases, the subj. is determined by context, but one should expect the subj. to occur before the pred. nom. more frequently.

VERSE 5

καὶ οἴδατε ὅτι ἐκεῖνος ἐφανερώθη, ἵνα τὰς ἁμαρτίας ἄρῃ,
And you all know that he was revealed so that he would take away our sins.

John appeals to his readers' knowledge of the reason for Jesus's coming to the world as an impetus for holiness. Οἴδατε is 2nd pl. pf. act. indic. of οἶδα, an old pf. form synonymous with the pres. tense forms of γινώσκω. Ὅτι introduces a content clause (indir. discourse). Ἐκεῖνος "that one," is the nom. sg. masc. of the far dem. pron., one of John's favorite forms to refer to Christ throughout this letter (cf. 2:6; 3:3, 5, 7, 16; 4:17). Ἐκεῖνος is translated as "he" above and serves as the subj. of ἐφανερώθη, the 3rd sg. aor. pass. indic. of φανερόω. Divine agency is implied (i.e., revealed *by God the Father*). Ἵνα introduces a purpose clause (Rogers and Rogers 595) and necessitates a subjunc. mood vb. Ἄρῃ is 3rd sg. aor. act. subjunc. of αἴρω. Ἁμαρτίας is the acc. pl. fem. of ἁμαρτία and serves as the dir. obj. of ἄρῃ. The idea of a subjective or poss. gen. ("*our* sins," NIV, KJV) is implied.

καὶ ἁμαρτία ἐν αὐτῷ οὐκ ἔστιν.
And there is no sin in him.

This phrase can be translated more literally, "And sin is not in him." Ἁμαρτία is nom. sg. fem. and functions as subj. of the negated vb. ἔστιν, the 3rd sg. pres. indic. of εἰμί. The prep. phrase ἐν αὐτῷ functions adv. in a metaphorical loc./spherical sense. John challenges his readers to consider that their Savior's ontological sinlessness is a reason they should shun sin.

VERSE 6

πᾶς ὁ ἐν αὐτῷ μένων οὐχ ἁμαρτάνει·
Everyone who remains in him does not keep on sinning.

Μένων is a nom. sg. masc. of pres. act. ptc. of μένω, here functioning as a subst. modified by πᾶς. We find here the common "participial sandwich," with the adverbial prepositional phrase ἐν αὐτῷ sandwiched between the art. and ptc. Πᾶς ὁ ἐν αὐτῷ μένων functions as the subj. of the negated vb. ἁμαρτάνει, a 3rd sg. pres. act. indic. of ἁμαρτάνω. The history of scholarship reflects diverse explanations for the potential tension reflected between John's words here (and 3:9) and his words elsewhere (cf. 1:8–2:1). Common views include:

*1. John is referring to habitual sin as a pattern of life, a reading based on immediate context and choice of present tense in light of lexical limitations of the vb. (Baugh 47, 50–52; ZG 730; see also Akin 143; Stott 129; cf. ESV "keeps on sinning"; sim. NIV, NLT). While the present tense vb. reflects imperfective aspect (encoded in the tense choice itself), it is the consideration of "pragmatic values" (lexeme and context) that ultimately supports viewing the vb. as iterative (so labeled by KMP 261; Young 108).

2. John is referring specifically to ἀνομία, understood broadly as rebellion against God and rejection of his authority—the sin of the devil (Jobes 147, following Kruse 130; cf. Yarbrough 182–84).
3. John is speaking in terms of an "eschatological reality," which is a possibility for the believer if he or she lives in Christ (Marshall 182; cf. Smalley 156, who states the verse reflects the "potential state of sinlessness . . . Christians can be sinless inasfar as they share now the life of eternity . . . but the completion of that process of perfection lies in the future"; Wallace 525 states John is speaking "in an absolute manner truths that are not yet true").
4. John's language should be understood as polemical/hyperbolic to address theological errors (Laws 224–28; cf. Stott 129).

Baugh helpfully points out why an English translation that highlights the imperfective aspect of the Gk. present tense is preferred (Baugh 47, 50–52). An abiding relationship with the Lord makes persistent, unrepentant sin impossible.

πᾶς ὁ ἁμαρτάνων οὐχ ἑώρακεν αὐτὸν οὐδὲ ἔγνωκεν αὐτόν.
Everyone who keeps on sinning has neither seen him nor known him.

Ἁμαρτάνων is a nom. sg. masc. of pres. act. ptc. of ἁμαρτάνω, here functioning as a subst. modified by πᾶς. Πᾶς ὁ ἁμαρτάνων serves as the subj. of the negated vbs. ἑώρακεν and ἔγνωκεν. Ἑώρακεν is 3rd sg. pf. act. indic. of ὁράω, with αὐτόν as the acc. sg. masc. dir. obj. Ἔγνωκεν is the 3rd sg. pf. act. indic. of γινώσκω, with αὐτόν as the acc. sg. masc. dir. obj.

VERSE 7

Παιδία, μηδεὶς πλανάτω ὑμᾶς
Dear children, let no one lead you astray.

Παιδία (see 2:14, 17) is the voc. pl. neut. of παιδίον, a diminutive form of παῖς, expressing affection or smallness (-ιον is the most common diminutive ending). Μηδείς, "no one," is nom. sg. masc. and functions as the subj. of πλανάτω, the 3rd sg. pres. act. impv. of πλανάω, "lead astray, cause to wander" (see 1:8). Ὑμᾶς is the acc. pl. of the 2nd pers. personal pron., functioning here as the dir. obj. of πλανάτω.

ὁ ποιῶν τὴν δικαιοσύνην δίκαιός ἐστιν,
The person practicing righteousness is righteous,

Ποιῶν is the nom. sg. masc. of pres. act. ptc. of ποιέω, here functioning as a subst. Δικαιοσύνην is the acc. sg. fem. of δικαιοσύνη, -ης, ἡ, serving as the dir. obj. of ποιῶν. Ὁ ποιῶν τὴν δικαιοσύνην serves as the subj. of ἐστιν, the 3rd sg. pres. indic. of εἰμί. Δίκαιός is nom. sg. masc. and serves as a pred. nom.

καθὼς ἐκεῖνος δίκαιός ἐστιν·
just as that one is righteous.

Καθώς introduces a comparison. Ἐκεῖνος, the nom. sg. masc. of the far dem. pron., refers to Jesus, as the form frequently does in this letter (cf. 2:6; 3:3, 5, 7, 16; 4:17). Ἐκεῖνος is the subj. of ἐστιν, the 3rd sg. pres. indic. of εἰμί. Δίκαιός is nom. sg. masc. and serves as a pred. nom. The righteousness of Jesus must be reflected in the behavior of his followers; that is a critical test of true discipleship. "You will know a tree by its fruits" (cf. Matt 12:33; Luke 6:43–45). As Law notes, "Doing is the test of Being" (220).

VERSE 8

ὁ ποιῶν τὴν ἁμαρτίαν ἐκ τοῦ διαβόλου ἐστίν,
The one practicing sin is of the devil,

Ποιῶν is the nom. sg. masc. of pres. act. ptc. of ποιέω, here functioning as a subst. Ἁμαρτίαν is the acc. sg. fem. of ἁμαρτία, -ας, ἡ, serving as the dir. obj. of ποιῶν. Ὁ ποιῶν τὴν ἁμαρτίαν (cf. 3:4) serves as the subj. of ἐστίν, the 3rd sg. pres. indic. of εἰμί (the vb. functioning in a gnomic sense; see KMP 261). In place of a pred. adj. or pred. nom., we find the prep. phrase ἐκ τοῦ διαβόλου (Marshall 184 n. 29 notes it "may express belonging to the devil or originating from him). Διαβόλου is the gen. sg. masc. subst. use of the adj. διάβολος, -η, -ον, "slanderer" (see *NIDNTTE* 1:692; on term, see also Foerster and Von Rad, *TDNT* 2:71–81; 37× in the GNT; as a subst., "Devil"). John challenges his readers to see sin for what it really is: devilish behavior (cf. Kruse 122).

Ὅτι ἀπ' ἀρχῆς ὁ διάβολος ἁμαρτάνει.
because from the beginning, the devil has been sinning.

Ὅτι introduces a causal clause. The plastic prep. phrase ἀπ' ἀρχῆς appears again (cf. 1:1; 2:7, 13, 14, 24; 3:11; see comments on 1:1), here mng. something like, "all along" (see Marshall 184 n. 30) or "from the beginning of his devilish career" (Stott 127). The prep. phrase functions adv., modifying ἁμαρτάνει, the 3rd sg. pres. act. indic. of ἁμαρτάνω (the vb. conveying a durative sense [KMP 258–59; Young 111] or possibly gnomic [BW 87; Yarbrough 187]). Διάβολος is the nom. sg. masc. subst. use of the adj. διάβολος, "slanderer" (see above), here functioning as the subj. of ἁμαρτάνει.

εἰς τοῦτο ἐφανερώθη ὁ υἱὸς τοῦ θεοῦ, ἵνα λύσῃ τὰ ἔργα τοῦ διαβόλου.
For this the Son of God was revealed—that he would destroy the works of the devil.

The prep. phrase εἰς τοῦτο expresses purpose (see BDAG 290d). Τοῦτο is the acc. sg. neut. of the near dem. pron. Ἐφανερώθη is 3rd sg. aor. pass. indic. of φανερόω, "reveal, manifest." Ὁ υἱὸς τοῦ θεοῦ functions as the subj. of ἐφανερώθη. Θεοῦ is gen. sg. masc. of θεός, here functioning as the gen. of relationship. Note the example of Apollonius's Canon (see 1:1), whereby both the head noun and gen. qualifier are articular (ὁ υἱὸς τοῦ θεοῦ). Ἵνα introduces an epex. or content clause (see BW 180; Wallace 471–77, 678, 762; Young 187; Z §410; cf. 3:1), clarifying what the τοῦτο in the earlier part of the verse is (see 3:1). Λύσῃ is 3rd sg. aor. act. subj. of λύω. Students who have memorized countless paradigms of λύω will be comforted to know the word actually occurs forty-two times in the GNT, here conveying the nuance of "destroy" ("to put an end to the works of the devil," LN §13.100) rather than "loosen." The dir. obj. of λύσῃ is τὰ ἔργα τοῦ διαβόλου. Ἔργα is the acc. pl. neut. of ἔργον, "work, deed." Διαβόλου is gen. sg. masc. subst. use of the adj. διάβολος, "slanderer" (see above). Here, διαβόλου functions as a subj. gen. (on topic, see KMP 98–100). Again, we note an example of Apollonius's Canon, whereby both the head noun and gen. qualifier are articular (τὰ ἔργα τοῦ διαβόλου).

VERSE 9

Πᾶς ὁ γεγεννημένος ἐκ τοῦ θεοῦ ἁμαρτίαν οὐ ποιεῖ,
Everyone who has been born of God does not keep practicing sin,

Γεγεννημένος is the nom. sg. masc. of pf. pass. ptc. of γεννάω, functioning subst., modified by πᾶς. Ἐκ τοῦ θεοῦ is an adv. prep. phrase modifying γεγεννημένος. The prep. phrase communicates source or origin (see BDAG 296c), occurring sixteen times from this point in the letter (22× in Johannine literature; 27× in GNT). Πᾶς ὁ γεγεννημένος ἐκ τοῦ θεοῦ (cf. 4:7; 5:1, 4, 18) functions as the subj. of the negated vb. ποιεῖ, the 3rd sg. pres. act. indic. of ποιέω. Baugh cogently argues for the progressive translation to emphasize a pattern of life (47, 50–52; see 3:6 for discussion). Ἁμαρτίαν is the acc. sg. fem. of ἁμαρτία, -ας, ἡ, here functioning as the dir. obj. of the vb.

ὅτι σπέρμα αὐτοῦ ἐν αὐτῷ μένει,
for his seed remains in him,

Ὅτι introduces a causal clause. Σπέρμα, -ατος, τό, "seed," is nom. sg. neut. and likely refers to the regenerative power and/or presence of God. The term has been interpreted by scholars as a reference to the word of God (Dodd 77–78), the Spirit of God (Brooke 89; Brown 410–11; Kruse 125), a combination of both word and Spirit (Marshall 186–87; Smalley 165), the divine principle of life or divine nature (Akin 149; Law 389), and the believers' status as God's offspring (Yarbrough 195). Αὐτοῦ is the gen. sg. masc. of the 3rd pers. personal pron., here expressing origin/source. Σπέρμα αὐτοῦ functions as the subj. of μένει, the 3rd sg. pres. act. indic. of μένω. The prep. phrase ἐν αὐτῷ communicates sphere or location, with overlapping physical and metaphorical senses.

καὶ οὐ δύναται ἁμαρτάνειν,
and he is not able to keep on sinning,

The negated vb. δύναται is the 3rd sg. pres. mid. indic. of δύναμαι. In the GNT, δύναται is followed by a pres. complementary inf. fifty-seven times and by an aor. complementary inf. 154 times (Baugh, *Tense Form Choice*, 69). Here, the complementary inf. (ἁμαρτάνειν) is a pres. act. inf. of ἁμαρτάνω. The vb. ἁμαρτάνω arguably has a preference for the aor. tense outside the ind. mood (6× as aor. subj., never as pres. subj.), so the choice of the pres. tense here seems deliberate to emphasize a pattern of life (trans. above: "keep on sinning," also ESV, NLT; cf. "not able to sin," CSB and NET). There are no other instances of ἁμαρτάνω as an inf. in the GNT. See Baugh's helpful discussion (Baugh 50–52).

ὅτι ἐκ τοῦ θεοῦ γεγέννηται.
because he has been born of God.
Ὅτι introduces a causal clause. Γεγέννηται is the 3rd sg. pf. pass. indic. of γεννάω. Ἐκ τοῦ θεοῦ is an adv. prep. phrase modifying γεγέννηται. The prep. phrase communicates source or origin.

VERSE 10

ἐν τούτῳ φανερά ἐστιν τὰ τέκνα τοῦ θεοῦ καὶ τὰ τέκνα τοῦ διαβόλου·
By this, the children of God and the children of the devil are evident:

The prep. phrase ἐν τούτῳ communicates instr. or means (see BDAG 328c; BDF §§195, 219), pointing forward to the following clause (πᾶς ὁ μὴ ποιῶν . . .). Τούτῳ is the dat. sg. neut. of the near dem. pron. Τὰ τέκνα τοῦ θεοῦ καὶ τὰ τέκνα τοῦ διαβόλου serves as compound subj. of ἐστιν, two neut. pl. subjs. conjugated with a sg. vb. Singular vbs. are frequently employed with neut. pl. subjs. in Koine Gk. Ἐστιν is 3rd sg. pres. indic. of εἰμί. Θεοῦ and διαβόλου are gens. of relationship. Διαβόλου is a gen. sg. masc. subst. use of the adj. διάβολος, "slanderer" (as a subst., "devil"; see 3:8). Both θεός and διάβολος are monadic (substantives of which there is "one" from the perspective of the writer; see BW 73–74; KMP 158; Wallace 223–24), and thus we expect them to appear more commonly as articular. Note that John conforms to Apollonius's Canon (see 1:1), with both head nouns and gen. qualifiers as articular (τὰ τέκνα τοῦ θεοῦ, τὰ τέκνα τοῦ διαβόλου). Φανερά is nom. pl. neut. of φανερός, -ά, -όν, "clearly revealed, evident" (BDAG 1047d: "evident so as to be really known, visible, clear"), here functioning as a pred. adj.

πᾶς ὁ μὴ ποιῶν δικαιοσύνην οὐκ ἔστιν ἐκ τοῦ θεοῦ καὶ ὁ μὴ ἀγαπῶν τὸν ἀδελφὸν αὐτοῦ.
Everyone who does not practice righteousness is not from God—and the one not loving his brother,

Ποιῶν is the negated nom. sg. masc. of pres. act. ptc. of ποιέω, here functioning substantively and modified by πᾶς. Δικαιοσύνην is the acc. sg. fem. of δικαιοσύνη (cf. 2:29; 3:7), here serving as the dir. obj. of ποιῶν. Πᾶς ὁ μὴ ποιῶν δικαιοσύνην is the subj. of the negated vb. ἔστιν, the 3rd sg. pres. indic. of εἰμί. In the "expected slot" of the pred. nom./adj., we find the prep. phrase ἐκ τοῦ θεοῦ. Τοῦ θεοῦ is in the gen. case because the prep. ἐκ always takes a gen. obj. John "expands" the subj. after having already conjugated a sg. subj. (πᾶς ὁ μὴ ποιῶν δικαιοσύνην) with a sg. vb. (οὐκ ἔστιν), an example of a Pindaric constr., after the poet Pindar, who not uncommonly used compound subjs. with sg. vbs. (cf. 2:17; on constr., see KMP 46; R 404–5; Wallace 399–400). The second part of the compound subj. is: ὁ μὴ ἀγαπῶν τὸν ἀδελφὸν αὐτοῦ. Ἀγαπῶν is the negated nom. sg. masc. of pres. act. ptc. of ἀγαπάω, here functioning substantively. The dir. obj. of ἀγαπῶν is τὸν ἀδελφὸν αὐτοῦ. Ἀδελφόν is the acc. sg. masc. of ἀδελφός, with αὐτοῦ as the gen. sg. masc. of the 3rd pers. personal pron., here serving as a gen. of relationship.

FOR FURTHER STUDY

27. Assurance (2:28)

Caneday, Ardel B. "Persevering in Christ and Tests of an Eternal Life." *SBJT* 10, no. 3 (2006): 40–56.
*Carson, D. A. "Reflections on Christian Assurance." *WTJ* 54, no. 1 (1992): 1–29.
Court, John M. "Blessed Assurance." *JTS* 33, no. 2 (1982): 508–17.
Frame, 1005–7.
Grudem, 803–6.
Johnson, D. H. *DLNT*, 102–4.
Gundry, Stanley N., J. Matthew Pinson, Michael S. Horton, Norman L. Geisler, Stephen M. Ashby, and Steve Harper. *Four Views on Eternal Security*. Grand Rapids: Zondervan, 2002.
Köstenberger, *Theology*, 480–81.
Kruse, 198–200 (see "A Note on the Bases of Assurance").
Rockwell, Stephen. "Assurance as the Interpretive Key to Understanding the Message of 1 John." *The Reformed Theological Review* 69, no. 1 (2010): 17–33.
Schreiner, Thomas R., and Ardel B. Caneday. *The Race Set before Us: A Biblical Theology of Perseverance and Assurance*. Downers Grove, IL: IVP Academic, 2001.
Stubblefield, Benjamin S. "That You May Know: Assurance of Salvation in 1 John." *JETS* 53, no. 1 (2010): 183–85.

28. Παρρησία/Boldness Word Study (2:28)

Balz, H. *EDNT,* 3:45–47.
BDAG 781b–82a.
Marrow, Stanley B. "Parrhēsia and the New Testament." *CBQ* 44, no. 3 (1982): 431–46.
NIDNTTE 3:657–60.
*Schlier, H. *TDNT,* 5:871–86.
Unnik, W. C. van. "The Semitic Background of παρρησία in the New Testament." Pages 290–306 in *Sparsa Collecta: The Collected Essays of W. C. van Unnik (Part 2)*. Edited by C. K. Barrett, A. F. J. Klijn, and J. Smit Sibinga. NovTSup 30. Leiden: Brill, 1980.

29. Παρουσία Word Study (2:28)

Berkouwer, G. C. *Studies in Dogmatics: The Return of Christ*. Translated by James Van Oosterom. Grand Rapids: Eerdmans, 1972.
Grudem, 109.
Kreitzer, L. J. *DLNT*, 856–75.
NIDNTTE 3:647–57.
Oepke, A. *TDNT,* 5:858–71.
Radl, W. *EDNT,* 3:43–44.

Vena, Osvaldo D. *The Parousia and Its Rereadings: The Development of the Eschatological Consciousness in the Writings of the New Testament.* New York: Lang, 2001.

30. Born of God/New Birth/Children of God (2:29; 3:2)

Büchsel, Friedrich. *TDNT,* 1:673–75.
Burkhardt, Helmut. *The Biblical Doctrine of Regeneration.* Edited by Klaus Bockmuehl. Translated by O. R. Johnston. Downers Grove, IL: InterVarsity, 1978.
Drane, J. W. *DNLT*, 1115–17.
Fortune, A. W. *ISBE,* 1:646–48.
Geoffrey, Bromily W. *ISBE,* 4:67–71.
Goldsworthy, G. *NDBT*, 720–23.
Jobes, 111–12 (see "IN DEPTH: Being of God (ἐκ) in John's Letters").
Köstenberger, *Theology*, 479–80.
Lieu, Judith. "'Authority to Become Children of God': A Study of 1 John." *NovT* 23, no. 3 (1981): 210–28.
Packer, J. I. *Knowing God.* Downers Grove, IL: InterVarsity, 1973 (see 200–229).
Porsch, Felix. *EDNT,* 1:76–77.
Smalley, 127–29.
Toon, Peter. *Born Again: A Biblical and Theological Study of Regeneration.* Grand Rapids: Baker, 1987.
Vellanickal, M. *The Divine Sonship of Christians in the Johannine Writings.* Analecta Biblica 72. Rome: Biblical Institute Press, 1977.
Wilkins, M. J. *DNLT*, 792–95.

31. Hope (3:3)

Ateek, N. S. "Hope in a Hopeless World." *Evangelical Review of Theology* 10 (1986): 33–38.
Banks, R., ed. *Reconciliation and Hope.* Grand Rapids: Eerdmans, 1974.
Beker, J. C. *Suffering and Hope: The Biblical Vision and the Human Predicament.* Philadelphia: Fortress, 1987.
Currie, S. D. "Hope in Its Biblical Settings." *Austin Seminary Bulletin* 84 (1969): 29–39.
Denbeaux, Fred J. "Biblical Hope." *Int* 5, no. 3 (1951): 285–303.
Gibbs, J. A. "Regaining Biblical Hope: Restoring the Prominence of the Parousia." *CJ* 27 (2001): 310–22.
Hebblethwaite, B. *The Christian Hope.* Grand Rapids: Eerdmans, 1984.
Hoffman, E. *NIDNTT,* 2:238–44.
Hubbard, David Allan. "Hope in the Old Testament." *TynBul* 34 (1983): 33–59.
Moule, C. F. D. *The Meaning of Hope.* Philadelphia: Fortress, 1963.

32. Sinless Perfection or a Pattern of Living? 1 John 3:4–9

Bogart, John L. *Orthodox and Heretical Perfectionism in Johannine Community as Evident in the First Epistle of John.* Missoula, MT: Scholars, 1977.
Kotzé, P. P. A. "The Meaning of 1 John 3:9 with Reference to 1 John 1:8 and 10." *Neot* 13 (1981): 68–83.

Kruse, 126–32 (see "A Note on Sinless Perfectionism").
Kubo, Sakae. "1 John 3:9: Absolute or Habitual?" *Andrews University Seminary Studies* 7, no. 1 (1969): 47–56.
———. "Sin and Perfection in 1 John," *SBJT* 10, no. 3 (2006): 58–66.
Marshall, 178–84.
Wallace, 524–25.

33. Son of God (3:8)

Bauckham, Richard. "Sonship of the Historical Jesus in Christology." *SJT* 31, no. 3 (1978): 245–60.
*Carson, D. A. *Jesus the Son of God: A Christological Title Often Overlooked, Sometimes Misunderstood, and Currently Disputed.* Wheaton, IL: Crossway, 2012.
Collins, Adela Yarbro, and John J. Collins. *King and Messiah as Son of God: Divine, Human, and Angelic Messianic Figures in Biblical and Related Literature.* Grand Rapids: Eerdmans, 2008.
Drane, J. W. *DLNT*, 1111–15.
Frame, 456–59.
Hahn, Ferdinand. *The Titles of Jesus in Christology: Their History in Early Christianity.* Cambridge: Clarke, 2002.
Hengel, Martin. *The Son of God: The Origin of Christology and the History of Jewish-Hellenistic Religion.* London: SCM, 1976.
Hurtado, L. W. *DPL*, 900–906.
Köstenberger, *Theology*, 380–93, 540–42.
Schreiner, *NT Theology*, 415–16.
Schweizer, E. *TDNT,* 8:385–88.
See also For Further Study 21 "World/Κόσμος in John's Letters and the New Testament"

HOMILETICAL SUGGESTIONS

The Children of God (2:28–3:10)

1. Identity of the children of God (2:28–3:3)
   a. Confidence in abiding in Christ (2:28)
   b. Eschatological hope (3:2)
2. Living like children of God (3:4–10)
   a. The nature and cost of sin (3:4–6)
   b. God's children practice righteousness as a pattern of life (3:7–9)
   c. Distinction between the children of God and the children of the devil (3:10)

Distinctive from the World (2:28–3:10)

1. God's children remain in Christ (2:28)
   a. Remaining in Christ means our lives reflect a pattern of holiness (3:6)
   b. Remaining in Christ now means no shame at his second coming (2:28)

2. God's children have a future hope that affects their present behavior (2:28; 3:2)
    a. Motivated by pain: Practicing righteousness in the present so that we may not be ashamed at Christ's future return
    b. Motivated by glory: Practicing righteousness now with our eyes on a future glory (3:2–3)
3. God's children practice righteousness (2:29)
    a. Because they are born of God (2:29; 3:9) (spiritual rebirth, see John 3:3)
    b. Not perfection, but a pattern of life (3:6)
    c. Growing in the image of Christ (3:7)
    d. Practicing righteousness is loving one another
4. God's children love fellow believers (3:10)

IX. Love One Another (3:11–18)

The ἵνα of v. 11 provides the content of the message heard from the beginning, "that we love one another," which introduces the fundamental theme of the section. The vb. ἀγαπάω and its cognate noun occur six times in the section (vv. 11, 14, 16, 18). As often encountered in the letter, we see a developed contrast at work between believers and the world and between those who love and those who hate. This contrast continues the focus of 3:7–10 (Jobes 154). The impv. of v. 13 (θαυμάζετε) warns the readers to not marvel if the world hates them. Verses 14–15 develop the contrast between those who love the brothers and those who hate. Verse 16 offers the supreme example of love, Christ laying down his life. Finally, the impv. of v. 18 exhorts the believers to love in deed and in truth.

11 Ὅτι αὕτη ἐστὶν ἡ ἀγγελία
ἣν ἠκούσατε
ἀπ' ἀρχῆς,
ἵνα ἀγαπῶμεν ἀλλήλους,

12 οὐ καθὼς Κάϊν ἐκ τοῦ πονηροῦ ἦν
καὶ ἔσφαξεν τὸν ἀδελφὸν αὐτοῦ·
καὶ χάριν τίνος ἔσφαξεν αὐτόν;
ὅτι τὰ ἔργα αὐτοῦ πονηρὰ ἦν,
τὰ δὲ τοῦ ἀδελφοῦ αὐτοῦ δίκαια.

13 Καὶ μὴ θαυμάζετε, ἀδελφοί,
εἰ μισεῖ ὑμᾶς ὁ κόσμος.

14 ἡμεῖς οἴδαμεν ὅτι μεταβεβήκαμεν
ἐκ τοῦ θανάτου
εἰς τὴν ζωήν,
ὅτι ἀγαπῶμεν τοὺς ἀδελφούς·
ὁ μὴ ἀγαπῶν μένει
ἐν τῷ θανάτῳ.

15 πᾶς ὁ μισῶν τὸν ἀδελφὸν αὐτοῦ ἀνθρωποκτόνος ἐστίν,
καὶ οἴδατε ὅτι πᾶς ἀνθρωποκτόνος οὐκ ἔχει ζωὴν αἰώνιον
ἐν αὐτῷ μένουσαν.

16 ἐν τούτῳ ἐγνώκαμεν τὴν ἀγάπην,
ὅτι ἐκεῖνος ὑπὲρ ἡμῶν τὴν ψυχὴν αὐτοῦ ἔθηκεν,
καὶ ἡμεῖς ὀφείλομεν ὑπὲρ τῶν ἀδελφῶν τὰς ψυχὰς θεῖναι.

17 ὃς δ᾽ ἂν ἔχῃ τὸν βίον
τοῦ κόσμου
καὶ θεωρῇ τὸν ἀδελφὸν αὐτοῦ χρείαν ἔχοντα
καὶ κλείσῃ τὰ σπλάγχνα αὐτοῦ ἀπ᾽ αὐτοῦ,
πῶς ἡ ἀγάπη τοῦ θεοῦ μένει ἐν αὐτῷ;

18 Τεκνία, μὴ ἀγαπῶμεν
λόγῳ
μηδὲ τῇ γλώσσῃ,
ἀλλ᾽ [ἀγαπῶμεν]
ἐν ἔργῳ
καὶ ἀληθείᾳ,

VERSE 11

Ὅτι αὕτη ἐστὶν ἡ ἀγγελία ἣν ἠκούσατε ἀπ᾽ ἀρχῆς,
because this is the message which you all heard from the beginning:

Both the punctuation of the UBS[5] and most EVV favor starting a new paragraph at v. 11, but it would be strange for ὅτι to begin a new section. Much more likely is a tight connection with the preceding verse (cf. Jobes 154; Yarbrough 97), with this ὅτι of v. 11 giving an additional reason why Christians should love their brothers and sisters (causal ὅτι). Αὕτη is the nom. sg. fem. of the near dem. pron., here as the subj. of ἐστίν, the 3rd sg. pres. indic. of εἰμί. Ἡ ἀγγελία, -ας, ἡ ("message"; see 1:5) is nom. sg. fem., serving as the predicate nom. Ἥν, with ἡ ἀγγελία as the antecedent, is the acc. sg. fem. rel. pron., functioning as the dir. obj. of ἠκούσατε, the 2nd pl. aor. act. indic. of ἀκούω. Ἀπ᾽ ἀρχῆς (see 1:1) is a prep. phrase functioning in an adverb. temp. way, modifying ἠκούσατε. The phrase occurs eight times in the letter, here likely referring to the founding of the Christian community (cf. 2:7; also Marshall 189). John appeals to the traditional nature of the love command in reminding his recipients to strive for fraternal love in the Christian community.

ἵνα ἀγαπῶμεν ἀλλήλους,
you should love one another,

Ἵνα here functions to introduce the content of ἡ ἀγγελία "the message," referenced in the previous clause. This is sometimes called the epex. function of ἵνα (see BW 180; Wallace 471–77, 678, 762; Young 187; Z §410; cf. 3:1). Ἀγαπῶμεν is the 1st pl. pres. act. subj. of ἀγαπάω (as Young 187 helpfully highlights, not every 1st pl. subjunc. vb. is hortatory). The procedural nature of the verbal activity of ἀγαπάω has a strong preference for imperfective aspect, so it is not surprising to find a pres. subj., even though ἵνα is more frequently followed by an aor. subj. In other words, in describing the verbal activity of "love," the author's presentation usually does not include a beginning or ending for the activity but presents it in progress (imperfective aspect). Ἀλλήλους, "one another," is the reciprocal pron., whose lexical form is ἀλλήλων. The lexical form is gen. pl. because the reciprocal pron. is always pl. and the nom. form does not exist (one does not use "one another" as the subject of a verb).

VERSE 12

οὐ καθὼς Κάϊν ἐκ τοῦ πονηροῦ ἦν καὶ ἔσφαξεν τὸν ἀδελφὸν αὐτοῦ·
not as Cain was of the evil one and slaughtered his brother.

The opposite of love is hate, of which Cain serves as an apropos prototype. Note that the two dots over the iota in Κάϊν is a diaeresis and alerts the reader to pronounce the alpha and iota as distinct sounds (i.e., not as a diphthong). Ἦν is the 3rd sg. impf. indic. of εἰμί, with Κάϊν as the subj. In the sentence slot where we might expect a pred. nom. or pred. adj., we find the prep. phrase ἐκ τοῦ πονηροῦ, likely expressing source or poss. Ἔσφαξεν is the 3rd sg. aor. act. indic. of σφάζω, "slay, slaughter, violently kill" or "to murder someone" (BDAG 979d). Τὸν ἀδελφόν is the acc. sg. masc. of ἀδελφός, -οῦ, ὁ, serving here as the dir. obj. of ἔσφαξεν. Αὐτοῦ is the gen. sg. masc. of the 3rd pers. sg. personal pron., here functioning as a gen. of relationship.

καὶ χάριν τίνος ἔσφαξεν αὐτόν;
And why did he slaughter him?

Literally: "On account of what did he slaughter him?" Χάριν (acc. of χάρις, mng. "on account of, because of"; LN §89.29, "a marker of reason"; see also Harris 250) is an improper prep. only occurring nine times in the GNT. Its obj. is in the gen. and usually precedes the prep. (unlike here, where the obj. follows; Moule 86). Improper preps. were originally adverbs (thus, only *improperly* preps.) and are never found as prepositional prefixes on compound vbs. Τίνος, "what," is the gen. sg. masc. of the interrogative pron. τίς (χάριν τίνος, "for what reason," so BDAG 1079a). Ἔσφαξεν is the 3rd sg. aor. act. indic. of σφάζω, "slay, slaughter, violently kill." Αὐτόν is the acc. sg. masc. of αὐτός, here functioning as the dir. obj. of ἔσφαξεν.

ὅτι τὰ ἔργα αὐτοῦ πονηρὰ ἦν, τὰ δὲ τοῦ ἀδελφοῦ αὐτοῦ δίκαια.
Because his deeds were evil, but the deeds of his brother were righteous.

The apostle John here teaches us that Cain's seething resentment of his brother's righteous deeds was the impetus for his murderous actions. Τὰ ἔργα is nom. pl. neut. of ἔργον, -ου, τό, and serves as the subj. of ἦν. (Neut. pl. subjects frequently take sg. vbs; see BDF §133; R 403–4; Wallace 399 notes, "Since the neuter usually refers to impersonal things (including animals), the singular verb regards the plural subject as a collective whole.") Αὐτοῦ is the gen. sg. masc. of the 3rd pers. personal pron., here functioning as a subj. gen. Ἦν is the 3rd sg. impf. indic. of εἰμί. Πονηρά is the nom. pl. neut. of πονηρός, -ά, -όν, here functioning as the pred. adj. There are ellipses of two words (ἔργα, ἦν) in the final clause. With the implied words provided, the clause reads: τὰ ἔργα δὲ τοῦ ἀδελφοῦ αὐτοῦ δίκαια ἦν (or, more commonly, δέ would occur between τά and ἔργα). Τά stands for τὰ ἔργα, which is the nom. pl. neut. of ἔργον and serves as the subj. of the implied ἦν. Τοῦ ἀδελφοῦ is the gen. sg. masc. of ἀδελφός, serving here as the subj. gen. Αὐτοῦ is the gen. sg. masc. of the 3rd pers. personal pron., here functioning as a gen. of relationship. Δίκαια is the nom. pl. neut. of δίκαιος, -αία, -ον (see 3:7), here functioning as the pred. adj.

VERSE 13

Καὶ μὴ θαυμάζετε, ἀδελφοί, εἰ μισεῖ ὑμᾶς ὁ κόσμος.
And do not marvel, brothers, if the world hates you.

The story of Cain and Abel is played out repeatedly in world history, with the wicked despising and persecuting the righteous. Θαυμάζετε is 2nd pl. pres. act. impv. of θαυμάζω, "marvel, be amazed, be astonished" or "Do not be surprised" (most EVV). The impv. should be understood as a general command, applicable through many stages of the recipients' experience. Ἀδελφοί is voc. pl. masc. of ἀδελφός. Context makes clear that the form is voc. and not nom. A nom. can sometimes function the same as the voc., but in such cases the art. is usually present (e.g., John 20:28). The negative command to not be surprised (μὴ θαυμάζετε) functions as the apod. of a first class cond. sentence. The prot. (εἰ μισεῖ ὑμᾶς ὁ κόσμος) is presented as assumed true for the sake of argument. And, based on John's other statements, we know the prot. to be true in reality (on first class cond., see BW 182; Wallace 690–94; cf. Young 228). Note that εἰ could be understood as "that" in this context (so BDAG 277d–78a, "marking an indirect question as content"; Burton §277, "nearly the force of a clause introduced by ὅτι"; Young 185, functioning as a "complementizer"; Smalley 178, noting use is "common after verbs of emotion or wonder") or the εἰ could be understood (as noted above) as part of a first class cond. clause (so Akin 156; Culy 83; Hiebert 155). Context and John's use elsewhere support the cond. sense. Μισεῖ is 3rd sg. pres. act. indic. of μισέω. Ὑμᾶς, the acc. pl. of the 2nd pers. personal pron., is the dir. obj. of μισεῖ. Ὁ κόσμος, the nom. sg. masc. form, functions as the subj. of μισεῖ.

VERSE 14

ἡμεῖς οἴδαμεν ὅτι μεταβεβήκαμεν ἐκ τοῦ θανάτου εἰς τὴν ζωήν,
We know that we have crossed over from death into life

Ἡμεῖς, the nom. pl. of the 1st pers. personal pron. and subj. of οἴδαμεν, is inclusive, referring to John, any of his associates, and the recipients of the letter, marking "the contrast between the world . . . and true believers" (Hiebert 155). Οἴδαμεν is 1st pl. pf. act. indic. of οἶδα (an old pf. form that John uses synonymously with γινώσκω). Ὅτι communicates the content (Marshall 191 n. 11) of what John affirms that he and his recipients know. Using slightly different language, Culy says that ὅτι "introduces the clausal complement of οἴδαμεν" (84). He explains, "Such complements may be thought of as introducing indirect discourse with a verb of cognition" (25; cf. R 1034–35; Wallace 456–58). Μεταβεβήκαμεν is the 1st pl. pf. act. indic. of μεταβαίνω, "cross over, pass over, transfer from one place to another" (BDAG 638c, "to change from one state or condition to another state"). The prep. phrase ἐκ τοῦ θανάτου expresses the location from which the transference began (see BDAG 295d) and εἰς τὴν ζωήν expresses the destination of the movement (see BDAG 290a). Greek frequently uses articles with abstract nouns (e.g., life, joy, peace, death) while such nouns are usually anar. in English. Θανάτου is the obj. of the prep. ἐκ and the gen. sg. masc. form of θάνατος, -ου, ὁ, "death." Ζωήν is the obj. of the prep. εἰς and the acc. sg. fem. form of ζωή, -ῆς, ἡ. "Death" and "life" are presented as two realms or categories of existence. All humans are found in one or the other.

ὅτι ἀγαπῶμεν τοὺς ἀδελφούς·
because we love our brothers.

Ὅτι is causal and gives the evidential reason that believers know they have crossed from the realm of death into life: because they love their Christian brothers and sisters. Ἀγαπῶμεν is the 1st pl. pres. act. indic. of ἀγαπάω. Students may well note that the subjunc. form is orthographically identical, but context here demands an indicative. Ἀδελφούς is the acc. pl. masc. of ἀδελφός, here serving as the dir. obj. of ἀγαπῶμεν.

ὁ μὴ ἀγαπῶν μένει ἐν τῷ θανάτῳ.
The person not loving remains in death.

Ἀγαπῶν is the nom. sg. masc. pres. act. ptc. of ἀγαπάω, here negated and as a subst. use of the ptc. functioning as the subj. of μένει, the 3rd sg. pres. act. indic. of μένω. The prep. phrase ἐν τῷ θανάτῳ communicates the metaphorical idea of sphere/realm. Θανάτῳ is the dat. sg. masc. of θάνατος, "death."

VERSE 15

πᾶς ὁ μισῶν τὸν ἀδελφὸν αὐτοῦ ἀνθρωποκτόνος ἐστίν,
Everyone who hates his brother is a murderer,

Μισῶν is the nom. sg. masc. pres. act. ptc. of μισέω, "hate, despise," here functioning substantively. Πᾶς functions as an attrib. adj. modifying ὁ μισῶν. Τὸν ἀδελφόν is the acc. sg. masc. of ἀδελφός, functioning here as the dir. obj. of μισῶν. Αὐτοῦ is the gen. sg. masc. of the 3rd pers. personal pron., functioning as a gen. of relationship. This entire phrase functions as an elongated subject: πᾶς ὁ μιςῶν τὸν ἀδελφὸν αὐτοῦ. Ἐστίν is 3rd sg. pres. indic. of εἰμί, with the pred. nom. ἀνθρωποκτόνος, "murderer" (LN §20.85; BDAG 81a; lit. "man-killer"; used 3× in GNT). Just as Jesus teaches that the lusting heart reveals embryonic adultery (Matt 5:27–28; cf. Matt 5:21–22), so hatred is embryonic murder. Stott notes v. 15a is a "faithful echo of the teaching of Jesus in the Sermon on the Mount" (144; see also Kruse 136).

καὶ οἴδατε ὅτι πᾶς ἀνθρωποκτόνος οὐκ ἔχει ζωὴν αἰώνιον ἐν αὐτῷ μένουσαν.
and you all know that no murderer has eternal life remaining in him.

John appeals to the traditional nature of his teaching and the community's knowledge of it. Οἴδατε is the 2nd pl. pf. act. indic. of οἶδα (used synonymous with the pres. tense forms of γινώσκω). Ὅτι introduces the content of what the community knows (see 3:14 for further discussion of this use of ὅτι). Ἀνθρωποκτόνος, "murderer, man killer" (see above), is nom. sg. masc. and is modified by the attrib. πᾶς. Πᾶς ἀνθρωποκτόνος serves as the subj. of the negated vb. ἔχει, the 3rd sg. pres. act. indic. of ἔχω. The text literalistically reads: "And you all know that every murderer does not have eternal life remaining in him" (Young 203–4 refers to this constr. as a universal negative; cf. 2:21; 4:3; 5:18). Ζωήν is the acc. sg. fem. of ζωή, -ῆς, ἡ, and is modified by the attrib. adj. αἰώνιον, acc. sg. fem. of αἰώνιος. Αἰώνιος (see 1:2) often appears as a two-termination adj. (on this topic, see BDF §59[1]; Decker 95; R 272–73), though sometimes (inconsistently) 1st decl. endings are employed with fem. forms (though not here). Μένουσαν is acc. sg. fem. pres. act. ptc. of μένω, here telling us more about the acc. sg. fem. ζωὴν αἰώνιον. Culy labels μένουσαν as the complement in a double acc. object-complement cstr., though perhaps the ptc. is supplementary (see "Supplementary Participles" in the introduction) or simply attrib. Ἐν αὐτῷ is a prep. phrase functioning adv. to modify μένουσαν. Αὐτῷ is the obj. of the prep. ἐν and is dat. sg. masc. of the 3rd pers. personal pron.

VERSE 16

ἐν τούτῳ ἐγνώκαμεν τὴν ἀγάπην, ὅτι ἐκεῖνος ὑπὲρ ἡμῶν τὴν ψυχὴν αὐτοῦ ἔθηκεν,
By this we know love: that one laid down his life for us.

The prep. phrase ἐν τούτῳ functions instr., pointing forward to the ὅτι clause (Marshall 192 n. 14; Smalley 183; Yarbrough 202). Τούτῳ is the dat. sg. neut. of the near dem. pron., here functioning as the obj. of the prep. ἐν. Ἐγνώκαμεν is 1st pl. pf. act. indic. of γινώσκω. The "we" is inclusive (see 2:18; 3:14); John states that he, his associates, and the recipients of the letter have come to know (in the past) what love is and now live with that knowledge/experience (stative aspect). Ἀγάπην is the acc. sg. fem. of ἀγάπη, functioning here as the dir. obj. of ἐγνώκαμεν. Abstract nouns are frequently art. in Gk. as here (τὴν ἀγάπην; see BW 74; R 794; see 1:4). Ὅτι introduces an epex. clause (see BDF 397[3]; cf. BDF 394). Ἐκεῖνος (a reference to Jesus in 2:6; 3:3, 5, 7; 4:17 and the subj. of the vb. ἔθηκεν) is the nom. sg. masc. of the far dem. pron. Ἔθηκεν is 3rd sg. aor. act. indic. of τίθημι, with ψυχήν, the acc. sg. fem. of ψυχή, as the dir. obj. Αὐτοῦ, the gen. sg. masc. of the 3rd pers. personal pron. is a gen. of poss. It is common for a head noun qualified by a gen. pron. to be art. (51× in 1 John) as here (τὴν ψυχὴν αὐτοῦ). Note the phrase τὴν ψυχὴν . . . ἔθηκεν conveys here the sense "to lay down or give (up) one's life" (BDAG 1003d; on this phrase, see also C. Maurer, *TDNT* 8:155–56; Marshall 193 n. 16). The prep. phrase ὑπὲρ ἡμῶν communicates advantage or benefit "in behalf of, for the sake of" (BDAG 1030c–d; cf. Harris 215–16). Contextually, the exemplary aspect of Christ's self-sacrifice is emphasized (Akin 159; Hiebert 160).

Yet, Smalley helpfully highlights the larger context of 1 John which explicitly affirms "Christ's vicarious suffering" (184). Ἡμῶν, the gen. pl. of the 1st pers. personal pron., is the obj. of the prep. ὑπέρ.

καὶ ἡμεῖς ὀφείλομεν ὑπὲρ τῶν ἀδελφῶν τὰς ψυχὰς θεῖναι.
We also ought to lay down our lives for our brothers.

Ἡμεῖς is nom. pl. of the 1st pers. personal pron. and serves as the subj. of ὀφείλομεν, the 1st pl. pres. act. indic. of ὀφείλω, "to owe, be obligated." The verb ὀφείλω is followed by a complementary inf. twenty-five times in the GNT (19× pres., 6× aor.) Perhaps John has chosen the aor. tense for the complementary inf. here (θεῖναι, aor. act. inf. of τίθημι) because laying down one's life (i.e., dying) more naturally lends itself to description with perfective aspect. Ψυχάς is the acc. pl. fem. of ψυχή, serving as the dir. obj. of θεῖναι. A poss. idea is implied (i.e., *our* lives). In cases where a poss. idea is implied, a noun is almost always art., as here (τὰς ψυχάς). The prep. phrase ὑπὲρ τῶν ἀδελφῶν communicates advantage or benefit (LN §90.36) and adv. modifies the inf. θεῖναι. Ἀδελφῶν is the gen. pl. masc. of ἀδελφός, employed here as the obj. of the prep. ὑπέρ.

VERSE 17

ὃς δ' ἂν ἔχῃ τὸν βίον τοῦ κόσμου καὶ θεωρῇ τὸν ἀδελφὸν αὐτοῦ χρείαν ἔχοντα καὶ κλείσῃ τὰ σπλάγχνα αὐτοῦ ἀπ' αὐτοῦ,
So, whoever has worldly possessions and sees his brother having need and closes his heart away from him,

The text more literalistically reads, "So whoever has the life of the world." The postpositive particle δέ carries the letter forward, here apparently drawing an implication about the need for practical, comparatively small sacrifices in light of our ultimate fraternal obligation to ultimate sacrifice (v. 16). The nom. sg. masc. indef. rel. ὃς ἄν serves as the subj. of ἔχῃ, the 3rd sg. pres. act. subj. of ἔχω. Βίον, "life, possessions" or "worldly goods" (BDAG 177b), is the acc. sg. masc. of βίος, -ου, ὁ, here as the dir. obj. of ἔχῃ. Κόσμου is gen. sg. masc. of κόσμος, functioning as a descriptive gen. or perhaps attrib. gen. ("world's goods," CSB, ESV, NASB; "material possessions," NIV). Θεωρῇ is the 3rd sg. pres. act. subj. of θεωρέω, "see, behold, look at." Ἀδελφόν is the acc. sg. masc. of ἀδελφός, -οῦ, ὁ, serving as the dir. obj. of θεωρῇ. Αὐτοῦ is the gen. sg. masc. of the 3rd pers. personal pron., functioning as a gen. of relationship. It is common for a head noun qualified by a gen. pron. to be articular, as here (τὸν ἀδελφὸν αὐτοῦ). Ἔχοντα is the acc. sg. masc. of pres. act. ptc. of ἔχω, here describing the acc. sg. masc. ἀδελφόν. Culy labels ἔχοντα as the complement in a double accusative object-complement constr., though perhaps the label "supplementary ptc." is more accurate (see "Supplementary Participles" in the introduction). Χρείαν is the acc. sg. fem. of χρεία, -ας, ἡ, "need, necessity" or "lack, want, difficulty" (BDAG 1088c) and serves as the dir. obj. of ἔχοντα. Κλείσῃ is the 3rd sg. aor. act. subj. of κλείω, "close, shut." Σπλάγχνα is the acc. pl. neut. of σπλάγχνον, -ου, τό (almost always pl., "guts, intestines, bowels, deepest seat of emotion" [i.e., "heart"]). The KJV renders τὰ σπλάγχνα as "bowels of compassion," a moniker that we recommend for your church group focused on benevolence. BDAG (938d) renders *κλείσῃ τὰ σπλάγχνα* as "to close one's heart" (sim. ESV, NASB; "to refuse to show compassion," LN §25.55; sim. CSB). Αὐτοῦ is the gen. sg. masc. of the 3rd pers. personal pron., functioning as a gen. of relationship. The prep. phrase *ἀπ' αὐτοῦ* expresses disassociation or separation. Αὐτοῦ is the obj. of the prep. *ἀπό*.

πῶς ἡ ἀγάπη τοῦ θεοῦ μένει ἐν αὐτῷ;
how is the love of God remaining in him?

John's rhetorical question functions the same as the assertion: "The love of God is not remaining in this sort of person." Ἡ *ἀγάπη τοῦ θεοῦ* functions as the subj. of *μένει*, the 3rd sg. pres. act. indic. of *μένω*. Ἀγάπη is nom. sg. fem. and θεοῦ is the gen. sg. masc. of θεός. While the gen. is likely functioning as an obj. gen. ("love for God"; so Culy 89; Young 30), some commentators support a subj. gen. ("God's love"; so Stott 145; Yarbrough 205 n. 18; so also Rogers and Rogers 596). Others support a sense reflecting "a love like God's" (Smalley 188; cf. Marshall 194; Law 245). As Hiebert helpfully notes, "in the operation of true Christian love both the subjective and objective aspects of 'the love of God' are involved" (162–63). Note that with the phrase *ἡ ἀγάπη τοῦ θεοῦ* Apollonius's Canon is followed, with both the head noun and gen. qualifier as art. (see 1:1). Ἐν *αὐτῷ* is a prep. phrase expressing a metaphorical spherical/loc. idea. Αὐτῷ is the dat. sg. masc. obj. of the prep. *ἐν*.

VERSE 18

Τεκνία, μὴ ἀγαπῶμεν λόγῳ μηδὲ τῇ γλώσσῃ,
Dear children, let us not love by word nor with tongue,

Τεκνία is a voc. pl. of *τεκνίον*, a diminutive form of *τέκνον* (see 2:1). Diminutive forms often express affection or smallness. Ἀγαπῶμεν is the 1st pl. pres. act. subj. of *ἀγαπάω*, a hortatory subjunc. (on this topic, see KMP 206; BDF §364). Although the indicative form is spelled the same, *μή* indicates a non-indicative is to be expected. Λόγῳ is dat. sg. masc. of *λόγος*, functioning here as an instr. dat. of means. Γλώσσῃ, the dat. sg. fem. of *γλῶσσα, -ης, ἡ* ("tongue, language"; "speech," CSB, NIV; "talk," ESV), is also an instr. dat. In light of John's other statements and the rest of the biblical canon, the apostle is certainly not against oral expressions of love but *mere* oral expressions with no accompanying deeds (e.g., "Let's not merely say that we love each other," NLT).

ἀλλ' ἐν ἔργῳ καὶ ἀληθείᾳ.
but by deed and in truth.

There is an ellipsis in this clause of the hortatory subjunc. *ἀγαπῶμεν* "let us love." Ἔργῳ is the dat. sg. neut. of *ἔργον, -ου, τό*, functioning here as obj. of the prep. *ἐν*. Harris rightfully warns against pressing a distinction with the added prep. *ἐν* (40). The entire prep. phrase (*ἐν ἔργῳ*) functions to communicate instr. or means (see BDAG 328c; BDF §§195, 219). Ἀληθείᾳ is the dat. sg. fem. of *ἀλήθεια, -ας, ἡ*, and communicates manner.

FOR FURTHER STUDY

See For Further Study 16 "Love/Ἀγαπάω/Ἀγάπη Word Study," 17 "The Love of God," and 19 "Loving One Another."

HOMILETICAL SUGGESTIONS

Loving Like Christ (3:11–18)

1. Love one another (vv. 12–13)
   a. Do not love like the world (v. 12)
   b. Do not be surprised if hated by the world (v. 13)
2. Love as evidence of our new life in Christ (vv. 14–15)
3. Love like Christ who laid down his life for us (vv. 16–18)
   a. Expressions of God's indwelling love (v. 17)
   b. Love in deed and in truth (v. 18)

X. Assurance and the Condemning Heart (3:19–24)

This section offers assurance to believers against the condemning heart by affirming the greatness of God (vv. 19–21). Based on this assurance before God, v. 22 affirms confidence in prayer. Verses 22–24 highlight the ethical element of the Christian life, introduced in v. 22 by the ὅτι clause "because we keep his commands." The ἵνα of v. 23 introduces the content of the command: to believe in Jesus Christ and to love one another. It is by loving others and believing in Christ that we experience mutual indwelling (v. 24). The presence of the Holy Spirit affirms this. The introduction of the Spirit functions as a transition to the following section (4:1–6).

19 Καὶ ἐν τούτῳ γνωσόμεθα ὅτι ἐκ τῆς ἀληθείας ἐσμέν.
καὶ ἔμπροσθεν αὐτοῦ πείσομεν τὴν καρδίαν ἡμῶν,

20 ὅτι
ἐὰν καταγινώσκῃ ἡμῶν ἡ καρδία,
ὅτι μείζων ἐστὶν ὁ θεὸς τῆς καρδίας ἡμῶν
καὶ γινώσκει πάντα.

21 Ἀγαπητοί,
ἐὰν ἡ καρδία ἡμῶν μὴ καταγινώσκῃ,
παρρησίαν ἔχομεν πρὸς τὸν θεὸν

22 καὶ ὃ ἐὰν αἰτῶμεν,
λαμβάνομεν ἀπ' αὐτοῦ,
ὅτι τὰς ἐντολὰς αὐτοῦ τηροῦμεν
καὶ τὰ ἀρεστὰ ἐνώπιον αὐτοῦ ποιοῦμεν.

23 Καὶ αὕτη ἐστὶν ἡ ἐντολὴ αὐτοῦ,
ἵνα | πιστεύσωμεν τῷ ὀνόματι τοῦ υἱοῦ αὐτοῦ Ἰησοῦ Χριστοῦ
| καὶ ἀγαπῶμεν ἀλλήλους,
καθὼς ἔδωκεν ἐντολὴν ἡμῖν.

24 καὶ ὁ τηρῶν τὰς ἐντολὰς αὐτοῦ ἐν αὐτῷ μένει
καὶ αὐτὸς [μένει] ἐν αὐτῷ·
καὶ ἐν τούτῳ
γινώσκομεν ὅτι μένει ἐν ἡμῖν,
ἐκ τοῦ πνεύματος
οὗ ἡμῖν ἔδωκεν.

VERSE 19

Καὶ ἐν τούτῳ γνωσόμεθα ὅτι ἐκ τῆς ἀληθείας ἐσμέν.
And by this, we will know that we are of the truth,

The initial conjunction is omitted in some mss. (A B 5 436 et al.) though supported by others (ℵ C Ψ 81 307 et al.). A decision for inclusion is difficult but its interpretive implications are not significant. Ἐν τούτῳ apparently points backward to the previous principle of loving by deed and in truth (ZG 730; most commentators, e.g., Jobes 165–66; Smalley 190; contra NIV). It is *by this* manifestation of love in action that believers will know that they are of the truth. The prep. phrase ἐν τούτῳ communicates means or instr. (BDAG 328c; BDF §§195, 219). Τούτῳ, the dat. sg. neut. of the near dem. pron., functions as the object of the prep. ἐν. Γνωσόμεθα is the 1st pl. fut. mid. indic. of γινώσκω. Not a few Gk. vbs. follow middle endings for their future forms. Ὅτι communicates the content (on this use, see BW 179–80; R 1034–35) of what John affirms that he and his recipients know. Using slightly different language to describe this type of constr., Culy says that ὅτι "introduces the clausal complement" of γνωσόμεθα (84); see note on 3:14. Ἐσμέν is the 1st pl. pres. indic. of εἰμί. The prep. phrase ἐκ τῆς ἀληθείας functions adv. answering the question, "from where?" (likely conveying origin or source [BDAG 296c; Akin 163; Hiebert 165] or possibly poss., "belong to the truth" [NIV; cf. Marshall 197 n. 2]). As Culy rightly notes, "the use of a prepositional phrase, headed by ἐκ, once again highlights identity" (92). Ἀληθείας, the gen. sg. fem. of ἀλήθεια, -ας, ἡ, functions as the obj. of the prep. ἐκ.

καὶ ἔμπροσθεν αὐτοῦ πείσομεν τὴν καρδίαν ἡμῶν,
and before him we will persuade our hearts,

Considering the transforming work of God in one's life can help quiet the condemning heart. Ἔμπροσθεν αὐτοῦ is a prep. phrase functioning adv., modifies πείσομεν, and answers the question "Where?" (location). Ἔμπροσθεν is one of the most common improper preps. in the GNT (48×). Improper preps. began as adverbs and only later came to be used as preps. (thus, *improper* preps.). Improper preps. are never used as prefixes on compound vbs. Πείσομεν is the 1st pl. fut. act. indic. of πείθω, "trust, persuade, convince, win over" (LN §25.166 notes πείσομεν τὴν καρδίαν as an idiom mng. "to convince the heart"; see Akin 163; Culy 93; cf. Kruse 140–41). The vb. can also convey the mng. of "conciliate," "pacify," or "set at ease" (BDAG 791d; NIV, "set our hearts at rest," so Smalley 191; Yarbrough 209; cf. CSB, ESV "reassure," which perhaps reflects aspects of both). Καρδίαν is the acc. sg. fem. of καρδία, -ας, ἡ, here employed as the dir. obj. of πείσομεν. Καρδία reflects the "seat of emotions" (Akin 164; cf. Hiebert 166; Marshall 198 n. 5;

and Smalley 192, who all render the noun as "conscience"; contra Kruse 139–41). The sense of καρδία in this context seems to be broader than "conscience," though, as Akin notes, "the part conscience plays in the seat of emotions . . . should not be completely dismissed" (164). Ἡμῶν is the gen. form of the 1st pers. pl. personal pron. (nom: ἡμεῖς), here expressing poss. Note how a head noun qualified by a gen. pron. is usually art. (τὴν καρδίαν ἡμῶν).

VERSE 20

ὅτι ἐὰν καταγινώσκῃ ἡμῶν ἡ καρδία,
(that is, if our hearts condemn us)

Commentators debate the syntax of this verse, and its challenges are reflected among EVV. (Law 391 notes vv. 19–20 "present an exegetical problem of no little complexity.") It is perhaps only slightly more likely that the first ὅτι in the verse is epex. (NET), restating and clarifying the situation in which one needs a reassured heart. If this reading is correct, then ἐάν introduces the prot. of a third class cond. sentence (on third class cond., see 1:6) and the previous clause should be understood as a fronted apod. Καταγινώσκῃ is the 3rd sg. pres. act. subjunc. of καταγινώσκω ("condemn," LN §30.118; BDAG 515d; "to give sentence against," Law 391), a vb. that takes a gen. obj. or complement (here: ἡμῶν, the gen. pl. of the 1st pers. personal pron.). The vb. occurs three times in the GNT: here, 3:21 in indic. form, and ptc. form in Gal 2:11. Καρδία (see 3:19), a distributive sg. with poss. implied, is the subj. of the vb. καταγινώσκῃ. Another possible (and popular) way of reading ὅτι ἐάν here is as ὅ τι ἐάν (an alternate form of the indef. rel. pron.), functioning as an adv. accusative of reference (i.e., "with reference to whatever situation our hearts condemn us"; "whatever," NASB; "whenever," CSB; commentators supporting the ὅ τι ἐάν reading include Akin 164; Hiebert 166; Smalley 192; Stott 149; Yarbrough 210 n. 4). Regardless of how one treats ὅτι ἐάν, it is possible for ἡμῶν to be either the dir. obj. of καταγινώσκῃ or the poss. gen. modifier of ἡ καρδία. A gen. qualifier more commonly follows the head noun, though perhaps John pulls ἡμῶν forward to create a chiasm with the closing part of the verse (καταγινώσκῃ ἡμῶν ἡ καρδία . . . τῆς καρδίας ἡμῶν . . . γινώσκει).

ὅτι μείζων ἐστὶν ὁ θεὸς τῆς καρδίας ἡμῶν καὶ γινώσκει πάντα.
for God is greater than our hearts and he knows all things.

"Even if our conscience makes us fainthearted and presents God as angry, still 'God is greater than our heart.' Conscience is one drop; the reconciled God is a sea of comfort. The fear of conscience, or despair, must be overcome, even though this is difficult. It is a great and exceedingly sweet promise that if our heart blames us, 'God is greater than our heart' and 'knows everything'" (Martin Luther, as cited by Baugh 61). Ὅτι here functions causally (Robertson, *Pictures* 6:226; CSB; Smalley 192; Stott 149; Yarbrough 208; contra NET, which reflects both instances of ὅτι as epex.) and looks back to the closing clause of v. 19. Ὁ θεός is the subj. of ἐστιν, the 3rd sg. pres. indic. of εἰμί. Μείζων is a pred. adj, here a nom. sg. masc. comparative form of μέγας, with καρδίας, the gen. sg. fem. of καρδία, as the gen. of comparison (BW 27; KMP 104;

Porter, *Idioms*, 96; ZG 731). Καρδίας is a distributive sg. (see above). Ἡμῶν is the gen. form of the 1st pers. personal pron., here expressing poss. In this compound sentence, ὁ θεός also serves as the subj. of γινώσκει, the 3rd sg. pres. act. indic. of γινώσκω. Πάντα, the acc. pl. neut. of πᾶς, functions as the dir. obj. of γινώσκει. John does not employ hyperbole here; God truly does know everything, and yet his knowledge is directed by a fatherly, loving heart that knows fully the righteous life his Son lived for us and the atoning death his Son died in our stead. The sense of the verses could be understood as negative, emphasizing the severe nature of God's judgment (i.e.,"If our hearts condemn us, how much more will God judge us?"). This view was held by some early Greek commentators and some of the Reformers, including Calvin (cf. Stott 149; see also Brown 459). Yet, assurance/comfort is the primary intent (a view popularized by Luther [Brown 459] and held by most commentators surveyed; though note the nuanced view of Kruse 141 followed by Akin 164–65). As Marshall notes concerning the passage, "its main purpose is to give assurance to the readers, on the basis of which they may have confidence to approach God in prayer" (196).

VERSE 21

Ἀγαπητοί, ἐὰν ἡ καρδία ἡμῶν μὴ καταγινώσκῃ,
Beloved ones, if our hearts do not condemn us,

Ἀγαπητοί is voc. pl. masc., a subst. use of the adj. ἀγαπητός. The apostle John, a disciple specially loved by the Lord Jesus (John 21:7, 20), constantly reminds the congregation to which he writes that they too are beloved (cf. 2:7; 3:2, 21; 4:1, 7, 11). Ἐάν introduces the prot. of a third class cond. sentence (on this topic, see 1:6). The negated vb. καταγινώσκῃ is a 3rd sg. pres. act. subjunc. of καταγινώσκω ("condemn"; see 3:20), with ἡ καρδία ἡμῶν functioning as the subj. Καρδία is a distributive sg. and ἡμῶν is a poss. gen. of the 1st pers. pl. personal pron. The dir. obj. "us" (ἡμᾶς) is implied. The ms. evidence that differs from the reading in UBS[5]/NA[28] (noted above) reflects variations in wording (see Metzger 643–44). Yet, ultimately there is no significant difference in meaning.

παρρησίαν ἔχομεν πρὸς τὸν θεὸν
we have confidence towards God,

This phrase introduces the apod. of the third class cond. sentence (on third class cond, see 1:6) that began in the previous clause. Παρρησίαν is the acc. sg. fem. of παρρησία, "boldness, confidence" (see 2:28), which is serving as the dir. obj. of ἔχομεν, the 1st pl. pres. act. indic. of ἔχω. The prep. phrase πρὸς τὸν θεόν functions adv. to narrow the frame of reference for which confidence is asserted (i.e., toward God, or in the presence of God, when in intercession; on πρός with the acc., see BDAG 874d–75a). A Christian reassured of his spiritual status before God will find renewed confidence expressed in bold, believing, Scripture-shaped prayer.

VERSE 22

καὶ ὃ ἐὰν αἰτῶμεν, λαμβάνομεν ἀπ' αὐτοῦ,
and whatever we ask, we receive from him,

The apod. of the third class cond. sentence (on third class cond., see 1:6) that began in v. 21 continues here. Ὃ ἐάν is the acc. sg. neut. indef. rel., functioning as the dir. obj. of αἰτῶμεν (BDF §107 notes, "Ἐάν appears very frequently instead of ἄν after relatives in the NT"). Αἰτῶμεν is the 1st pl. pres. act. subjunc. of αἰτέω. Λαμβάνομεν is 1st pl. pres. act. indic. of λαμβάνω. The prep. phrase ἀπ' αὐτοῦ expresses source/origin. Αὐτοῦ is the obj. of the prep. ἀπό and is the gen. sg. masc. of the 3rd pers. personal pron. In this verse, John speaks hyperbolically, as sinful requests (among others outside the divine will) shall not be answered positively by God.

ὅτι τὰς ἐντολὰς αὐτοῦ τηροῦμεν καὶ τὰ ἀρεστὰ ἐνώπιον αὐτοῦ ποιοῦμεν.
because we are keeping his commandments and doing that which pleases him.

Ὅτι introduces a causal clause. Ἐντολάς, the dir. obj. of τηροῦμεν, is the acc. pl. fem. of ἐντολή, -ῆς, ἡ. Αὐτοῦ is a gen. sg. masc. of the 3rd pers. personal pron., here functioning as a subj. gen. Τηροῦμεν is the 1st pl. pres. act. indic. of τηρέω. Ἀρεστά, the subst. use of the adj. ἀρεστός, -ή, -όν, "pert. to being satisfying" or "pleasing" (LN §25.92), functioning as the dir. obj. of ποιοῦμεν, is acc. pl. neut. Ποιοῦμεν is the 1st pl. pres. act. indic. of ποιέω. The prep. phrase ἐνώπιον αὐτοῦ functions in a loc./spherical sense. Αὐτοῦ, the obj. of the prep. ἐνώπιον, is the gen. sg. masc. of the 3rd pers. personal pron. Ἐνώπιον is an improper prep., having originally been an adverb and then only later became "improperly" employed as an prep. The entire clause reads more literalistically, "because his commandments we keep and the pleasing things before him we do" ("what is pleasing *in his sight*," CSB; cf. BDAG 342c; BDF §214[6]). This causal clause should not be understood as an example of *quid pro quo*. On the contrary, "obedience is the indispensable condition, not the meritorious cause, of answered prayer" (Stott 150). The qualification here can be understood as another way of saying that a petition confidently offered must be offered according to the will of God (5:14).

VERSE 23

Καὶ αὕτη ἐστὶν ἡ ἐντολὴ αὐτοῦ,
And this is his commandment:

Αὕτη is the fem. sg. nom. of the near dem. pron., here functioning as the subj. of ἐστίν, the pres. indic. of εἰμί. Αὕτη points forward to the following ἵνα clause. Ἐντολή is nom. sg. fem. and the pred. nom. of ἐστίν. Αὐτοῦ, the gen. sg. masc. of the 3rd pers. personal pron., is a subj. gen.

ἵνα πιστεύσωμεν τῷ ὀνόματι τοῦ υἱοῦ αὐτοῦ Ἰησοῦ Χριστοῦ καὶ ἀγαπῶμεν ἀλλήλους,
that we believe in the name of his Son, Jesus Christ, and that we love one another,

Ἵνα introduces a "content clause," giving the content of "this commandment" (v. 23a; on similar uses of ἵνα, see 3:1, 8, 11; 4:21; 5:3; 2 John 6; 3 John 4; cf. Wallace 475–76, who labels this an "appositional ἵνα"; R 992 notes that in John "the appositional use is very frequent"; on this topic, see also BW 180; Wallace 471–77, 678, 762; Young 187; Z §410; cf. 3:1). Interestingly, the singular commandment is explicated as two distinct injunctions, demonstrating the inseparability of belief and behavior. Πιστεύσωμεν is the 1st pl. aor. act. subjunc. of πιστεύω. Ὀνόματι, the dat. sg. neut. of ὄνομα, functions as a dat. obj. or dat. complement of πιστεύσωμεν. Υἱοῦ, the gen. sg. masc. of υἱός, communicates poss. Αὐτοῦ is a gen. of relationship. Ἰησοῦ Χριστοῦ is gen. in appos. to υἱοῦ. Ἀγαπῶμεν is the 1st pl. pres. act. subj. of ἀγαπάω (subjunc. because it is a vb., along with πιστεύσωμεν, in the ἵνα clause). Ἀλλήλους, the acc. pl. masc. of the reciprocal pron. ἀλλήλων, functions as the dir. obj. of ἀγαπῶμεν.

καθὼς ἔδωκεν ἐντολὴν ἡμῖν.
just as he commanded us.

Verse 23 ends pleonastically to emphasize both the divine and personal nature of the central imperative behind the Christian life. Ἔδωκεν is the 3rd sg. aor. act. indic. of δίδωμι. Ἐντολήν is the acc. sg. fem. of ἐντολή, serving as the dir. obj. of ἔδωκεν. Ἡμῖν is the dat. form of the 1st pers. personal pron., functioning as the indir. obj. of ἔδωκεν.

VERSE 24

καὶ ὁ τηρῶν τὰς ἐντολὰς αὐτοῦ ἐν αὐτῷ μένει καὶ αὐτὸς ἐν αὐτῷ·
And the person who keeps his commandments remains in him, and he remains in him.

Τηρῶν is the nom. sg. masc. pres. act. ptc. of τηρέω, functioning here as a subst. Ἐντολάς is the acc. pl. fem. of ἐντολή, functioning as the dir. obj. of τηρῶν. Αὐτοῦ, a subj. gen., is the gen. sg. masc. of the 3rd pers. personal pron., here referring to God (NIV). Ἐν αὐτῷ is a prep. phrase functioning adv. in a metaphorical loc./spherical sense, also referring to God (reflected in ESV, NET), and modifying μένει. The phrase τηρῶν τὰς ἐντολὰς αὐτοῦ ἐν αὐτῷ functions as the subj. of μένει, the 3rd sg. pres. act. indic. of μένω. There is an ellipsis of μένει at the end of the clause above; αὐτός, here referring to God, is the nom. subj. of the implied vb. μένει. The final prep. phrase ἐν αὐτῷ also functions adv. in a metaphorical loc. sense to modify the implied vb. The final αὐτῷ refers to the believer.

καὶ ἐν τούτῳ γινώσκομεν ὅτι μένει ἐν ἡμῖν,
And by this, we know that he remains in us:

The prep. phrase ἐν τούτῳ functions to communicate instr./means. Τούτῳ is the dat. sg. neut. of the near dem. pron. and the obj. of the prep. ἐν. The instr. expression points forward to the ἐκ clause at the end of the verse (NIV; most commentators, e.g.,

Smalley 201). Γινώσκομεν is the 1st pl. pres. act. indic. of γινώσκω. Ὅτι introduces the content of what is known. In cstrs. like this, Culy says that ὅτι "introduces the clausal complement of [γινώσκομεν]" (84); see note on 3:14. Μένει is the 3rd sg. pres. act. indic. of μένω. Ἐν ἡμῖν is a prep. phrase expressing a metaphorical loc./spherical sense (see BDAG 326c; R 585–86). Ἡμῖν, the obj. of the prep. ἐν, is the dat. of the 1st pers. personal pron.

ἐκ τοῦ πνεύματος οὗ ἡμῖν ἔδωκεν.
from the Spirit whom he gave to us.

The prep. phrase ἐκ τοῦ πνεύματος communicates instr./means. Πνεύματος, the obj, of the prep. ἐκ, is the gen. sg. neut. of πνεῦμα, here referring to the Holy Spirit, the Third Person of the triune God. The rel. pron. οὗ refers back to the antecedent πνεύματος. One would have expected the acc. sg. neut. rel. pron. ὅ (as the dir. obj. of ἔδωκεν), but the rel. pron. is in the gen. case by attraction to the case of the antecedent (on this topic, see BDF §294). Ἡμῖν is the indir. obj. of ἔδωκεν and dat. of the 1st pers. personal pron. Ἔδωκεν is the 3rd sg. aor. act. indic. of δίδωμι.

FOR FURTHER STUDY

34. Belief/Faith (3:23)

Barth, G. *EDNT* 3:91–98.
Bavinck 4:96–135.
Botha, J. E. "The Meanings of πιστεύω in the Greek New Testament." *Neot* 21 (1987): 225–40.
Bultmann R. *TDNT* 6:174–228.
Eastman, B. *DLNT*, 366.
Frame 951–58.
Lindsay, Dennis R. "The Roots and Development of the Pist- Word Group as Faith Terminology." *JSNT* 15 (1993): 103–18.
Lürhman, D. *ABD* 2:749–58.
Machen, J. G. *What is Faith?* Grand Rapids: Eerdmans, 1962.
Michel, O. *NIDNTT* 1:587–605.
NIDNTTE 3:759–72.
Schreiner, *NT Theology*, 566–69.
See also For Further Study 7 "Obedience/Christian Growth" and 27 "Assurance"

HOMILETICAL SUGGESTIONS

Assurance for the Christian Heart (3:19–24)

1. The condemning heart and the greatness of God (vv. 19–20)
2. Confidence in prayer (vv. 21–22)
3. The commandment of God (vv. 23–24)

   a. Believe and love (v. 23)
   b. Obedience and mutual indwelling (v. 24)

Reassuring Our Hearts (3:19–24)

1. Reassuring our hearts (vv. 19–20)
   a. The small voice of conscience versus the knowledge of the cross
   b. Our merciful God knows our hearts
2. Praying in confidence (vv. 21–22)
   a. Confident prayer is a result of a heart consoled by the truth of God's love
   b. Asking in accord with God's will
   c. Asking from the context of obedience
3. Keeping his commandments (vv. 23–24)
   a. The overarching commandment (v. 23)
      (1) Believe in the name of Jesus Christ, the Son of God
      (2) Love one another
   b. Assurance of mutual indwelling (v. 24)
      (1) In our obedience
      (2) By the gift of God's Spirit

XI. The Spirit of Truth and the Spirit of Deception (4:1–6)

This section, beginning again with the voc. ἀγαπητοί, picks up the theme of the Spirit introduced in 3:24. The two impvs. of v. 1, which provide the exhortations to not believe every spirit (μὴ . . . πιστεύτε) and to test the spirits (δοκιμάζετε), introduce the theme of the Spirit of God and the spirit of the Antichrist (vv. 1–3). The ὅτι clause of v. 1 provides the reason for the need for discernment, highlighting the false prophets who have come into the world. Verses 2–3 offer the criteria for discernment to heed the exhortations of v. 1. The confession of Jesus as having come in the flesh once again underscores the doctrinal test of the letter. Specifically, the confession of Jesus Christ having come in the flesh delineates those who are of God (ἐκ τοῦ θεοῦ) and those who are not. Verses 4–6 convey the contrast between the believers who are of God and the false prophets who are from the world and provide criteria for discernment. Verse 6 further defines the boundaries between the contrasting groups: those who are of God receive their gospel message; those who are not of God, reject it (v. 6b).

1 Ἀγαπητοί,
μὴ παντὶ πνεύματι πιστεύετε
ἀλλὰ δοκιμάζετε τὰ πνεύματα
εἰ ἐκ τοῦ θεοῦ ἐστιν,
ὅτι πολλοὶ ψευδοπροφῆται ἐξεληλύθασιν εἰς τὸν κόσμον.

2 ἐν τούτῳ
γινώσκετε τὸ πνεῦμα
τοῦ θεοῦ·
πᾶν πνεῦμα,
ὃ ὁμολογεῖ Ἰησοῦν Χριστὸν ἐν σαρκὶ
ἐκ τοῦ θεοῦ ἐστιν,

3 καὶ πᾶν πνεῦμα
ὃ μὴ ὁμολογεῖ τὸν Ἰησοῦν
ἐκ τοῦ θεοῦ οὐκ ἔστιν
καὶ τοῦτό ἐστιν τὸ τοῦ ἀντιχρίστου

ὃ ἀκηκόατε ὅτι ἔρχεται,
καὶ νῦν ἐν τῷ κόσμῳ ἐστὶν ἤδη.

4 Ὑμεῖς ἐκ τοῦ θεοῦ ἐστε, τεκνία,
καὶ νενικήκατε αὐτούς,
ὅτι μείζων ἐστὶν ὁ ἐν ὑμῖν
ἢ ὁ ἐν τῷ κόσμῳ.

5 αὐτοὶ ἐκ τοῦ κόσμου εἰσίν,
↓διὰ τοῦτο
ἐκ τοῦ κόσμου λαλοῦσιν
καὶ ὁ κόσμος αὐτῶν ἀκούει.

6 ἡμεῖς ἐκ τοῦ θεοῦ ἐσμεν·
ὁ γινώσκων τὸν θεὸν ἀκούει ἡμῶν·
↓ὃς οὐκ ἔστιν ἐκ τοῦ θεοῦ
[οὗτος] οὐκ ἀκούει ἡμῶν.
↓ἐκ τούτου
γινώσκομεν τὸ πνεῦμα
τῆς ἀληθείας
καὶ τὸ πνεῦμα
τῆς πλάνης.

VERSE 1

Ἀγαπητοί, μὴ παντὶ πνεύματι πιστεύετε ἀλλὰ δοκιμάζετε τὰ πνεύματα εἰ ἐκ τοῦ θεοῦ ἐστιν,
Beloved ones, do not believe every spirit, but test the spirits—to see if they are from God,

A mention of the Spirit (v. 24) leads to a warning against not gullibly believing everyone who claims to speak under spiritual inspiration. Ἀγαπητοί is voc. pl. masc. of ἀγαπητός, here used substantively (see 2:7; 3:2, 21; 4:1, 7, 11), alerting the readers that the author is transitioning to a new section of the letter. The nonindicative negation word (μή) and the dative obj./complement (παντὶ πνεύματι) are pulled forward for emphasis: "*not every spirit . . .*" Παντί is the dat. sg. neut. of πᾶς, an attrib. use of the adj. modifying πνεύματι, dat. sg. neut., from πνεῦμα, -ατος, τό. Πιστεύετε is the 2nd pl. pres. act. impv. of πιστεύω. Δοκιμάζετε is 2nd pl. pres. act. impv. of δοκιμάζω ("put to the text, examine," BDAG 255c; "to try to determine the genuineness of," LN §27.45), with τὰ πνεύματα (acc. pl. neut. of πνεῦμα) as the dir. obj. (Smalley [208] notes the pl. πνεύματα "is used here because John sees that the spirit of truth or error can operate in a number of people at any one time.") There is an ellipsis of the idea of "to see/determine." The prep. phrase ἐκ τοῦ θεοῦ communicates source/origin (occurring 16× in 1 John), with τοῦ θεοῦ as the obj. of the prep. ἐκ. Θεοῦ is the gen. sg. masc. of θεός.

ὅτι πολλοὶ ψευδοπροφῆται ἐξεληλύθασιν εἰς τὸν κόσμον.
for many false prophets have gone out into the world.

Ὅτι is causal. Πολλοί is the nom. pl. masc., from πολύς, πολλή, πολύ, used as an attrib. adj. modifying ψευδοπροφῆται, the nom. pl. masc. of ψευδοπροφήτης, "false prophet" (11× in GNT). Πολλοὶ ψευδοπροφῆται is the subj. of ἐξεληλύθασιν, the 3rd pl. pf. act. indic. of ἐξέρχομαι, "to go out; indication of goal" (BDAG 347d–48a). The prep. phrase εἰς τὸν κόσμον communicates spatial progression, with κόσμον as the obj. of the prep. εἰς.

VERSE 2

ἐν τούτῳ γινώσκετε τὸ πνεῦμα τοῦ θεοῦ
By this, you all know the Spirit of God:

The prep. phrase ἐν τούτῳ communicates instr./means (see BDAG 328c; BDF §§195, 219) and looks forward to the following clause (ZG 731; most EVV; Marshall 204 n. 5; Yarbrough 223). Τούτῳ, the obj. of the prep. ἐν, is the dat. sg. neut. of the near dem. pron. Γινώσκετε is the 2nd pl. pres. act. indic. of γινώσκω (note that the indic. and impv. share the same form, but context supports viewing the vb. as an indic. here, see most EVV and commentators surveyed; contra Law 396). Πνεῦμα is acc. sg. neut. and serves as the dir. obj. of γινώσκετε. Θεοῦ is the gen. sg. masc. of θεός, functioning to communicate source or perhaps poss.

πᾶν πνεῦμα ὃ ὁμολογεῖ Ἰησοῦν Χριστὸν ἐν σαρκὶ ἐληλυθότα ἐκ τοῦ θεοῦ ἐστιν,
Every spirit which confesses Jesus Christ having come in the flesh is from God.

Πᾶν, the nom. sg. neut. of πᾶς, functions as an attrib. adj. modifying πνεῦμα, also nom. sg. neut. Ὅ, the nom. sg. neut. rel. pron., refers back to the antecedent πνεῦμα. Ὁμολογεῖ is the 3rd sg. pres. act. indic. of ὁμολογέω ("profess, confess," LN §33.274; "acknowledge," NIV), followed by the dir. obj. Ἰησοῦν Χριστόν (both forms, acc. sg. masc.) and the supplementary ptc. ἐληλυθότα, communicating indir. discourse (see "Supplementary Participles" in the introduction). BDF (§157) refers to this double acc. constr. as "an accusative of object and a predicate accusative" (also BDF §416[3]; on constr., see also Turner, *Syntax*, 246; R 480; cf. Moule 35; BW 151 addresses the double accusative structure within their grammar, understood to reflect an appositional sense, but labels this ptc. in 4:2 under the category of ptc. in indir. discourse; also KMP 343; sim. Burton §460; cf. Young 149, who highlights the entire noun phrase as the direct object of the vb. of speaking). With the intent for more specificity, Wallace labels this double acc. constr. as object-complement (181–89). Culy, using the object-complement terminology, views Ἰησοῦν Χριστόν as the direct object and ἐληλυθότα as the acc. complement (101). Grammatically, Ἰησοῦν could be understood as the direct object and Χριστὸν ἐληλυθότα as the complement. In this understanding, a break is seen between Ἰησοῦν and Χριστόν; the direct object is understood as "Jesus" and the complement as "the Christ come in the flesh," the focus being placed on Jesus being confessed as the Christ (NET; Stott 154). The vb. can be understood as having only one object, in contrast to the above views that understand the vb. as having two objects. This understanding views the entire phrase after the vb. as a single unit (i.e., "Jesus Christ come in the flesh"), placing the focus on the person who "must be understood in terms of his career in the flesh" (Brown 492–93; see also Smalley 212, who views the phrase as "a connected and descriptive unit"). Note that the "ptc. in indirect discourse" label referenced above fundamentally views the confession Ἰησοῦν Χριστὸν ἐν σαρκὶ ἐληλυθότα as a single obj. of the vb. (see esp. Young 149). Yet, this label reflects more of a grammatical observation while the examples of Brown and Smalley are governed more by observation of the phrase's intended christological emphasis. Ἐληλυθότα is the acc. sg. masc. of pf. act. ptc. of ἔρχομαι. The prep. phrase ἐν σαρκί expresses manner. The eternal Son of God, the Messiah Jesus, came incarnate on his saving mission. Σαρκί is the dat. sg. fem. of σάρξ and the obj. of the prep. ἐν.

This entire phrase functions as the subj. of ἐστιν: πᾶν πνεῦμα ὃ ὁμολογεῖ Ἰησοῦν Χριστὸν ἐν σαρκὶ ἐληλυθότα. Ἐστιν is the 3rd sg. pres. indic. of εἰμί. The prep. phrase ἐκ τοῦ θεοῦ communicates source/origin (see BDAG 296c). Θεοῦ is the gen. sg. masc. of θεός, here functioning as the obj. of the prep. ἐκ.

VERSE 3

καὶ πᾶν πνεῦμα ὃ μὴ ὁμολογεῖ τὸν Ἰησοῦν ἐκ τοῦ θεοῦ οὐκ ἔστιν·
And every spirit which does not confess Jesus is not from God.

Πᾶν, the nom. sg. neut. of πᾶς, functions as an attrib. adj. modifying πνεῦμα, also nom. sg. neut. (on the cstr. πᾶς + negation, see 2:21). Ὅ, the nom. sg. neut. rel. pron., refers to the antecedent πνεῦμα. The negated vb. ὁμολογεῖ is 3rd sg. pres. act. indic. of ὁμολογέω "profess, confess," followed by the dir. obj. τὸν Ἰησοῦν. Μή is used here as negation with the indic. vb. where οὐ is normally expected. Law notes the rarity of μή in a rel. clause with the indic. in the NT and adds that it is used here "with classical correctness" to emphasize the author's conviction "that there are no exceptions to the statement he is making" (396; followed by Smalley 213; cf. Porter, *Idioms*, 284, who notes these instances of exceptions to the expectations regarding negation "may simply be grammatical slips"). The article (τόν) likely has an anaphoric function, referring back to the more explicit confession in v. 2 above (i.e., to confess this Jesus *as the Christ and as having come in the flesh*). The negated vb. ἐστιν is the 3rd sg. pres. indic. of εἰμί. The prep. phrase ἐκ τοῦ θεοῦ communicates source/origin. Θεοῦ is the gen. sg. masc. of θεός, here functioning as the obj. of the prep. ἐκ.

καὶ τοῦτό ἐστιν τὸ τοῦ ἀντιχρίστου ὃ ἀκηκόατε ὅτι ἔρχεται,
And this is the spirit of the Antichrist, which you have heard is coming,

Τοῦτό is the nom. sg. neut. of the near dem. pron., functioning here as the subj. of ἐστιν, the 3rd sg. pres. indic. of εἰμί. Τό stands for τὸ πνεῦμα, with the ellipsis of the noun. Τοῦ ἀντιχρίστου is the gen. sg. masc. of ἀντίχριστος, "Antichrist" (see 2:18), functioning as a gen. of source/origin and the art. specifying *the* end-times arch-opponent of Christ (on the "par excellence" article, see BDF §263; Wallace 222–23; KMP 158). Ὅ, the dir. obj. of ἀκηκόατε, is an acc. sg. neut. rel. pron. and refers to the implied πνεῦμα as the antecedent. Ἀκηκόατε is the 2nd pl. pf. act. indic. of ἀκούω. Ὅτι introduces the content of what the congregation heard (indir. discourse; see BDAG 731d; R 1034–35). Ἔρχεται is the 3rd sg. pres. mid. indic. of ἔρχομαι, a vb. of motion communicating imminent future, sim. to English: "I am going to the store tomorrow."

καὶ νῦν ἐν τῷ κόσμῳ ἐστὶν ἤδη.
and now is already in the world.

John reveals the surprising news that already, even now, the spirit of the end-times opponent of Christ is operative in the world. The implied subject of ἐστίν is τὸ πνεῦμα τοῦ ἀντιχρίστου. Ἐστίν is the 3rd sg. pres. indic. of εἰμί. The two adverbs (νῦν, ἤδη) modify ἐστίν. The prep. phrase ἐν τῷ κόσμῳ communicates location/sphere (see BDAG 326c; R 585–86; Moule 75–76). Κόσμῳ is the dat. sg. masc. of κόσμος, functioning here as the obj. of the prep. ἐν.

VERSE 4

Ὑμεῖς ἐκ τοῦ θεοῦ ἐστε, τεκνία, καὶ νενικήκατε αὐτούς,
You all are from God, dear children, and you have conquered them,

Ὑμεῖς is the nom. of the 1st pers. personal pron. and the subj. of ἐστε, the 2nd pl. pres. indic. of εἰμί. The prep. phrase ἐκ τοῦ θεοῦ communicates source/origin (Marshall 208 n. 14). Θεοῦ is the gen. sg. masc. of θεός, here functioning as the obj. of the prep. ἐκ (the phrase ἐκ τοῦ θεοῦ occurring 16× in the letter; see 3:9). Τεκνία is the voc. pl. neut. of τεκνίον, "little children, dear children," a diminutive form of τέκνον expressing affection or smallness (see 2:1). Νενικήκατε is the 2nd pl. pf. act. indic. of νικάω, "conquer, overcome." Αὐτούς, the dir. obj, of νενικήκατε, is the acc. pl. masc. form of the 3rd pers. personal pron.

ὅτι μείζων ἐστὶν ὁ ἐν ὑμῖν ἢ ὁ ἐν τῷ κόσμῳ.
for the one in you is greater than the one in the world.

Ὅτι introduces a causal clause. Μείζων, "greater," the nom. sg. masc. comparative form of μέγας, is pulled forward for emphasis. Ἐστίν is the 3rd sg. pres. indic. of εἰμί. The subj. of ἐστίν is ὁ ἐν ὑμῖν. The art. (ὁ) substantivizes/nominalizes the prep. phrase ἐν ὑμῖν (see BDF §266). Ὑμῖν is the dat. of the 2nd pers. pl. personal pron., functioning here as the obj. of the prep. ἐν. The particle ἤ, "than" (see KMP 173), introduces the person being compared, ὁ ἐν τῷ κόσμῳ. Again, the art. here substantivizes/nominalizes the prep. phrase. Κόσμῳ is the dat. sg. masc. of κόσμος, functioning here as the obj. of the prep. ἐν.

VERSE 5

αὐτοὶ ἐκ τοῦ κόσμου εἰσίν,
They are from the world.

Αὐτοί is the nom. pl. masc. of the 3rd pers. personal pron., functioning here as the subj. of εἰσίν, the 3rd pl. pres. indic. of εἰμί. The prep. phrase ἐκ τοῦ κόσμου communicates source/origin (cf. 2:16; occurring 13× in John's Gospel). Κόσμου is the gen. sg. masc. of κόσμος and serves as the obj. of the prep. ἐκ. (on the term κόσμος and its various mngs., see Marshall 209 n.15.)

διὰ τοῦτο ἐκ τοῦ κόσμου λαλοῦσιν
Because of this, they speak from the world

Τοῦτο is the acc. sg. neut. of the near dem. pron., functioning here as the obj. of the prep. διά. The prep. phrase refers back to the previous clause (Yarbrough 228 n. 2; cf. 3:1). It is *because* the schismatics find their origin in the rebellious world that they are worldly in speech and that the wicked world welcomes them. Λαλοῦσιν is the 3rd pl. pres. act. indic. of λαλέω. As above, the prep. phrase ἐκ τοῦ κόσμου communicates source/origin. Κόσμου is the gen. sg. masc. of κόσμος and serves as the obj. of the prep. ἐκ.

καὶ ὁ κόσμος αὐτῶν ἀκούει.
and the world listens to them.

The nom. sg. masc. κόσμος serves as the subj. of ἀκούει, the 3rd sg. pres. act. indic. of ἀκούω (here conveying "a receptive hearing of the speaker's message," Hiebert 190). Αὐτῶν, the gen. pl. masc. of the 3rd pers. personal pron., serves as the dir. obj. or gen. complement of ἀκούει. The vb. ἀκούω frequently takes a gen. dir. obj., though ἀκούω also can take a dir. obj. in the acc. case (e.g., Luke 1:4; Acts 5:24; Rev 5:11; on topic, see KMP 107).

VERSE 6

ἡμεῖς ἐκ τοῦ θεοῦ ἐσμεν
We are from God.

Ἡμεῖς is the nom. sg. of the 1st pers. personal pron., here likely referring to John and his coworkers who convey the apostolic gospel (see 1:1). Other views include understanding the "we" as reference to the apostles (Stott 158), all Christians (Akin 175; Smalley 218), or the author and his community (Kruse 149–51). Ἡμεῖς serves as the subject of ἐσμεν, the 1st pl. pres. indic. of εἰμί. The prep. phrase ἐκ τοῦ θεοῦ communicates source/origin (see 3:9). Θεοῦ is the gen. sg. masc. of θεός, here functioning as the obj. of the prep. ἐκ.

ὁ γινώσκων τὸν θεὸν ἀκούει ἡμῶν
The person who knows God listens to us.

Γινώσκων is nom. sg. masc. of pres. act. ptc. of γινώσκω, functioning subst. Θεόν (with a monadic art.; see Young 61) is the acc. sg. masc. of θεός and the dir. obj. of γινώσκων. The entire phrase ὁ γινώσκων τὸν θεόν serves as the subj. of ἀκούει, the 3rd sg. pres. act. ind. of ἀκούω. Ἡμῶν, the gen. pl. of the 1st pers. personal pron., is the gen. obj. or gen. complement of ἀκούει.

ὃς οὐκ ἔστιν ἐκ τοῦ θεοῦ οὐκ ἀκούει ἡμῶν.
He who is not from God does not listen to us.

Ὅς, the nom. sg. masc. rel. pron., begins a headless rel. clause (Culy 105; cf. Young 76) and serves as the subj. of the negated vb. ἔστιν, the 3rd sg. pres. indic. of εἰμί.

The prep. phrase ἐκ τοῦ θεοῦ communicates source/origin (see 3:9). Θεοῦ is the gen. sg. masc. of θεός, here functioning as the obj. of the prep. ἐκ. The entire phrase ὃς οὐκ ἔστιν ἐκ τοῦ θεοῦ functions as the subj. of the negated vb. ἀκούει, the 3rd sg. pres. act. indic. of ἀκούω. Ἡμῶν, the gen. pl. of the 1st pers. personal pron., is the gen. obj. or gen. complement of ἀκούει.

ἐκ τούτου γινώσκομεν τὸ πνεῦμα τῆς ἀληθείας καὶ τὸ πνεῦμα τῆς πλάνης.
By this, we know the Spirit of truth and the spirit of error.

The prep. phrase ἐκ τούτου expresses instr. (Moule 73) or means. Τούτου is the gen. sg. neut. of the near dem. pron. and serves here as the obj. of the prep. ἐκ (on the mng. of the prep. here, see LN §89.77; BDAG 297b). By one's receptive attention to the apostolic proclamation, a person reveals that he is led by the Spirit of God (τὸ πνεῦμα τῆς ἀληθείας = "Holy Spirit," so most surveyed commentators, e.g., Akin 175; Marshall 209). On the other hand, rejection of the gospel proclamation shows one is led by the spirit of error. Γινώσκομεν is the 1st pl. pres. act. indic. of γινώσκω. The vb. γινώσκομεν takes a compound dir. obj., τὸ πνεῦμα τῆς ἀληθείας and τὸ πνεῦμα τῆς πλάνης. In both cases τὸ πνεῦμα is acc. sg. neut. Ἀληθείας is the gen. sg. fem. of ἀλήθεια, -ας, ἡ (see 1:6), here functioning as a descriptive gen. The Spirit of truth is the Spirit of God (not a counterfeit) who reveals and confirms the truth. Πλάνης, the gen. sg. fem. of πλάνη, -ης, ἡ, "error, deceit" (see BDAG 822b; H. Braun, *TDNT* 6:245–46), is also a descriptive gen. The spirit of error is a deceitful, wicked spirit that leads others into error. This verse has two examples of Apollonius's Canon (see 1:1). In both cases the head nouns and qualifying gens. are art., τὸ πνεῦμα τῆς ἀληθείας and τὸ πνεῦμα τῆς πλάνης.

FOR FURTHER STUDY

See For Further Study 22 "Antichrist."

HOMILETICAL SUGGESTIONS

Testing the Spirits (4:1–6)

1. Listen to the message of the speaker (vv. 1–3)
    a. The Spirit of God confesses that Jesus Christ has come in the flesh
    b. The spirit of Antichrist does not confess Jesus Christ
2. Look at the audience of the speaker (vv. 4–6)
    a. The world listens to the message of the world (v. 5)
    b. Those of God listen to and receive the gospel message (v. 6)

Believers Beware (4:1–6)

1. Two commands in the passage that call us to be discerning to "spiritual scams" (v. 1)
    a. Do not believe every spirit
    b. Test the spirits

2. They're here: False teachers are in the world (v. 1)
3. "Red Flag" Alerts
    a. False teachers do not profess a biblical understanding of Jesus Christ (v. 3)
        (1) Protection by knowing your Bible
        (2) Protection by studying the multifaceted message of the gospel
    b. False teachers are worldly (v. 5)
        (1) They echo the talking points of the world
        (2) They are mouthpieces of the coming Antichrist (v. 3)
4. "Identity check": Encouragement for God's children (v. 4)
    a. Those who trust in the finished work of Christ for their salvation are "of God"
    b. He who is in you is greater than he who is in the world

XII. The Love of God (4:7–12)

In this section, after addressing his readers as ἀγαπητοί, "beloved," John returns to the exhortation to "love one another" with the hortatory subjunc. The subordinate ὅτι clause provides the reason for the appeal. In v. 8, the ὅτι clause provides the fundamental theme for the section: "God is love." The fullest expression of God's love is reflected in the sending of his only begotten Son into the world to be the propitiation for sin (vv. 9–10). In v. 11, after the repeated voc. ἀγαπητοί, the first class cond. clause offers further appeal to love in response to such divine love as revealed in Christ. In v. 12, ἐάν introduces a third class cond. clause that allows the author to affirm to the readers what happens "if" they love one another: God remains in them and his love is perfected in them.

7 Ἀγαπητοί,
ἀγαπῶμεν ἀλλήλους,
ὅτι ἡ ἀγάπη ἐκ τοῦ θεοῦ ἐστιν,
καὶ πᾶς ὁ ἀγαπῶν ἐκ τοῦ θεοῦ γεγέννηται
καὶ γινώσκει τὸν θεόν.

8 ὁ μὴ ἀγαπῶν οὐκ ἔγνω τὸν θεόν,
ὅτι ὁ θεὸς ἀγάπη ἐστίν.

9 ἐν τούτῳ
ἐφανερώθη ἡ ἀγάπη τοῦ θεοῦ ἐν ἡμῖν,
ὅτι τὸν υἱὸν αὐτοῦ τὸν μονογενῆ ἀπέσταλκεν ὁ θεὸς εἰς τὸν κόσμον,
ἵνα ζήσωμεν
δι᾽ αὐτοῦ.

10 ἐν τούτῳ
ἐστὶν ἡ ἀγάπη,
οὐχ ὅτι ἡμεῖς ἠγαπήκαμεν τὸν θεόν,
ἀλλ᾽ ὅτι αὐτὸς ἠγάπησεν ἡμᾶς
καὶ ἀπέστειλεν τὸν υἱὸν αὐτοῦ ἱλασμὸν
περὶ τῶν ἁμαρτιῶν ἡμῶν.

11 Ἀγαπητοί,
↓εἰ οὕτως ὁ θεὸς ἠγάπησεν ἡμᾶς,
καὶ ἡμεῖς ὀφείλομεν ἀλλήλους ἀγαπᾶν.

12 θεὸν οὐδεὶς πώποτε τεθέαται.
↓ἐὰν ἀγαπῶμεν ἀλλήλους,
ὁ θεὸς ἐν ἡμῖν μένει
καὶ ἡ ἀγάπη αὐτοῦ ἐν ἡμῖν τετελειωμένη ἐστίν.

VERSE 7

Ἀγαπητοί, ἀγαπῶμεν ἀλλήλους, ὅτι ἡ ἀγάπη ἐκ τοῦ θεοῦ ἐστιν,
Beloved ones, let us love one another because love is from God,

Ἀγαπητοί is the voc. pl. masc. of ἀγαπητός, -ή, -όν, "beloved." John's recipients are loved by him, by God, and by one another. Even so, they must be encouraged not to let their love flag. Ἀγαπῶμεν is 1st pl. pres. act. subjunc. of ἀγαπάω, here functioning as a hortatory subjunct. (Porter, *Idioms*, 118; Young 140). The acc. pl. masc. reciprocal pron. ἀλλήλους (lexical form, ἀλλήλων) serves as the dir. obj. of ἀγαπῶμεν. Stott (161) notes the verse begins with "striking assonance"—Ἀγαπητοί, ἀγαπῶμεν ἀλλήλους. Ὅτι introduces a causal clause, giving a reason why believers must love one another. Ἀγάπη is nom. sg. fem. and the subj. of ἐστιν, the 3rd sg. pres. indic. of εἰμί. The prep. phrase ἐκ τοῦ θεοῦ communicates source/origin (see 3:9). Θεοῦ is the gen. sg. masc. of θεός, here functioning as the obj. of the prep. ἐκ.

καὶ πᾶς ὁ ἀγαπῶν ἐκ τοῦ θεοῦ γεγέννηται καὶ γινώσκει τὸν θεόν.
and everyone who loves has been born from God and knows God.

Ἀγαπῶν is the nom. sg. masc. pres. act. ptc. of ἀγαπάω, modified attrib. by the nom. sg. masc. πᾶς. Πᾶς ὁ ἀγαπῶν serves as the subj. of γεγέννηται and γινώσκει. Γεγέννηται is the 3rd sg. pf. pass. indic. of γεννάω. The prep. phrase ἐκ τοῦ θεοῦ communicates source/origin. Θεοῦ is the gen. sg. masc. of θεός, here functioning as the obj. of the prep. ἐκ. Γινώσκει is the 3rd sg. pres. act. indic. of γινώσκω, with τὸν θεόν as the dir. obj. Θεόν is the acc. sg. masc. of θεός. As a monadic noun (on this topic, see Young 61), θεός is frequently art. (about 80 percent of the time).

VERSE 8

ὁ μὴ ἀγαπῶν οὐκ ἔγνω τὸν θεόν,
The person not loving has not come to know God,

The negated ptc. ἀγαπῶν is a nom. sg. masc. pres. act. ptc. of ἀγαπάω functioning as the subj. of the negated vb. ἔγνω (on vb., see 3:1). Note how nonindicative verbal forms are negated with μή and indicative vbs. are negated with οὐ (or οὐκ or οὐχ). Nevertheless, dozens of exceptions are found in the GNT. Ἔγνω is the 3rd sg. aor. act. indic. of γινώσκω. Stative vbs. (e.g., γινώσκω) frequently convey an inceptive sense in the aor. tense, as reflected in the translation above (on inceptive, see KMP 293; also referred to as "ingressive," see BDF §331; BW 99–100; Wallace 558–59). A gnomic/proverbial nuance is also possible: "The person not loving does not know God." Θεόν is acc. sg. masc. from θεός and serves as the dir. obj. of ἔγνω.

ὅτι ὁ θεὸς ἀγάπη ἐστίν.
for God is love.

Ὅτι introduces a causal clause. Θεός is nom. sg. masc. and serves as the subj. of ἐστίν, the 3rd sg. pres. indic. of εἰμί. Ἀγάπη, the nom. sg. fem., functions as the pred. nom. Although abstract nouns normally are art., perhaps ἀγάπη here lacks the art. to communicate a qualitative nuance: God is, in essence, loving (cf. Hiebert 199; Marshall 213; cf. John 9:24; 1 John 1:5). To come into relationship with the God who is ontologically loving is to necessitate one's transformation into a loving person.

VERSE 9

ἐν τούτῳ ἐφανερώθη ἡ ἀγάπη τοῦ θεοῦ ἐν ἡμῖν,
In this the love of God was revealed among us:

The prep. phrase ἐν τούτῳ expresses instr. or means (see BDAG 328c; BDF §§195, 219) and points forward to the ὅτι clause (Culy 107; NET Translation Notes; Yarbrough 237). Τούτῳ is the dat. sg. neut. of the near dem. pron. and the obj. of the prep. ἐν. Ἐφανερώθη is the 3rd sg. aor. pass. indic. of φανερόω. Ἀγάπη, nom. sg. fem., is the subj. of ἐφανερώθη. Θεοῦ is the gen. sg. masc. of θεός, functioning here as a subj. gen. (e.g., CSB, NIV; KMP 99; most commentators surveyed, e.g., Hiebert 200; Marshall 213; Stott 162). The prep. phrase ἐν ἡμῖν is an adv. modifier of ἐφανερώθη and communicates a loc./spatial idea (Culy 107; "in us," NASB, NET; "among us," CSB, NIV, ESV; e.g., Culy 107; Kruse 157; Marshall 213 n. 5; Smalley 229; Stott 162; on the various interpretations, see Brown 516). Ἡμῖν is the dat. pl. of the 1st pers. personal pron. and obj. of the prep. ἐν.

ὅτι τὸν υἱὸν αὐτοῦ τὸν μονογενῆ ἀπέσταλκεν ὁ θεὸς εἰς τὸν κόσμον,
God sent his only begotten Son into the world

Ὅτι introduces a content clause, synonymously labeled as a clause epex. to τούτῳ (Culy 108; so most EVV, though cf. KJV). Υἱόν is the acc. sg. masc. of υἱός and dir. obj. of ἀπέσταλκεν. Αὐτοῦ, the gen. sg. masc. of the 3rd pers. personal pron., is a gen. of relationship. Μονογενῆ, acc. sg. masc. of μονογενής, -ές, is the attrib. modifier of υἱόν. The adj. either means (1) only begotten (KJV, NASB; ZG 731) or (2) unique, one of a kind (CSB, NET, NIV; BDAG 658a–b; J. A. Fitzmyer, *EDNT* 2:439d–40c; *NIDNTTE* 3:335–36; all commentators surveyed, e.g., Hiebert 200; Jobes 192; Kruse 158–60; Marshall 214 and n. 8; Smalley 230–31; Stott 163). For many years, scholars assumed the textual data favored heavily option 2, but recent scholarship has arguably provided significant data in favor of option 1, which is the wording provided in the translation above (see the series of posts on the term at Seumas Macdonald, The Patrologist, "The Siblingless Son: μονογενής in Greek literature (1)," September

9, 2021, https://thepatrologist.com/2021/09/09/the-siblingless-son-%ce%bc%ce%bf%ce%bd%ce%bf%ce%b3%ce%b5%ce%bd%e1%bd%b5%cf%82-in-greek-literature-1/). Ἀπέσταλκεν is the 3rd sg. pf. act. indic. of ἀποστέλλω. Θεός is the nom. sg. masc. subj. of ἀπέσταλκεν. The prep. phrase εἰς τὸν κόσμον communicates location/direction. Κόσμον is the acc. sg. masc. of κόσμος and serves as the obj. of the prep. εἰς.

ἵνα ζήσωμεν δι᾽ αὐτοῦ.
so that we may live through him.

Ἵνα communicates purpose (Rogers and Rogers 597). Ζήσωμεν is the 1st pl. aor. act. subj. of ζάω, "live." The prep. phrase δι᾽ αὐτοῦ communicates intermediate agency (Culy 108). Αὐτοῦ is the gen. sg. masc. of the 3rd pers. personal pron. and serves here as the obj. of the prep. διά.

VERSE 10

ἐν τούτῳ ἐστὶν ἡ ἀγάπη,
In this is love:

The prep. phrase ἐν τούτῳ points forward to the two ὅτι clauses later in the verse (most EVV; so Culy 108; Yarbrough 239). Τούτῳ is the dat. sg. neut. of the near dem. pron. and the obj. of the prep. ἐν. Ἐστίν is the 3rd sg. pres. indic. of εἰμί. Ἀγάπη is nom. sg. fem. and the subj. of ἐστίν.

οὐχ ὅτι ἡμεῖς ἠγαπήκαμεν τὸν θεόν,
Not that we loved God,

This is the first of two ὅτι clauses that are epex. to τούτῳ (i.e., content clauses). Οὐχ is pulled forward for emphasis. Ἡμεῖς is the nom. of the 1st pers. pl. personal pron. and the subj. of ἠγαπήκαμεν. The explicit pron. subj. ἡμεῖς is included to highlight the contrast with αὐτός below. Ἠγαπήκαμεν is the 1st pl. pf. act. indic. of ἀγαπάω. About 11 percent of pf. forms in the GNT are indistinguishable in nuance from the aor. and perhaps this is one such pf. as we find the aor. in parallel below. Eventually, in the late Koine period, the pf. overlapped fully in meaning with the aor. and the tense became superfluous and fell out of usage. While the aor. tense of the vb. (ἠγαπήσαμεν) reflects strong ms. support (including the corrector of ℵ, A, 5, 436, 1175), Metzger rightly notes (645) that it seems more likely a scribe would have changed the pf. (supported by B Ψ and others) to assimilate to the following vbs. Θεόν is the acc. sg. masc. of θεός and the dir. obj. of ἠγαπήκαμεν.

ἀλλ᾽ ὅτι αὐτὸς ἠγάπησεν ἡμᾶς καὶ ἀπέστειλεν τὸν υἱὸν αὐτοῦ ἱλασμὸν περὶ τῶν ἁμαρτιῶν ἡμῶν.
but that he loved us and sent his Son as a propitiation for our sins.

This is the second of two ὅτι clauses that are epex. to τούτῳ (i.e., content clauses). Αὐτός is the nom. sg. masc. of the 3rd pers. personal pron. and subj. of the vbs. ἠγάπησεν and ἀπέστειλεν. The explicit pron. subj. αὐτός is included to highlight the contrast with ἡμεῖς above. Ἠγάπησεν is the 3rd sg. aor. act. indic. of ἀγαπάω. Ἡμᾶς, acc. of the 1st pers. pl. personal pron., is the dir. obj. of ἠγάπησεν. Ἀπέστειλεν is the 3rd sg. aor. act. indic. of ἀποστέλλω. We find here a double acc. constr. with the object τὸν υἱὸν αὐτοῦ and complement ἱλασμόν (Wallace 185 n. 33). Υἱόν is the acc. sg. masc. of υἱός. Αὐτοῦ, a gen. of relationship, is the gen. sg. masc. of the 3rd pers. personal pron. Ἱλασμόν, "propitiation, atoning sacrifice," is the acc. sg. masc. of ἱλασμός. See 2:2 for more discussion on the debated meaning of ἱλασμὸν. The prep. phrase περὶ τῶν ἁμαρτιῶν ἡμῶν limits the frame of reference for Jesus's propitiatory death. Ἁμαρτιῶν is the gen. pl. fem. of ἁμαρτία, functioning here as the obj. of the prep. περί. Ἡμῶν, the gen. form of the 1st pers. plural personal pron., functions here as a subj. gen. Marshall muses concerning this verse on ἡ ἀγάπη writing, "This is what God has done for rebellious mankind: he pardons their sins against himself at his own cost" (215).

VERSE 11

Ἀγαπητοί, εἰ οὕτως ὁ θεὸς ἠγάπησεν ἡμᾶς,
Beloved ones, if God loves us in this way,

Ἀγαπητοί is the voc. pl. masc. of ἀγαπητός, -ή, -όν, "beloved" (see 2:7). John's recipients are loved by him, by God, and by one another. Even so, they must be reminded of their ongoing obligation to love their Christian brothers and sisters. Εἰ introduces a first class cond. sentence (i.e., the prot. is presented as true for consideration and *is* obviously true in this case; cf. Young 185; on this topic, see 3:13). Οὕτως, "in this way, thus, so," adv. modifies ἠγάπησεν, the 3rd sg. aor. act. indic. of ἀγαπάω. Θεός, nom. sg. masc., functions as the subj. of ἠγάπησεν. Ἡμᾶς, acc. of the 1st pers. pl. personal pron., serves as the dir. obj. of ἠγάπησεν.

καὶ ἡμεῖς ὀφείλομεν ἀλλήλους ἀγαπᾶν.
we also ought to love one another.

Ἡμεῖς is nom. of the 1st pers. personal pron. and the subj. of ὀφείλομεν, 1st pl. pres. act. ind., "ought, should." Ἀγαπᾶν is the pres. act. inf. of ἀγαπάω and functions as a complementary inf. (completing the idea began by ὀφείλομεν; on this topic, see BDF §392; KMP 365–66). The acc. pl. masc. reciprocal pron. ἀλλήλους serves as the dir. obj. of the inf. ἀγαπᾶν.

VERSE 12

θεὸν οὐδεὶς πώποτε τεθέαται.
No one has ever seen God.

Θεόν is the acc. sg. masc. of θεός and functions as the dir. obj. of τεθέαται. Οὐδείς, "no one," is nom. sg. masc. and serves as the subj. of τεθέαται. Τεθέαται is the 3rd sg. pf. mid. indic. of θεάομαι, "see, behold" (see 1:1). The vb. θεάομαι often conveys the sense of viewing with a sense of surprise or amazement. Τεθέαται is modified adv. with πώποτε ("ever, at any time," BDAG 900c; 6× in GNT).

ἐὰν ἀγαπῶμεν ἀλλήλους,
If we love one another,

Ἐάν introduces the prot. of a third class cond. sentence, setting up a situation for consideration ("Let's consider this . . . what if . . ."; on third class cond., see 1:6). Ἀγαπῶμεν is the 1st pl. pres. act. subjunc. of ἀγαπάω. The indic. form is identical in orthography, but context makes clear that ἀγαπῶμεν is subjunc. (i.e., following ἐάν). Ἀλλήλους, "one another," is the acc. pl. masc. of the reciprocal pron. and functions as the dir. obj. of ἀγαπῶμεν. The lex. form of the reciprocal pron. is ἀλλήλων (gen. pl.).

ὁ θεὸς ἐν ἡμῖν μένει
God remains in us,

Θεός is nom. sg. masc. and the subj. of μένει, the 3rd sg. pres. act. indic. of μένω. The prep. phrase ἐν ἡμῖν communicates location/sphere (see BDAG 326c; R 585–86; Moule 75–76) and modifies μένει adv.

καὶ ἡ ἀγάπη αὐτοῦ ἐν ἡμῖν τετελειωμένη ἐστίν.
and his love is perfected in us.

Ἀγάπη is nom. sg. masc. and functions as the subj. of the periph. constr. τετελειωμένη ἐστίν (periphrasis: form of εἰμί + ptc.; on this topic, see BDF §352; KMP 343–46; R 374–76). Nouns qualified by a gen. personal pron. are often art. (as here: ἡ ἀγάπη αὐτοῦ). Αὐτοῦ, a subj. gen. (so Culy 111; Kruse 162 n. 24; Stott 165; cf. Marshall 217), is the gen. sg. form of the 3rd pers. personal pron. Ἐστίν is the 3rd sg. pres. indic. of εἰμί. Τετελειωμένη is the nom. sg. fem. pf. pass. ptc. of τελειόω, "complete, finish, accomplish" (see 2:5), here as part of a periph. constr. ("is made complete," CSB, NIV; "is perfected," ESV, NASB, NET; "is brought to full expression," NLT). The prep. phrase ἐν ἡμῖν communicates location/sphere and modifies adv. τετελειωμένη ἐστίν. Although God is invisible, in the loving community of his people, his reality becomes visible.

FOR FURTHER STUDY

35. "Completed Love" (4:11–18)

Rensberger, David. "Completed Love: 1 John 4:11–18 and the Mission of the New Testament Church." Pages 237–71 in *Communities in Dispute: Current Scholarship on the Johannine Epistles*. Edited by R. Alan Culpepper and Paul N. Anderson. Atlanta: SBL Press, 2014.

See also For Further Study 16 "Love/Ἀγαπάω/Ἀγάπη Word Study," 17 "The Love of God," 19 "Abiding/Remaining/Μένω"

HOMILETICAL SUGGESTIONS

The Love of God (4:7–12)

1. God is love (v. 8)
2. God's love is expressed within the church (v. 7)
3. God's love is revealed in his Son (vv. 9–10)
    a. The Father sent the Son to be the propitiation for our sins
    b. Eternal life is through the Son (v. 9)
4. God's love is perfected in us (v. 12)

Knowing God: God's Love and Our Love (4:7–12)

1. The definition of God's love (vv. 7–10)
    a. God sent his Son into the world (v. 9)
    b. God sent his Son to be the propitiation for our sins (v. 10)
2. The response to God's love: love one another (v. 11)
3. The expression of God's love by the church (vv. 11–12)
    a. God is unseen and transcendent
    b. Yet, by loving one another, God dwells within us, and his love is made complete in us

XIII. Assurance for Believers and the Love of God (4:13–21)

This section contributes to John's overarching goal of offering assurance to the believers. Note, in vv. 13–16 the vb. *μένω* occurs five times. The causal ὅτι clause of v. 13 provides the reason for the knowledge of this mutual abiding: because of the Holy Spirit. The content ὅτι of v. 14 conveys the witnessed and testified fact that the Father sent his Son. John's assurance is founded on both the objective reality of Christ's coming and the subjective experience of the Holy Spirit (Stott 167). The indef. rel. pron. of v. 15 reveals who has this mutual abiding: the one who confesses Jesus. Verse 16 emphasizes God's love and affirms mutual abiding for the one who abides in love. A shift in vv. 17–21 highlights the believers' "perfected" love and the implications of this love: confidence in the day of judgment (indicated by the purpose ἵνα in v. 17). Verses 19–21 return to the theme of love for one another as a product of God's love for us and ours for him.

13 Ἐν τούτῳ
γινώσκομεν ὅτι ἐν αὐτῷ μένομεν
καὶ αὐτὸς ἐν ἡμῖν,
ὅτι ἐκ τοῦ πνεύματος αὐτοῦ δέδωκεν ἡμῖν.

14 καὶ ἡμεῖς τεθεάμεθα
καὶ μαρτυροῦμεν
ὅτι ὁ πατὴρ ἀπέσταλκεν τὸν υἱὸν σωτῆρα τοῦ κόσμου.

15 ὃς ἐὰν ὁμολογήσῃ ὅτι Ἰησοῦς ἐστιν ὁ υἱὸς τοῦ θεοῦ,
ὁ θεὸς ἐν αὐτῷ μένει
καὶ αὐτὸς ἐν τῷ θεῷ.

16 καὶ ἡμεῖς ἐγνώκαμεν
καὶ πεπιστεύκαμεν τὴν ἀγάπην
ἣν ἔχει ὁ θεὸς ἐν ἡμῖν.

Ὁ θεὸς ἀγάπη ἐστίν,

καὶ ὁ μένων ἐν τῇ ἀγάπῃ ἐν τῷ θεῷ μένει,
καὶ ὁ θεὸς ἐν αὐτῷ μένει.

17 ἐν τούτῳ
τετελείωται ἡ ἀγάπη μεθ᾽ ἡμῶν,
ἵνα παρρησίαν ἔχωμεν ἐν τῇ ἡμέρᾳ τῆς κρίσεως,
ὅτι καθὼς ἐκεῖνός ἐστιν,
καὶ ἡμεῖς ἐσμεν
ἐν τῷ κόσμῳ τούτῳ.

18 φόβος οὐκ ἔστιν ἐν τῇ ἀγάπῃ,
ἀλλ᾽ ἡ τελεία ἀγάπη ἔξω βάλλει τὸν φόβον,
ὅτι ὁ φόβος κόλασιν ἔχει,
ὁ δὲ φοβούμενος οὐ τετελείωται ἐν τῇ ἀγάπῃ.

19 ἡμεῖς ἀγαπῶμεν,
ὅτι αὐτὸς πρῶτος ἠγάπησεν ἡμᾶς.

20 ἐάν τις εἴπῃ ὅτι ἀγαπῶ τὸν θεὸν καὶ τὸν ἀδελφὸν αὐτοῦ μισῇ,
ψεύστης ἐστίν·
ὁ γὰρ μὴ ἀγαπῶν τὸν ἀδελφὸν αὐτοῦ
ὃν ἑώρακεν,
τὸν θεὸν
ὃν οὐχ ἑώρακεν
οὐ δύναται ἀγαπᾶν.

21 καὶ ταύτην τὴν ἐντολὴν ἔχομεν ἀπ᾽ αὐτοῦ,
ἵνα ὁ ἀγαπῶν τὸν θεὸν ἀγαπᾷ καὶ τὸν ἀδελφὸν αὐτοῦ.

VERSE 13

Ἐν τούτῳ γινώσκομεν ὅτι ἐν αὐτῷ μένομεν καὶ αὐτὸς ἐν ἡμῖν,
By this we know that we remain in him and he in us:

The prep. phrase ἐν τούτῳ communicates means/instr. Τούτῳ, dat. sg. neut. of the near dem. pron., is the obj. of the prep. ἐν. Ἐν τούτῳ points forward to the clause below (ὅτι ἐκ τοῦ πνεύματος αὐτοῦ δέδωκεν ἡμῖν; CSB, NET, NIV; so most commentators surveyed). Γινώσκομεν is the 1st pl. pres. act. indic. of γινώσκω. Ὅτι introduces a content clause or "the clausal complement" of γινώσκομεν (Culy 84). Culy explains, "Such complements may be thought of as introducing indirect discourse with a verb of cognition" (25; on use, see also Wallace 456–58; R 1034). The prep. phrase ἐν αὐτῷ conveys the idea of loc./sphere and adv. modifies μένομεν, the 1st pl. pres. act. indic. of μένω. Αὐτός is the nom. sg. masc. of the 3rd pers. personal pron. and serves as the subj.

of the implied vb. μένει. The prep. phrase ἐν ἡμῖν communicates location/sphere and modifies adv. the implied vb. μένει. On mutual indwelling/abiding, cf. 3:24.

ὅτι ἐκ τοῦ πνεύματος αὐτοῦ δέδωκεν ἡμῖν.
he has given to us from his Spirit.

The function of ὅτι is communicated by the colon at the end of the last clause. The ὅτι resumes the idea of τούτῳ above ("continuative," Yarbrough 246 n. 6; epex. to τούτῳ, so Culy 112; NET Translation Notes). John's wording here is a bit unusual, and commentators struggle to discern the exact nuance. The apostle does not say here that God has given us his Spirit; he says that God has given us ἐκ τοῦ πνεύματος, "from his Spirit." The unexpected wording perhaps reminds the reader of the Lord's gracious will in distributing apportionments, fillings, and giftings of the Spirit. Perhaps, too, the reader is to conclude that the Spirit is the one who empowers believers to display the evidences of regeneration previously discussed in the letter (i.e., love, faith, and obedience). The prep. phrase ἐκ τοῦ πνεύματος might best be labeled as expressing the idea of source/origin (Lenski 507). A partitive labeling is also suggested by commentators (Brown 522; Culy 112; Hiebert 206–7; Marshall 219 and n. 3, who understands the prep. phrase as conveying "a share in the Spirit." Yet, he adds that this may be reflected through various experiences such as inward conviction of assurance and charismatic gifts; NET Translation Notes, which argue the phrase "portrays God as 'apportioning' his Spirit to individual believers" and that assurance comes from the giving of the Spirit as opposed to the Spirit's ongoing witness; Smalley 238–39; cf. Kruse 163; Jobes 195–96; also see Moule 72). Πνεύματος is the gen. sg. neut. of πνεῦμα and serves as the obj. of the prep. ἐκ. Nouns qualified by a gen. personal pron. are often art. (as here: τοῦ πνεύματος αὐτοῦ). Αὐτοῦ, a subj. gen., is the gen. sg. form of the 3rd pers. personal pron. Δέδωκεν is the 3rd sg. pf. act. ind. of δίδωμι. Ἡμῖν is dat. of the 1st pers. plural personal pron., here functioning as a dat. of indir. obj. John challenges his readers to remember that the Spirit (or apportionments of the Spirit) have definitively been given to them in the past, and the immediate relevance of that reality is that the letter recipients can now know they remain in intimate relationship with God.

VERSE 14

καὶ ἡμεῖς τεθεάμεθα καὶ μαρτυροῦμεν
And we have beheld and are testifying

Although it's poor English style to frequently begin sentences with καί, it's a normal Koine Gk. pattern that structurally communicates continuity of the discourse. Ἡμεῖς is nom. of the 1st pers. pl. personal pron. and serves as the subj. of τεθεάμεθα and μαρτυροῦμεν. Τεθεάμεθα is the 1st pl. pf. mid. indic. of θεάομαι, "see, behold" (see 1:1). The vb. θεάομαι often conveys the nuance of seeing something with surprise, interest, or amazement. Perhaps the vb. θεάομαι prefers the mid. voice because of this emotional (subject-affected) element (on this topic, see KMP 196–99). John, speaking for the unified apostolic witness (see 1:1), avers that the saving event they historically witnessed fits them to be authoritative testifiers up to and at the time of his writing. Μαρτυροῦμεν is the 1st pl. pres. act. indic. of *μαρτυρέω*.

ὅτι ὁ πατὴρ ἀπέσταλκεν τὸν υἱὸν σωτῆρα τοῦ κόσμου.
that the Father sent his Son as Savior of the world.

Ὅτι introduces a content clause (ind. discourse) of what John and the other apostles have beheld and now bear witness to. Πατήρ is nom. sg. masc. and the subj. of *ἀπέσταλκεν*, the 3rd sg. pf. act. indic. of *ἀποστέλλω*. The pf. is perhaps chosen because of the ongoing and immediate relevance (relevant state) of salvation tied to the sending. Υἱόν is the acc. sg. masc. of *υἱός* and the first of two accusatives (the object) in a double acc. constr. (Culy 113; Young 17). The second acc. (the complement) is *σωτῆρα*, the sg. masc. of *σωτήρ*, -ῆρος, ὁ, "savior" (derivative of *σῴζω*; on the term, see H. Schelkle, *EDNT* 3:325d–327a; G. Fohrer, *TDNT* 7:1003–23; LN §21.22; for discussion on the title *σωτήρ*, see Smalley 241; the phrase "savior of the world" is found only here and John 4:42 in NT). Note in English how "as" or "to be" are usually provided between the translation of two accusatives in a double acc. constr. Κόσμου is the gen. sg. masc. of *κόσμος* and functions as an obj. gen. Note that vv. 13 and 14 reflect an example of the author's emphasis of two aspects of Christian assurance. As Stott writes, "Christian certainty rests on this combination of . . . the historical and the experiential, the Son's mission and the Spirit's testimony" (167).

VERSE 15

ὃς ἐὰν ὁμολογήσῃ ὅτι Ἰησοῦς ἐστιν ὁ υἱὸς τοῦ θεοῦ,
Whoever confesses that Jesus is the Son of God—

Ὃς ἐάν is the nom. sg. masc. indef. rel. pron. (an alternate synonymous form is ὅς ἄν). Ὃς ἐάν functions in a headless rel. clause as the subj. of the vb. ὁμολογήσῃ, the 3rd sg. aor. act. subjunc. of ὁμολογέω, "confess, publicly profess" (see 2:23). Ὅτι introduces either dir. or indir. discourse (above conveyed as indir. along with most EVV). Ἰησοῦς, nom. sg. masc., is the subj. of ἐστιν, the 3rd sg. pres. indic. of εἰμί. Υἱός, nom. sg. masc., is the pred. nom. Θεοῦ is the gen. sg. masc. of θεός, here serving as a gen. of relationship. Ὁ υἱὸς τοῦ θεοῦ follows Apollonius's Canon (see 1:1), with both the head noun and qualifying gen. as articular. Although it is grammatically possible that ὁ υἱὸς τοῦ θεοῦ serves as subject and Ἰησοῦς functions as the pred. nom., it is more likely that the proper name Ἰησοῦς is the subject of the copulative vb. (on determining the subject in a copulative sentence, see 2:22; Wallace 42–46; Young 64–65).

ὁ θεὸς ἐν αὐτῷ μένει καὶ αὐτὸς ἐν τῷ θεῷ.
God remains in him and he in God.

Θεός is nom. sg. masc. and the subj. of *μένει*, the 3rd sg. pres. act. indic. of *μένω*. The prep. phrase *ἐν αὐτῷ* adv. modifies *μένει* and communicates a loc./spherical idea (see BDAG 326c; R 585–86; Moule 75–76). The antecedent of *αὐτῷ* (and also of *αὐτός*, which is found later in the verse) is ὃς ἐὰν ὁμολογήσῃ ὅτι Ἰησοῦς ἐστιν ὁ υἱὸς τοῦ θεοῦ. Αὐτῷ is the dat. sg. masc. of the 3rd pers. personal pronoun, here serving as the obj.

of the prep. ἐν. Αὐτός is nom. sg. masc. of the 3rd pers. personal pron. and subj. of the implied vb. μένει (there is an ellipsis in the final clause). The prep. phrase ἐν τῷ θεῷ adv. modifies the implied vb. μένει and communicates a loc./spherical notion. Θεῷ is the dat. sg. masc. of θεός and functions as the obj. of the prep. ἐν. The noun is articular (τῷ θεῷ), as expected of monadic nouns (BW 73–74; KMP 158; Young 67).

VERSE 16

καὶ ἡμεῖς ἐγνώκαμεν καὶ πεπιστεύκαμεν τὴν ἀγάπην ἣν ἔχει ὁ θεὸς ἐν ἡμῖν.
And we know and have come to trust in the love which God has for us.

Ἡμεῖς, nom. pl. of the 1st pers. personal pron., is probably emphatic ("we" as opposed to the unbelieving world) and serves as the subj. of ἐγνώκαμεν and πεπιστεύκαμεν, both parsed as 1st pl. pf. act. ind., respectively from γινώσκω and πιστεύω (cf. NET Translation Notes and Yarbrough 165, who view the two vbs. as a hendiadys; also Law 269: "two verbs form one compound idea"). The pf. forms (ἐγνώκαμεν and πεπιστεύκαμεν) imply past actions (having come into relationship with, having trusted in), with the emphasis on the ongoing states which have resulted (see KMP 300, who label this use "Intensive Perfect"; Burton §74: "the Perfect of Completed Action"; see also BW 104; R 894–95; Wallace 574–76). Ἀγάπην is acc. sg. fem. of ἀγάπη, -ης, ἡ, and the dir. obj. of πεπιστεύκαμεν. The acc. sg. fem. rel. pron. ἥν refers back to the antecedent ἀγάπην and functions as the obj. of the vb. ἔχει, the 3rd sg. pres. act. indic. of ἔχω. Θεός, nom. sg. masc., serves as the subj. of ἔχει. Ἡμῖν is dat. pl. of the 1st pers. personal pron. and functions as the obj. of the prep. ἐν. The exact nuance/function of the prep. phrase ἐν ἡμῖν is in dispute. In broad terms, the phrase is often understood in the following ways:

*1. The phrase is rendered as "God's love *to/for* us" (i.e., God's love revealed in the ministry of Christ); "for us" (CSB, NASB, NIV; among commentators, see Kruse 162; Law 401).
2. The phrase is rendered as "God's love *in* us" (locally, i.e, God's love, experienced by the work of the Spirit within the life of the believer); "in us" (NET; among commentators, see Brown 516; Hiebert 211).
3. Marshall notes both senses may be reflected in that John is thinking "not merely of the love for us shown by God in the cross but also of the personal experience of his love in our hearts created by the Spirit" (221; so also Smalley 243).

The prep. phrase likely communicates reference/respect. Culy helpfully highlights that "the [unusual] choice of ἐν was probably dictated by stylistic concerns, in anticipation of the threefold use of the preposition at the end of the verse" (114).

Ὁ θεὸς ἀγάπη ἐστίν,
God is love,

Θεός is nom. sg. masc. and the subj. of ἐστίν, the 3rd sg. pres. indic. of εἰμί, with ἀγάπη, nom. sg. fem., as the pred. nom. Other persons can be described as loving, but only of God can it be said, "He is love (cf. 4:8)." Pause, ponder, and praise.

καὶ ὁ μένων ἐν τῇ ἀγάπῃ ἐν τῷ θεῷ μένει,
and the person remaining in love remains in God,

Μένων is the nom. sg. masc. pres. act. ptc., functioning as a subst. from μένω. The prep. phrase ἐν τῇ ἀγάπῃ communicates sphere/location. Ἀγάπῃ is the dat. sg. fem. of ἀγάπη, -ης, ἡ, and serves as the obj. of the prep. ἐν. The entire phrase ὁ μένων ἐν τῇ ἀγάπῃ functions as the subj. of the vb. μένει, the 3rd sg. pres. act. indic. of μένω. The prep. phrase ἐν τῷ θεῷ communicates location/sphere. Θεῷ is the dat. sg. masc. of θεός, here serving as the obj. of the prep. ἐν.

καὶ ὁ θεὸς ἐν αὐτῷ μένει.
and God remains in him.

Θεός is nom. sg. masc. and the subj. of μένει, the 3rd sg. pres. act. indic. of μένω. The prep. phrase ἐν αὐτῷ adv. modifies μένει and communicates a loc./spherical idea. Αὐτῷ is dat. sg. masc. of the 3rd pers. personal pron., here serving as the obj. of the prep. ἐν.

VERSE 17

ἐν τούτῳ τετελείωται ἡ ἀγάπη μεθ' ἡμῶν,
By this love has been perfected among us,

The prep. phrase ἐν τούτῳ, communicating instr., likely refers to the aforementioned mutual indwelling. The dem. is understood broadly in the following ways:

*1. Pointing backward to v. 16 (Brown 526–27; Jobes 204; Marshall 223 n. 17; Yarbrough 257).
2. Pointing forward to the ἵνα clause (Harris 167; Lenski 510).
3. Pointing forward to the ὅτι clause (Akin 185 n. 137).
4. Functioning transitionally, pointing back to the previous verse while also pointing forward to the remainder of v. 17 (Smalley 244–45, who argues for similar ambiguity in 2:5; 3:10, 19).

Τούτῳ is dat. sg. neut. of the near dem. pron. and serves as the obj. of the prep. ἐν. Τετελείωται is the 3rd sg. pf. pass. indic. of τελειόω, "complete, perfect" (see 2:5); "love is made complete" (CSB); "love is perfected" (ESV, NASB, NET); "love finds its fullest expression" (Harris 168). God is the implied agent of the passive vb. Ἀγάπη is nom. sg. fem. and serves as the subj. of τετελείωται. The prep. phrase μεθ' ἡμῶν communicates association, "among us" (NIV; Moule 61; "with us," most EVV; on prep., see BDAG 636b). Ἡμῶν is gen. pl. of the 1st pers. personal pron. and the obj. of the prep. μετά.

ἵνα παρρησίαν ἔχωμεν ἐν τῇ ἡμέρᾳ τῆς κρίσεως,
so that we would have boldness in the day of judgment,

Ἵνα introduces a result clause. Παρρησίαν is the acc. sg. fem. of παρρησία, "boldness, confidence" (see 2:28), and serves as the dir. obj. of ἔχωμεν, the 1st pl. pres. act. subj. of ἔχω. The prep. phrase ἐν τῇ ἡμέρᾳ τῆς κρίσεως is temporal, communicating a point of time in the future. Ἡμέρᾳ is the dat. sg. fem. of ἡμέρα, -ας, ἡ, and functions as the obj. of the prep. ἐν. The gen. qualifier τῆς κρίσεως is perhaps best labeled as a descriptive gen. The phrase "day of judgment" has a rich biblical history and was certainly understood by the letter's recipients to refer to the day in which God enacts final judgment of each person's eternal destiny (cf. Culy 116; on this topic, see For Further Study 37 "Judgment").

ὅτι καθὼς ἐκεῖνός ἐστιν, καὶ ἡμεῖς ἐσμεν ἐν τῷ κόσμῳ τούτῳ.
for just as that one is, we also are in this world.

Ὅτι introduces a causal clause, giving a reason that believers can have confidence in the day of judgment (i.e., because they stand in the same filial relational status to God the Father as his one and only Son). Καθώς introduces the comparison. Ἐκεῖνός, nom. sg. masc. of the far dem. pron., serves as the subj. of ἐστιν, the 3rd sg. pres. indic. of εἰμί. Ἡμεῖς is nom. pl. of the 1st pers. personal pron. and the subj. of ἐσμεν, the 1st pl. pres. indic. of εἰμί. The prep. phrase ἐν τῷ κόσμῳ τούτῳ communicates location/sphere. Τούτῳ, dat. sg. masc. of the near dem. pron., attrib. modifies κόσμῳ, the dat. sg. masc. of κόσμος. When a dem. pron. modifies a noun attrib., the dem. pron. occurs in the predicate position, as here. Κόσμῳ is the obj. of the prep. ἐν.

VERSE 18

φόβος οὐκ ἔστιν ἐν τῇ ἀγάπῃ,
There is no fear in love,

More literalistically, the text reads, "Fear is not in love." An impersonal subject "there," has been provided in the English translation above for readability. Φόβος, "fear," nom. sg. masc., serves as the subj. of the negated vb. ἔστιν, the 3rd sg. pres. indic. of εἰμί. The prep. phrase ἐν τῇ ἀγάπῃ depicts love as a realm/sphere (on prep., see BDAG 326c; Moule 81; R 589) in which the fearful expectation of judgment cannot coexist. Alternately, the prep. phrase could be understood as communicating reference/respect (Culy 117; on this contextual sense of the prep., see Young 96). Ἀγάπῃ is the dat. sg. fem. of ἀγάπη and functions here as the obj. of the prep. ἐν.

ἀλλ' ἡ τελεία ἀγάπη ἔξω βάλλει τὸν φόβον,
but perfect love casts out fear,

The advers. ἀλλά introduces a strong contrast with erroneous idea that fearful expectation of judgment and loving acceptance can coexist. Τελεία, the nom. sg. fem. of τέλειος, -α, -ον, "perfect" (see 2:5), attrib. modifies ἀγάπη, also nom. sg. fem. Ἡ τελεία ἀγάπη ("perfect love," most EVV; "genuine love," LN §73.6) functions as the subj. of βάλλει, the 3rd sg. pres. act. indic. of βάλλω. Ἔξω, "out, outside," adv. modifies βάλλει. Φόβον, the acc. sg. masc. of φόβος, "fear," serves as the dir. obj. of βάλλει. Abstract nouns are commonly art., as here (ἡ . . . ἀγάπη, τὸν φόβον; see BW 74; R 758; cf. Young 57).

ὅτι ὁ φόβος κόλασιν ἔχει,
for fear has to do with punishment.

Ὅτι introduces a causal clause. Φόβος, "fear," nom. sg. masc., serves as the subj. of the vb. ἔχει, the 3rd sg. pres. act. indic. of ἔχω. Κόλασιν, the acc. sg. fem. of κόλασις, "punishment" (BDAG 555c; LN §38.2; occurring only here and Matt 25:46 in GNT), functions as the dir. obj. of ἔχει. The clause literalistically reads, "For fear has punishment," but, from context, the somewhat puzzling sentence must mean something like, "Cringing fear has to do with the expectation of punishment." The phrase could reflect a fear of future punishment or that the fear itself is an endurance of pain. Smalley sees elements of both, noting that "fear anticipates and makes real the future punishment it contemplates" (Smalley 248). Regardless of the nuance (for discussions, see Smalley 248–49; Marshall 224–25; NET Translation Notes), this destructive fear is not consistent with "a full understanding of the nature of redemptive love which has removed our sins and established a living relationship with God in this life" (Hiebert 218).

ὁ δὲ φοβούμενος οὐ τετελείωται ἐν τῇ ἀγάπῃ.
The person fearing has not been perfected in love.

The postpositive particle δέ carries the passage forward, alerting the reader that additional information (usually favoring something new or different), is coming. Δέ is left untranslated above. Φοβούμενος is the nom. sg. masc. pres. mid. ptc. of φοβέομαι, functioning as a subst. and the subj. of the negated vb. τετελείωται. Verbs expressing emotion (e.g., φοβούμενος) often prefer the middle voice. Τετελείωται is the 3rd sg. pf. pass. indic. of τελειόω ("perfect, complete"; "has not been perfected," ESV, NET; on term, see 2:5). God is the implied agent of the passive vb. The prep. phrase ἐν τῇ ἀγάπῃ is probably best understood as communicating reference/respect, though it is possible that the author is speaking of love as a realm/sphere. Ἀγάπῃ is the dat. sg. fem. of ἀγάπη and serves here as the obj. of the prep. ἐν.

VERSE 19

ἡμεῖς ἀγαπῶμεν,
We love

Ἡμεῖς, nom. pl. of the 1st pers. personal pron., is probably included for more explicit contrast with αὐτός below (i.e., "we" love derivatively; "he" loves originally) and serves as the subj. of ἀγαπῶμεν, the 1st pl. pres. act. indic. of ἀγαπάω. (Though the vb. could read as a subjunc. [hortatory: "let us love"; so Law 402], the vb. is rightly understood contextually as indic. by most EVV and commentators surveyed.) The NET Bible Translation Notes observe, "No object is supplied for the verb *love* (the author with his propensity for obscurity has left it to the readers to supply the object). The obvious objects that could be supplied from the context are either God himself or other believers (the brethren). It may well be that the author has *both* in mind at this point; the statement is general enough to cover both alternatives, although the following verse puts more emphasis on love for the brethren." The lack of a direct object is well supported by Gk. mss.; yet, some mss. add τὸν θεόν or αὐτόν (cf. KJV) after ἀγαπῶμεν.

ὅτι αὐτὸς πρῶτος ἠγάπησεν ἡμᾶς.
because he first loved us.

Ὅτι introduces a causal clause. Αὐτός is the nom. sg. masc. of the 3rd pers. personal pron. and the subj. of ἠγάπησεν, the 3rd sg. aor. act. indic. of ἀγαπάω. Based on the sense of the passage (and all EVV), a reader might expect to find the neut. sg. πρῶτον, "first," used as an adv. here. Instead, one finds the nom. sg., πρῶτος. Similar constructions are found in extrabiblical Greek. For example, in Xenophon's *Anabasis* 2.3.19, we read, Κῦρον ἐπιστρατεύοντα πρῶτος ἤγγειλα, "I was the first to report that Cyrus was marching against them" (see BDAG 893b; on the term, see BDF §62; R 662–63). Ἡμᾶς is the acc. pl. masc. of the 1st pers. personal pron., functioning here as the dir. obj. of ἠγάπησεν.

VERSE 20

ἐάν τις εἴπῃ ὅτι ἀγαπῶ τὸν θεὸν καὶ τὸν ἀδελφὸν αὐτοῦ μισῇ, ψεύστης ἐστίν·
If anyone says, "I love God" and he hates his brother, he is a liar.

Ἐάν introduces the prot. of a third class cond. sentence (on topic, see 1:6). It is as if the author is saying, "Let's consider a situation. Think about this . . . what if . . ." (that is, there is a distancing of the considered situation from reality; this distancing can be for a variety of reasons, e.g., indefiniteness about the certainty or timing of fulfillment, politeness, etc.). Τις is nom. sg. of the indef. pron. and the subj. of both εἴπῃ (3rd sg. aor. act. subjunc. from λέγω) and μισῇ (3rd sg. pres. act. subjunc. from μισέω). Ὅτι here introduces direct discourse, as indicated by the translation/punctuation above (so most EVV; on ὅτι as recitative, see R 1027–28; Wallace 454–55). Ἀγαπῶ is the 1st sg. pres. act. indic. of ἀγαπάω. Θεόν, the acc. sg. masc. of θεός, functions as the dir. obj. of ἀγαπῶ. Ἀδελφόν, the acc. sg. masc. of ἀδελφός, serves as the dir. obj. of μισῇ. Αὐτοῦ, gen. sg. masc. of the 3rd pers. personal pron., acts as a gen. of personal relationship. A head noun qualified by a gen. personal pron. is expected to be art. (as here: τὸν ἀδελφὸν αὐτοῦ). Ψεύστης, nom. sg. masc., serves as pred. nom. of ἐστίν, the 3rd sg. pres. indic. of εἰμί. If the context favored ψεύστης as definite (and it does not), anarthrous ψεύστης would still appear as expected (on Colwell's Rule; see KMP 163; Moule 115–17; Young 65–66).

ὁ γὰρ μὴ ἀγαπῶν τὸν ἀδελφὸν αὐτοῦ ὃν ἑώρακεν,
For, the person not loving his brother, whom he has seen,

Postpositive γάρ is explanatory/causal. Ἀγαπῶν is the nom. sg. masc. pres. act. ptc. of ἀγαπάω. The ptc. ἀγαπῶν is negated (with μή) and functions as a subst. (and ultimately as the subj. of δύναται below). Ἀδελφόν, the acc. sg. masc. of ἀδελφός, serves as the dir. obj. of ἀγαπῶν. Αὐτοῦ, gen. sg. masc. of the 3rd pers. personal pron., acts as a gen. of personal relationship. Ὅν, acc. sg. masc. rel. pron., refers to the antecedent ἀδελφὸν and functions as the dir. obj. (thus acc. case) of ἑώρακεν, 3rd sg. pf. act. indic. of ὁράω.

τὸν θεὸν ὃν οὐχ ἑώρακεν οὐ δύναται ἀγαπᾶν.
is not able to love God, whom he has not seen.

Following the Gk. word order more rigidly, an English translation would read: "God, whom he has not seen, he is not able to love." Θεόν, the acc. sg. masc. of θεός, serves as the dir. obj. of the pres. act. inf. ἀγαπᾶν. Ὅν, acc. sg. masc. rel. pron., refers to the antecedent θεόν and functions as dir. obj. of the negated vb. ἑώρακεν, the 3rd sg. pf. act. ind. of ὁράω. Ὁ . . . μὴ ἀγαπῶν τὸν ἀδελφὸν serves as the subject of the negated vb. δύναται, the 3rd sg. pres. mid. indic. of δύναμαι. One expects δύναμαι to be followed by a complementary inf.; in the GNT, 72 percent of complementary infs. following δύναμαι are aor. tense (Baugh, *Tense Form Choice*, 69). Here, however, the complementary inf. is pres. act. inf., ἀγαπᾶν, from ἀγαπάω. The inherent procedural nature of the verbal activity of ἀγαπάω strongly favors an imperfective presentation (without the beginning and ending in the frame of presentation). Some mss. (including A K L) reflect the variant reading πῶς δῦναται ἀγαπᾶν ("how can he love?" KJV). The reading οὐ δύναται ἀγαπᾶν (followed here and by most EVV) is witnessed by a number of mss. (א B Ψ 442 1243 et al.). The UBS[5] follows the *Editio Critica Maior* and identifies the variant with a black diamond (the highest level of uncertainty, meaning it could equally be adopted).

VERSE 21

καὶ ταύτην τὴν ἐντολὴν ἔχομεν ἀπ᾽ αὐτοῦ,
And this commandment we have from him:

Ταύτην, acc. sg. fem. of the near dem. pron., attrib. modifies τὴν ἐντολήν, the acc. sg. fem. of ἐντολή and dir. obj. of ἔχομεν. When a dem. pron. attrib. modifies a noun, it occurs in the predicate position, as here (ταύτην τὴν ἐντολήν; see KMP 397). Ἔχομεν is 1st pl. pres. act. indic. of ἔχω. The prep. phrase ἀπ᾽ αὐτοῦ communicates source/origin (see R 575–76) and functions adv. to modify the vb. ἔχομεν. Αὐτοῦ, the gen. sg. masc. of the 3rd pers. personal pron., is obj. of the prep. ἀπό.

ἵνα ὁ ἀγαπῶν τὸν θεὸν ἀγαπᾷ καὶ τὸν ἀδελφὸν αὐτοῦ.
the one loving God should love also his brother.

Ἵνα introduces a content clause (Rogers and Rogers 598), epex. defining what ταύτην τὴν ἐντολήν is (on this use of ἵνα, see BW 180; R 991–92; Wallace 471–77, 678, 762; Young 187; Z §410; cf. 3:1). This syntactical relationship is communicated by a colon at the end of the previous clause. Ἀγαπῶν is the nom. sg. masc. pres. act. ptc. of ἀγαπάω, functioning substantively. Θεόν, acc. sg. masc. of θεός, -οῦ, ὁ, is the dir. obj. of ἀγαπῶν. The phrase ὁ ἀγαπῶν τὸν θεόν functions as the subj. of ἀγαπᾷ, the 3rd sg.

pres. act. subjunc. of ἀγαπάω. From context, the subjunc. form takes on an imperatival/obligatory sense (see Smalley 253). Wescott notes, "That which is a spiritual necessity is also an express injunction" (162). Ἀδελφόν, acc. sg. masc. of ἀδελφός, -οῦ, ὁ, serves as the dir. obj. of ἀγαπᾷ (translated with the sense "should love" above, also NASB, NET; "must love," CSB). Αὐτοῦ, a gen. of relationship, is the masc. sg. of the 3rd pers. personal pron. When a head noun is qualified by a gen. personal pron., one expects the head noun to be art., as here (τὸν ἀδελφὸν αὐτοῦ). Concerning John's words here, Hiebert succinctly notes they "underline the close union of the outward and the upward dimensions of Christian love. The two aspects cannot be separated" (222).

FOR FURTHER STUDY

36. Judgment (4:17)

Erickson, Millard J. *Christian Theology.* Grand Rapids: Baker, 1985 (see esp. 1185–204).
Hiers, Richard H. *ABD* 2:79–82.
Hoekema, Anthony A. *The Bible in the Future*. Grand Rapids: Eerdmans, 1979.
Morris, Leon. *The Biblical Doctrine of Judgment*. London: Tyndale, 1960.
Moule, Charles F. D. *Essays in New Testament Interpretation.* Cambridge: Cambridge University Press, 1982 (see 235–49).
Schreiner, *NT Theology*, 827–35.
Seifrid, Mark A. *DLNT*, 621–25.
Travis, S. H. *Christ and the Judgment of God: The Limits of Divine Retribution in New Testament Thought*. 2nd ed. Grand Rapids: Baker Academic, 2009.
See also For Further Study 16 "Love/Ἀγαπάω/Ἀγάπη Word Study," 17 "The Love of God," 18 "Abiding/Remaining/Μένω," 19 "Loving One Another," and 29 "Παρουσία Word Study"

HOMILETICAL SUGGESTIONS

Assurance and the Perfect Love of God (4:13–21)

1. Assurance based on the gift of the Spirit (v. 13)
2. Assurance based on the apostolic witness (v. 14)
3. Mutual indwelling (v. 15–16)
4. Perfect love casts out fear (vv. 17–18)
5. Loving God is expressed in loving others (vv. 20–21)

Assurance and Action (4:13–21)

1. Assurance of salvation
   a. Assurance of "mutual indwelling": We abide in God and he in us (vv. 13, 15)
      (1) The giving and experience of the Holy Spirit (v. 13)
      (2) The confession of Jesus Christ as the Son of God

            1. Profession of a biblical understanding of Christ
            2. Profession of trust in his saving work
    b. Assurance from the apostolic witness of the Son of God and his ministry (v. 14)
    c. Assurance of God's nature (vv. 17, 19)
    d. Assurance of our future (v. 18)
2. Action: Proclamation in Practice (vv. 19–21)
    a. Loving God and hating a fellow believer is incompatible (v. 20)
    b. God's command: "love one another" (v. 21)

XIV. Belief, Love, and Obedience (5:1–5)

Because this section continues to develop the theme of love, the passage could be seen as part of 4:13–21. Yet, the emphasis on believing (vv. 1, 5), as well as the "begotten" language (vv. 2, 4) seem to warrant a shift, albeit a subtle one. Verses 1–5 as a whole reflect the three characteristics of one begotten by God that texture the letter: belief in Jesus Christ as the Son of God (vv. 1, 4, 5), obedience (vv. 2–3), and love for one another (vv. 1, 2).

1 Πᾶς ὁ πιστεύων ὅτι Ἰησοῦς ἐστιν ὁ Χριστὸς ἐκ τοῦ θεοῦ γεγέννηται,
καὶ πᾶς ὁ ἀγαπῶν τὸν γεννήσαντα ἀγαπᾷ καὶ τὸν γεγεννημένον ἐξ αὐτοῦ.

2 ἐν τούτῳ γινώσκομεν ὅτι ἀγαπῶμεν τὰ τέκνα τοῦ θεοῦ,
ὅταν τὸν θεὸν ἀγαπῶμεν
καὶ τὰς ἐντολὰς αὐτοῦ ποιῶμεν.

3 αὕτη γάρ ἐστιν ἡ ἀγάπη τοῦ θεοῦ,
ἵνα τὰς ἐντολὰς αὐτοῦ τηρῶμεν,
καὶ αἱ ἐντολαὶ αὐτοῦ βαρεῖαι οὐκ εἰσίν.

4 ὅτι πᾶν τὸ γεγεννημένον ἐκ τοῦ θεοῦ νικᾷ τὸν κόσμον·
καὶ αὕτη ἐστὶν ἡ νίκη ἡ νικήσασα τὸν κόσμον = ἡ πίστις ἡμῶν.

5 Τίς δέ ἐστιν ὁ νικῶν τὸν κόσμον
εἰ μὴ ὁ πιστεύων ὅτι Ἰησοῦς ἐστιν ὁ υἱὸς τοῦ θεοῦ;

VERSE 1

Πᾶς ὁ πιστεύων ὅτι Ἰησοῦς ἐστιν ὁ Χριστὸς ἐκ τοῦ θεοῦ γεγέννηται,
Everyone who believes that Jesus is the Christ has been born from God,

Πιστεύων is the nom. sg. masc. pres. act. ptc. of πιστεύω, functioning as a subst. and modified attrib. by πᾶς. Note how πᾶς occurs in the pred. position when functioning attrib. to mean "every." Ὅτι introduces indir. discourse (i.e., the content of what a person believes; Baugh 71). Ἰησοῦς, nom. sg. masc., is the subj. of ἐστιν, the 3rd sg. pres. indic. of εἰμί. Χριστός, nom. sg. masc., serves as the pred. nom. The entire phrase πᾶς ὁ πιστεύων ὅτι Ἰησοῦς ἐστιν ὁ Χριστὸς (cf. Ἰησοῦς ἐστιν ὁ Χριστὸς in John 20:31) functions as the subj. of γεγέννηται, the 3rd sg. pf. pass. indic. of γεννάω. The prep. phrase ἐκ τοῦ θεοῦ communicates source/origin (R 598; cf. Young 95) and adv. modifies the vb. γεγέννηται. Θεοῦ, the gen. sg. masc. of θεός, is obj. of the prep. ἐκ (cf. 2:29; 3:9).

καὶ πᾶς ὁ ἀγαπῶν τὸν γεννήσαντα ἀγαπᾷ καὶ τὸν γεγεννημένον ἐξ αὐτοῦ.
and everyone who loves the one who begat loves also the one having been begotten from him.

An extraliteral English translation has been provided above to help the reader follow the Gk. text. This clause gives us the generally observed principles that people who love a man who is a father will love his child(ren) as well. This truism is applied in the next verse to the relationship of Christians to God as their Father (i.e., believers should love all of God's children if they really love God the Father). Ἀγαπῶν is the nom. sg. masc. pres. act. ptc. of ἀγαπάω, functioning as a subst. and modified attrib. by πᾶς. The subst. ptc. γεννήσαντα, acc. sg. masc. of aor. act. ptc. of γεννάω, serves as the dir. obj. of ἀγαπῶν. The entire phrase πᾶς ὁ ἀγαπῶν τὸν γεννήσαντα serves as the subj. of ἀγαπᾷ, the 3rd sg. pres. act. indic. of ἀγαπάω. The subst. ptc. γεγεννημένον, acc. sg. masc. pf. pass. ptc., functions as the dir. obj. of ἀγαπᾷ. The prep. phrase ἐξ αὐτοῦ communicates source/origin (R 598; or possibly agency; on use, see Young 95) and adv. modifies γεγεννημένον. Αὐτοῦ, the gen. sg. masc. of the 3rd pers. personal pron. is obj. of the prep. ἐκ.

VERSE 2

ἐν τούτῳ γινώσκομεν ὅτι ἀγαπῶμεν τὰ τέκνα τοῦ θεοῦ,
By this principle, we know that we ought to love the children of God—

A word corresponding directly to the English word "principle" (see above) is not present in the Gk. text, but it has been added to the translation above to make clearer that the initial prep. phrase refers back to the principle enunciated at the end of v.1 above (so Marshall 227; Dodd 125). In contrast to the affirmed view, the prep. phrase could also be understood as pointing forward to the ὅταν clause: "We know we love God's children when we love God and obey his commands." This view is held by many commentators (Akin 190–91; Brown 537; Culy 121; Kruse 171; Law 403; Smalley 255; Stott 173; Yarbrough 271) as well as most EVV (e.g., CSB, NET, NIV). Τούτῳ is dat. sg. neut. of the near dem. pron. and functions as obj. of the prep. ἐν. The prep. phrase ἐν τούτῳ communicates instr./means (on this use of ἐν, see BDAG 328c; BDF §219). Γινώσκομεν is the 1st pl. pres. act. indic. of γινώσκω. Ὅτι introduces the content of what is known (i.e., indir. discourse; see BDAG 731d; R 1034–35; Wallace 456–58). Ἀγαπῶμεν is 1st pl. pres. act. indic. of ἀγαπάω. It is not normal for the indic. to communicate an imperatival sense (as ἀγαπῶμεν is translated above), but Marshall is correct to note that the literary context calls for this nuance (227–28). Τέκνα is the acc.

pl. neut. of τέκνον and the dir. obj. of ἀγαπῶμεν. Θεοῦ, a gen. of relationship (see BW 9; KMP 94–95, 108), is the sg. masc. of θεός. Note here the example of Apollonius's Canon (see 1:1), with both the head noun and gen. qualifier as art. (τὰ τέκνα τοῦ θεοῦ).

ὅταν τὸν θεὸν ἀγαπῶμεν καὶ τὰς ἐντολὰς αὐτοῦ ποιῶμεν.
whenever we love God and do his commandments.

Ὅταν introduces an indef. temp. clause that demands subjunc. mood vbs. Θεόν, the acc. sg. masc. of θεός, is the dir. obj. of ἀγαπῶμεν, the 1st pl. pres. act. subjunc. of ἀγαπάω. Ἐντολάς is the acc. pl. fem. of ἐντολή, -ῆς, ἡ, and the dir. obj. of ποιῶμεν, the 1st pl. pres. act. subjunc. of ποιέω. Some mss. read τηρῶμεν (א A K L P 048 et al.). Yet, ποιῶμεν (B Ψ 81 436 et al.) is the harder reading and so it seems likely scribes would replace it with the more natural sounding vb. τηρῶμεν. UBS[5] committee assigns the decision a "B" rating (mng. the text is almost certain). Regardless, both convey the same sense in this context, so the choice reflects little interpretive significance ("obey," CSB, NET; "observe," NASB). Αὐτοῦ, the gen. sg. masc. of the 3rd pers. personal pron., acts here as a subj. gen.

VERSE 3

αὕτη γάρ ἐστιν ἡ ἀγάπη τοῦ θεοῦ,
For this is the love of God:

Postpositive γάρ introduces an explanatory clause. Αὕτη, the nom. sg. fem. of the near dem. pron., serves as the subj. of ἐστιν, the 3rd sg. pres. indic. of εἰμί. Ἀγάπη, nom. sg. fem., functions as the predicate nom. Θεοῦ, the gen. sg. masc. of θεός, functions as an obj. gen. (KMP 99–100; NET Translation Notes; Rogers and Rogers 598; Wallace 121, 136). Note here the example of Apollonius's Canon (see 1:1), with both the head noun and gen. qualifier as art. (ἡ ἀγάπη τοῦ θεοῦ).

ἵνα τὰς ἐντολὰς αὐτοῦ τηρῶμεν,
that we keep his commandments,

Ἵνα introduces a content or epex. clause (see BW 180; Wallace 471–77, 678, 762; Young 187; Z §410; cf. 3:1), as communicated by the colon in the English translation above. Ἐντολάς, the acc. pl. fem. of ἐντολή, -ης, ἡ, functions as the dir. obj. of τηρῶμεν, the 1st pl. pres. act. subjunc. of τηρέω. Αὐτοῦ is the gen. sg. masc. of the 3rd pers. personal pron. and acts as a subj. gen.

καὶ αἱ ἐντολαὶ αὐτοῦ βαρεῖαι οὐκ εἰσίν.
and his commandments are not burdensome.

Ἐντολαί, nom. pl. fem. of ἐντολή, serves as the subj. of the negated vb. εἰσίν, the 3rd sg. pres. indic. of εἰμί. Αὐτοῦ is the gen. sg. masc. of the 3rd pers. personal pron. and acts as a subj. gen. Βαρεῖαι, the nom. pl. fem. from the adj. βαρύς, -εῖα, -ύ (occurring 6× in GNT mng. "heavy," BDAG 167d; "burdensome," LN §22.30; also ESV, NASB, NIV) functions here as a pred. adj.

VERSE 4

ὅτι πᾶν τὸ γεγεννημένον ἐκ τοῦ θεοῦ νικᾷ τὸν κόσμον·
Because everyone who has been born of God conquers the world,

Ὅτι introduces a causal clause (CSB, NET). The subst. ptc. γεγεννημένον is a nom. sg. neut. pf. pass. ptc. of γεννάω modified by the acc. sg. neut. attrib. πᾶν (from πᾶς). A masc. subst. is more naturally expected. Smalley asserts that the neuter generalizes the reference (257–58; so also Marshall 227 n. 37; BDF §138[1] states, "the neuter is sometimes used with reference to persons if it is not the individuals but a general quality that is to be emphasized"). The prep. phrase ἐκ τοῦ θεοῦ adv. modifies γεγεννημένον and communicates the idea of source/origin (see 3:9). Θεοῦ is the gen. sg. masc. from θεός and functions as the object of the prep. ἐκ. The phrase πᾶν τὸ γεγεννημένον ἐκ τοῦ θεοῦ serves as the subj. of the vb. νικᾷ, the 3rd sg. pres. act. ind. of νικάω ("conquer," CSB, NET; "overcome," NASB, NIV, ESV; a word that occurs 6× in the letter, once in John's Gospel, 17× in John's Apocalypse, and only 4× outside of these occurrences in GNT: Rom 3:4; 12:21; Luke 11:22). Κόσμον, the acc. sg. masc. of κόσμος, -ου, ὁ, is the dir. obj. of νικᾷ.

καὶ αὕτη ἐστὶν ἡ νίκη ἡ νικήσασα τὸν κόσμον, ἡ πίστις ἡμῶν.
And this is the victory which has overcome the world—our faith.

Αὕτη, nom. sg. fem. of the near dem. pron., serves as the subj. of ἐστίν, the 3rd sg. pres. indic. of εἰμί. Νίκη, "victory" (most EVV), is nom. sg. fem. and functions as the pred. nom. Νικήσασα, the nom. sg. fem. of aor. act. ptc. of νικάω (in context, "has conquered," CSB; "has overcome," ESV, NASB, NIV), attrib. modifies νίκη. Κόσμον, acc. sg. masc. of κόσμος, is the dir. obj. of νικήσασα. Πίστις, nom. sg. fem., is in appos. to νίκη. Ἡμῶν, the gen. of the 1st pers. pl. personal pron., functions as a subj. gen.

VERSE 5

Τίς δέ ἐστιν ὁ νικῶν τὸν κόσμον
And who is the one conquering the world

Postpositive particle δέ cues the reader that additional information is forthcoming. Context here favors translating δέ with a continuative function ("and" or "now"; on function of δέ, see Runge 31–36). Τίς is nom. sg. masc. of the interr. pron. and functions here as the subj. of ἐστιν, the 3rd sg. pres. indic. of εἰμί. The interr. "asks for the personal identification of the one characterized as overcoming the world" (Hiebert 230). Νικῶν, the nom. sg. masc. pres. act. ptc. of νικάω, functions subst. as a pred. nom. Κόσμον, acc. sg. masc. of κόσμος, -ου, ὁ, is the dir. obj. of the ptc. νικῶν. Smalley notes the term κόσμον "has a definite negative connotation. It represents all that is at enmity with God and his children" (263). Literary context favors understanding νικάω as conveying primarily a figurative military nuance rather than an athletic metaphor.

εἰ μὴ ὁ πιστεύων ὅτι Ἰησοῦς ἐστιν ὁ υἱὸς τοῦ θεοῦ;
except the person who believes that Jesus is the Son of God?

Εἰ μή means "except, if not" (BDAG 278d) or "but" (CSB, NASB, KJV). Πιστεύων, nom. sg. masc. pres. act. ptc. of πιστεύω, serves as a subst. ptc. followed by ὅτι introducing the content of what is believed. Ἰησοῦς, nom. sg. masc., serves as the subj. of ἐστιν, the 3rd sg. pres. indic. of εἰμί. Υἱός, nom. sg. masc., functions as the pred. nom. Θεοῦ, the gen. sg. masc. of θεός, serves as a gen. of relationship. The apostle John reminds his readers that trusting in Jesus as the Son of God is the *sine qua non* of resisting the lies and temptations of a world at war with heaven (cf. Rom 8:37).

FOR FURTHER STUDY

37. Messiah/Χριστός (5:1)

Bird, Michael F. *Are You the One Who Is to Come? The Historical Jesus and the Messianic Question*. Grand Rapids: Baker Academic, 2009.
Evans, C. A. *DNTB*, 698–707.
Frame 459–60.
Grundman, W. *TDNT* 9:527–80 (see esp. 566–71).
Hurtado, Larry W. *Lord Jesus Christ: Devotion to Jesus in Earliest Christianity*. Grand Rapids: Eerdmans, 2003.
Jobes 54–56 (see "IN DEPTH: Messiah or Christ?").
Jonge, M. de. *ABD* 1:914–21.
———. "The Earliest Christian Use of Christos: Some Suggestions." *NTS* 32, no. 3 (1986): 321–43.
———. "The Use of the Word Christos in the Johannine Epistles." Pages 66–74 in *Studies in John*. Edited by C. K. Barrett. NovTSup 24. Leiden: Brill, 1970.
Köstenberger, *Theology*, 311–23.
NIDNTTE 4:688–97.
Piper, O. A. *ISBE* 3:330–38.
Pollard, T. E. *Johannine Christology and the Early Church*. Cambridge: Cambridge University Press, 2005.
Schreiner, *NT Theology*, 413–15.
*Witherington, B. *DLNT*, 152–59.

HOMILETICAL SUGGESTIONS

A True Follower of Christ (5:1–5)

1. A child of God believes Jesus is the Christ (vv. 1, 5)
2. A child of God loves God's children (vv. 1–2)
3. A child of God obeys his commandment (vv. 2–3)
4. A child of God overcomes the world (vv. 4–5)

XV. Eternal Life and God's Testimony concerning His Son (5:6–12)

This section addresses God's testimony concerning the Son. A combination of the noun *μαρτυρία* and the vb. *μαρτυρέω* occurs nine times in the section. Verses 6–8 highlight the witness of the water and blood (Jesus's baptism and death on the cross) and that of the Holy Spirit. The subst. ptc. *οἱ μαρτυροῦντες* of v. 7 and the witnesses of *τὸ πνεῦμα καὶ τὸ ὕδωρ καὶ τὸ αἷμα* in v. 8 are in apposition. Again, we see John emphasizing the obj. (baptism and event of the cross) and the subj. (inward testimony of the Spirit; see Stott 179). Verses 9–10 affirm that the testimony is the testimony of God (causal *ὅτι* clause, v. 9). By means of the first class cond. clause, John conveys that the testimony of God is greater than that of man. The content *ὅτι* of v. 11 provides a succinct understanding of the testimony: God has given them the gift of eternal life in his Son. Verse 12 develops v. 11, offering a typical Johannine contrast, emphasizing that to have the Son is to have life.

6 οὗτός ἐστιν ὁ ἐλθὼν δι' ὕδατος καὶ αἵματος = Ἰησοῦς Χριστός,
οὐκ [*ἦλθεν*] ἐν τῷ ὕδατι μόνον,
ἀλλ' [*ἦλθεν*] ἐν τῷ ὕδατι
καὶ ἐν τῷ αἵματι·
καὶ τὸ πνεῦμά ἐστιν τὸ μαρτυροῦν,
ὅτι τὸ πνεῦμά ἐστιν ἡ ἀλήθεια.

7 ὅτι τρεῖς εἰσιν οἱ μαρτυροῦντες, =

8 τὸ πνεῦμα
καὶ τὸ ὕδωρ
καὶ τὸ αἷμα,
καὶ οἱ τρεῖς εἰς τὸ ἕν εἰσιν.

9 εἰ τὴν μαρτυρίαν τῶν ἀνθρώπων λαμβάνομεν,
ἡ μαρτυρία τοῦ θεοῦ μείζων ἐστίν·
ὅτι αὕτη ἐστὶν ἡ μαρτυρία τοῦ θεοῦ,
ὅτι μεμαρτύρηκεν περὶ τοῦ υἱοῦ αὐτοῦ.

10 ὁ πιστεύων εἰς τὸν υἱὸν τοῦ θεοῦ ἔχει τὴν μαρτυρίαν ἐν αὐτῷ,
ὁ μὴ πιστεύων τῷ θεῷ ψεύστην πεποίηκεν αὐτόν,
ὅτι οὐ πεπίστευκεν εἰς τὴν μαρτυρίαν
ἣν μεμαρτύρηκεν ὁ θεὸς
περὶ τοῦ υἱοῦ αὐτοῦ.

11 καὶ αὕτη ἐστὶν ἡ μαρτυρία,
ὅτι ζωὴν αἰώνιον ἔδωκεν ἡμῖν ὁ θεός,
καὶ αὕτη ἡ ζωὴ ἐν τῷ υἱῷ αὐτοῦ ἐστιν.

12 ὁ ἔχων τὸν υἱὸν ἔχει τὴν ζωήν·
ὁ μὴ ἔχων τὸν υἱὸν τοῦ θεοῦ τὴν ζωὴν οὐκ ἔχει.

VERSE 6

οὗτός ἐστιν ὁ ἐλθὼν δι' ὕδατος καὶ αἵματος, Ἰησοῦς Χριστός,
This is the one who came through water and blood, Jesus Christ.

Οὗτός, nom. sg. masc. of the near dem. pron., serves as the subj. of ἐστιν, the 3rd sg. pres. indic. of εἰμί. Ἐλθών, nom. sg. masc. aor. act. ptc. of ἔρχομαι, functions subst. as a pred. nom. The prep. phrase δι' ὕδατος καὶ αἵματος adv. modifies ἐλθών. Serving as the compound obj. of the prep. διά are ὕδατος, gen. sg. neut. of ὕδωρ, τό, and αἵματος, gen. neut. sg. of αἷμα, τό. The nom. sg. masc. forms Ἰησοῦς Χριστός are in apposition to ὁ ἐλθὼν δι' ὕδατος καὶ αἵματος. Many different views have been offered for the mysterious phrase δι' ὕδατος καὶ αἵματος. The following reflect four main views:

1. A reference to the water and blood from Jesus's side at the crucifixion (e.g., Augustine).
2. A reference to Jesus's *birth* and death (e.g., Witherington, "Waters of Birth"; see For Further Study 39 "Water and Blood")
3. A reference to the sacraments of baptism and the Lord's Supper (see Strecker 183).

*4. A reference to Jesus's *baptism* and his death on the cross (the most accepted view, though with nuances of understanding; see Akin 196; Hiebert 235–36; Marshall 231; Stott 178; Yarbrough 282; cf. Brown 578, who notes John is emphasizing the salvific nature of Christ's death with the phrase; sim. Smalley 266–67).

John is likely referring to Jesus's baptism and death/resurrection and how those historical events testify to his person and work. In other words, Jesus came (i.e., he came on the scene of human history), revealing his identity in an anticipatory fashion by his baptism and in a climatic way through his death and resurrection.

οὐκ ἐν τῷ ὕδατι μόνον,
He came not by the water only,

The Gk. phrase above literally reads, "Not in/by the water only." The English translation above reflects an ellipsis of the vb. ἔρχομαι. Οὐκ negates an implied form of ἔρχομαι. The prep. phrase ἐν τῷ ὕδατι adv. modifies the implied form of ἔρχομαι and conveys means/instr. (Harris 79–80). The variation in preps. (δία in the initial part of verse and ἐν in the latter) may reflect stylistic variation (Young 92; Kruse 174 n. 201; Marshall 232 n. 6; note most EVV translate both preps. with "by," e.g., CSB, NIV, KJV, NLT; on a possible intended distinction, see Culy 126; Lenski 525–26). Μόνον also adv. modifies the implied form of ἔρχομαι.

ἀλλ' ἐν τῷ ὕδατι καὶ ἐν τῷ αἵματι·
but by the water and by the blood.

A form of ἔρχομαι is implied in the clause above. Both prep. phrases (ἐν τῷ ὕδατι and ἐν τῷ αἵματι) adv. modify the implied form of ἔρχομαι and denote the explicit means by which Jesus's identity and mission were unveiled. Ὕδατι, the dat. sg. neut. of ὕδωρ, ὕδατος, τό, serves as object of the preposition ἐν. Αἵματι, the dat. sg. neut. of αἷμα, serves as the object of the prep. ἐν.

καὶ τὸ πνεῦμά ἐστιν τὸ μαρτυροῦν,
And the Spirit is the one bearing witness,

In addition to the historical incidents of Jesus's baptism and death/resurrection as witnesses to Jesus's identity and mission, the apostle John marshals the inner witness of the Holy Spirit. Τὸ πνεῦμά, nom. sg. neut., serves as the subj. of ἐστιν, 3rd sg. pres. indic. of εἰμί. Functioning as the pred. nom. is τὸ μαρτυροῦν, the nom. sg. neut. of pres. act. ptc. of μαρτυρέω.

ὅτι τὸ πνεῦμά ἐστιν ἡ ἀλήθεια.
for the Spirit is the truth.

Ὅτι introduces a causal clause "because" (most EVV). Τὸ πνεῦμά, nom. sg. neut., serves as the subj. of ἐστιν, the 3rd sg. pres. indic. of εἰμί. Functioning as the pred. nom. is ἡ ἀλήθεια, the nom. sg. fem. form.

VERSE 7

ὅτι τρεῖς εἰσιν οἱ μαρτυροῦντες,
For the witnesses are three in number,

The text reads more literally, "for three are those bearing witness." Ὅτι introduces a causal clause "for" (most EVV; NET Translation Notes regard it as "not strictly causal but inferential in sense"). Μαρτυροῦντες, the nom. pl. masc. pres. act. ptc. of μαρτυρέω, acts as the subj. of εἰσιν, the 3rd pl. pres. indic. of εἰμί. Τρεῖς, "three," nom. pl. masc., functions as a pred. adj. The use of the masc. ptc. in relation to the three neut. nouns that follow (v. 8) is likely governed by the author's intent to personalize or personify the water and blood and highlight them as witnesses along with the Spirit (see Wallace 332 n. 44; Kruse 179 n. 209). Some late mss. include the following wording after μαρτυροῦντες: (1) ἐν τῷ οὐρανῷ (2) ὁ πατήρ (3) ὁ λόγος (4) καὶ τὸ ἅγιον πνεῦμα (5) καὶ οὗτοι οἱ τρεῖς ἕν εἰσιν (6) καὶ τρεῖς εἰσιν οἱ μαρτυροῦντες ἐν τῇ γῇ. This section, the so-called Johannine Comma ("comma" in this context mng. "clause" from Latin *comma*; Gk. κόμμα), is witnessed only by eight Gk. mss. (61 88[v.r.] 221[v.r.] 429[v.r.] 629 636[v.r.] 918 2318), none of which can be dated earlier than the fourteenth century (see Brown 776). The addition is never cited by Greek or Latin church fathers in the first four centuries, a significant fact in light of the various Trinitarian debates of that era. The Comma was included in the third edition of Erasmus's Gk. NT and later in the Textus Receptus, which led to its inclusion in today's KJV. Though the Comma is theologically true (and supported elsewhere in Scripture), ms. evidence does not support viewing it as authentic (on the subject, see discussions in Akin 198–200; Brown 775–86; Marshall 236 n. 19; Smalley 260–61).

VERSE 8

τὸ πνεῦμα καὶ τὸ ὕδωρ καὶ τὸ αἷμα,
the Spirit and the water and the blood,

This entire clause is in appos. to τρεῖς above. The three witnesses are τὸ πνεῦμα καὶ τὸ ὕδωρ καὶ τὸ αἷμα. All three noun forms are nom. sg. neut. While some have proposed a different reference here than in v. 6 (e.g., seeing the water and blood as reference to the sacraments of baptism and the Eucharist, so Law 121–23), the most straightforward reading is to see the same reference as in v. 6 (Marshall 238; Smalley 269; see Marshall 237–40 for discussion).

καὶ οἱ τρεῖς εἰς τὸ ἕν εἰσιν.
and these three are in agreement.

More literally, the text reads, "And the three are 'in the one.'" Εἰς τὸ ἕν "in the one," is a Gk. idiom meaning "in agreement" (most EVV, e.g., CSB, NIV, NET). Τρεῖς, nom. pl. masc., is the subst. use of the adj. as the subj. of εἰσιν, the 3rd pl. pres. indic. of εἰμί. The entire prep. phrase εἰς τὸ ἕν functions similarly to a pred. nom. or pred. adj. The article τό makes clear that the acc. sg. neut. ἕν, "one," functions as a subst. Τὸ ἕν is the obj. of the prep. εἰς.

VERSE 9

εἰ τὴν μαρτυρίαν τῶν ἀνθρώπων λαμβάνομεν,
If we receive the testimony of men,

Εἰ introduces the prot. of a first class cond. sentence (i.e., a condition assumed to be true, if only for the sake of argument; see 3:13). Μαρτυρίαν is acc. sg. fem. from μαρτυρία, -ας, ἡ, "testimony" (on term, see *NIDNTTE* 3:234–46; LN §33.262), and functions as the dir. obj. of λαμβάνομεν, the 1st pl. pres. act. indic. of λαμβάνω. Ἀνθρώπων is the gen. pl. masc. of ἄνθρωπος, -ου, ὁ, functioning as a subj. gen. The clause above offers a generally observed truth in life. Humans do, in fact, generally receive eyewitness testimony of other humans, especially when in plurality from reliable sources.

ἡ μαρτυρία τοῦ θεοῦ μείζων ἐστίν
the testimony of God is greater,

There appears to be an ellipsis between the first two clauses of v. 9. The flow of thought is: "If we receive the testimony of men . . . *we should certainly receive the testimony of God* . . . for the testimony of God is greater." Μαρτυρία, nom. sg. fem. is the subj. of ἐστίν, the 3rd sg. pres. indic. of εἰμί. Θεοῦ is the gen. sg. masc. of θεός, functioning as a subj. gen. (on use, see KMP 99–100). Μείζων, the nom. sg. fem. comparative form of μέγας, serves as a predicate nom.

ὅτι αὕτη ἐστὶν ἡ μαρτυρία τοῦ θεοῦ,
for this is the testimony of God,

Ὅτι introduces a causal clause. Αὕτη, nom. sg. fem. of the near dem. pron., serves as the subj. of ἐστίν, the 3rd sg. pres. indic. of εἰμί. Μαρτυρία, nom. sg. fem., is the pred. nom. Θεοῦ is the gen. sg. masc. of θεός, functioning as a subj. gen. (Culy 128; Yarbrough 205).

ὅτι μεμαρτύρηκεν περὶ τοῦ υἱοῦ αὐτοῦ.
that he has testified concerning his Son.

Ὅτι introduces a content clause (Porter, *Idioms*, 238; cf. Jobes 223, who regards it as epex.; NET Translation Notes who view it as equivalent to a rel. pron.). Μεμαρτύρηκεν is the 3rd sg. pf. act. indic. of μαρτυρέω, with God the Father as the implied subj. The prep. phrase περὶ τοῦ υἱοῦ αὐτοῦ adv. modifies μεμαρτύρηκεν, communicating reference or respect. Υἱοῦ, the gen. sg. masc. of υἱός, serves as the obj. of the prep. Περί αὐτοῦ, gen. sg. masc. of the 3rd pers. personal pron., is a gen. of relationship.

VERSE 10

ὁ πιστεύων εἰς τὸν υἱὸν τοῦ θεοῦ ἔχει τὴν μαρτυρίαν ἐν αὐτῷ,
The person who believes in the Son of God has this testimony in himself;

Πιστεύων is the nom. sg. masc. pres. act. ptc. of πιστεύω, functioning here as a subst. ptc. and subject of ἔχει, the 3rd sg. pres. act. indic. of ἔχω. The prep. phrase εἰς τὸν υἱὸν τοῦ θεοῦ adv. modifies πιστεύων and is synonymous in meaning with a dat. obj. for πιστεύω (on πιστεύω + εἰς, see BDAG 816c). Υἱόν, the acc. sg. masc. of υἱός, is the obj. of the prep. εἰς. Θεοῦ, the gen. sg. masc. of θεός, serves as a gen. of relationship. Τὴν μαρτυρίαν (see 5:9) functions as the acc. direct object of the vb. Following the *Editio Critica Maior*, the NA[28]/UBS[5] read ἐν αὐτῷ (witnessed by א Ψ et al.), in contrast to ἐν ἑαυτῷ of the NA[27]/UBS[4] (witnessed by B[2] *Byz* et al.). The adv. prep. phrase is loc. and the personal pron. αὐτῷ conveys a reflexive sense in this context (note BDF §283; R 680–81, 687; Young 75).

ὁ μὴ πιστεύων τῷ θεῷ ψεύστην πεποίηκεν αὐτόν,
the person who is not believing God has made him out to be a liar,

The negated subst. ptc. πιστεύων, nom. sg. masc. pres. act. ptc. of πιστεύω, serves as the subj. of πεποίηκεν, the 3rd sg. pf. act. indic. of ποιέω. Θεῷ, the dat. sg. masc. of θεός, serves as the dat. obj. or dat. complement of πιστεύων. Αὐτόν, the acc. sg. masc. of the 3rd pers. personal pron. functions as the obj. in a double acc. cstr. (see BW 51–52; Wallace 181–88). The complement in the double acc. cstr. is ψεύστην, "liar," the acc. sg. masc. of ψεύστης, -ου, ὁ. More literalistically, the text above reads, "has made him a liar." God is completely truthful and incapable of lying, but when a sinful human refuses to believe him, that person is acting as if God's revelation is not reliable. The rebellious human implies that God is a liar—an implication that the apostle John brings out here.

ὅτι οὐ πεπίστευκεν εἰς τὴν μαρτυρίαν ἣν μεμαρτύρηκεν ὁ θεὸς περὶ τοῦ υἱοῦ αὐτοῦ.
because he has not believed in the testimony which God has testified about his Son.

Ὅτι introduces a causal clause (most EVV). Ὁ μὴ πιστεύων τῷ θεῷ, "The person who is not believing in God," from the previous clause is the subj. of πεπίστευκεν, the 3rd sg. pf. act. indic. of πιστεύω. The prep. phrase εἰς τὴν μαρτυρίαν delineates the object of belief (interchangeable with a dat. complement with the vb. πιστεύω). Μαρτυρίαν, acc. sg. fem. of μαρτυρία (see 5:9), functions as the obj. of the prep. εἰς. Ἥν, the acc. sg. fem. form of the rel. pron., refers back to the antecedent μαρτυρίαν and functions as the dir. obj. of μεμαρτύρηκεν, the 3rd sg. pf. act. indic. of μαρτυρέω. Nom. sg. masc. θεός serves as the subj. of μεμαρτύρηκεν. The prep. phrase περὶ τοῦ υἱοῦ αὐτοῦ communicates reference or respect. Υἱοῦ, the gen. sg. masc. of υἱός, acts as the obj. of the prep. περί. Αὐτοῦ, gen. sg. masc. of the 3rd pers. personal pron., is a gen. of relationship.

VERSE 11

καὶ αὕτη ἐστὶν ἡ μαρτυρία, ὅτι ζωὴν αἰώνιον ἔδωκεν ἡμῖν ὁ θεός,
And this is the testimony: God gave us eternal life,

Αὕτη, nom. sg. fem. of the near dem. pron., functions as the subj. of ἐστίν, the 3rd sg. pres. indic. of εἰμί. Μαρτυρία (see 5:9), nom. sg. fem., is the pred. nom. Ὅτι introduces an epex. clause (most EVV; Smalley 271). Ζωήν, acc. sg. fem. of ζωή, -ῆς, ἡ, which is modified by αἰώνιον "eternal," serves as the dir. obj. of ἔδωκεν, the 3rd sg. aor. act. indic. of δίδωμι. Ἡμῖν, dat. pl. of the 1st pers. personal pron., functions as the indir. obj. Θεός, nom. sg. masc., is the subj. of ἔδωκεν.

καὶ αὕτη ἡ ζωὴ ἐν τῷ υἱῷ αὐτοῦ ἐστιν.
and this life is in his Son.

Modified attrib. by the near dem. pron. αὕτη, the nom. sg. fem. ζωή serves as the subj. of ἐστιν, the 3rd sg. pres. indic. of εἰμί. The prep. phrase ἐν τῷ υἱῷ αὐτοῦ adverb. modifies ἐστιν and communicates a metaphorical loc./spherical idea (see BDAG 326c; R

585–86, 589; Moule 75–76). Υἱῷ, dat. sg. masc. of υἱός, functions as the obj. of the prep. ἐν. Αὐτοῦ, gen. sg. masc. of the 3rd pers. personal pron., is a gen. of relationship. As Law succinctly summarizes concerning this verse, "The witness of God is not only that He gave us Eternal Life, but that the sole medium of its bestowal is His Son" (405).

VERSE 12

ὁ ἔχων τὸν υἱὸν ἔχει τὴν ζωήν
The one who has the Son has life.

Ἔχων, the nom. sg. masc. pres. act. ptc. of ἔχω, serves as the subj. of the vb. ἔχει, the 3rd sg. pres. act. ind. of ἔχω. Υἱόν, acc. sg. masc. of υἱός, -οῦ, ὁ, is the dir. obj. of the subst. ptc. ἔχων. Ζωήν, the acc. sg. fem., of ζωή, -ῆς, ἡ, is dir. obj. of ἔχει.

ὁ μὴ ἔχων τὸν υἱὸν τοῦ θεοῦ τὴν ζωὴν οὐκ ἔχει.
The one who does not have the Son of God does not have life.

Here we find a rare example of asyndeton (no connecting particle) in 1 John. Asyndeton "indicates that the writer did not find the need to specify any kind of relationship between the clauses" (Runge 20). The negated ptc. (nom. sg. masc. pres. act. ptc. of ἔχων) serves as the subj. of the negated vb. ἔχει, the 3rd sg. pres. act. indic. of ἔχω. Υἱόν, acc. sg. masc. of υἱός, functions as the dir. obj. of the ptc. ἔχων. Θεοῦ, gen. sg. masc. of θεός, is a gen. of relationship. Ζωήν, acc. sg. fem. of ζωή, is the dir. obj. of the negated vb. ἔχει.

FOR FURTHER STUDY

38. "Water and Blood" (5:6–8)

Michaels, J. Ramsey. "By Water and Blood: Sin and Purification in John and First John." Pages 149–62 in *Dimensions of Baptism: Biblical and Theological Studies*. Edited by Stanley E. Porter and Anthony R. Cross. London: Sheffield Academic, 2002.

Thatcher, Tom. "'Water and Blood' in AntiChrist Christianity (1 John 5:6)." *Stone-Campbell Journal* 4, no. 2 (2001): 235–48.

Witherington, Ben. "The Waters of Birth: John 3:5 and 1 John 5:6–8." *NTS* 35, no. 1 (1989): 155–60.

HOMILETICAL SUGGESTIONS

The Testimony of God concerning His Son (5:6–12)

1. The testimony of three: the water, the blood, and the Spirit (vv. 6–8)
2. The testimony of God; the highest authority (v. 9)
3. The testimony within us (v. 10)
4. The testimony defined (vv. 11–12)
   (a) God has given us eternal life (v. 11)
   (b) This life is in the Son of God, Jesus Christ (vv. 11–12)

The Divine Testimony (5:6–12)

1. The Context: a church impacted by false teaching
   a. Those who have left the church teach a distorted understanding of Christ and his atoning work (possibly related to Cerinthianism, the belief that the Christ descended on Jesus only at his baptism and left him before his death on the cross).
   b. John affirms the apostolic witness of Jesus Christ's baptism and death on a cross.
   c. John's words offer needed assurance of salvation to troubled hearts in the church and offer a clear distinction between those who trust in God's testimony and those who do not.
2. The Testimony: God has testified concerning his Son (vv. 6–8)
   a. The importance of multiple witnesses
      (1) Deut. 19:15
      (2) John 8:17–18
   b. The agreement of three
      (3) The water (Jesus's baptism witnesses to him and his ministry)
      (2) The blood (Jesus's atoning death witnesses to him and his ministry)
      (3) The Holy Spirit
         1. "What the Spirit says can be trusted because he speaks God's truth" (Marshall 234)
         2. The Spirit testifies in our "inward hearts" or through the preaching of God's Word (Marshall 234)
   c. "The three witnesses form, in fact, a single divine testimony to Jesus Christ, which God has given" (Stott 181)
3. The Response (vv. 9–10)
   a. Those who believe
      (1) They have this testimony in themselves.
      (2) They have trusted in the apostolic witness and the truth of the Holy Spirit which testifies to Christ's work.
   b. Those who do not believe
      (1) They reject the testimony of God himself.
      (2) God has made them "liars."
4. The Result (vv. 11–12)
   a. The testimony is that God has given us eternal life in his Son.
   b. Those who accept the testimony of God, who trust in the Son of God, have eternal life.
   c. Those who do not have the Son do not have eternal life.

XVI. Conclusion (5:13–21)

This section provides concluding thoughts to the letter. The ἵνα clause of v. 13 provides the fundamental purpose for why John has written to his readers (τοῖς πιστεύουσιν εἰς τὸ ὄνομα τοῦ υἱοῦ τοῦ θεοῦ is in appos. to the indir. object ὑμῖν): that they may know that they have eternal life. Verses 14–17 address the confidence the readers may have in praying for a fellow believer. To those sinning a sin not leading to death, the brother should ask and God will give him life (τοῖς ἁμαρτάνουσιν μὴ πρὸς θάνατον standing in appos. to the dat. sg. masc. 3rd pers. personal pron.). Verses 18–20 each begin with the familiar "we know" (οἴδαμεν, occurring 7× in the latter half of the letter), affirming three things known by the author and readers: (1) everyone born of God does not sin (v. 18); (2) they are of God in contrast to the world that lies in the evil one's embrace (v. 19); (3) the Son of God has come and given understanding. The ἵνα provides the purpose of the understanding: to know the true one.

Verse 21 begins with a final voc. (τεκνία) and a final impv. (φυλάξατε), exhorting the community to guard themselves from idols.

13 Ταῦτα ἔγραψα ὑμῖν =
ἵνα εἰδῆτε ὅτι ζωὴν ἔχετε αἰώνιον,
τοῖς πιστεύουσιν
εἰς τὸ ὄνομα τοῦ υἱοῦ τοῦ θεοῦ.

14 καὶ αὕτη ἐστὶν ἡ παρρησία
ἣν ἔχομεν πρὸς αὐτόν,
ὅτι ἐάν τι αἰτώμεθα
κατὰ τὸ θέλημα αὐτοῦ
ἀκούει ἡμῶν

15 καὶ ἐὰν οἴδαμεν ὅτι ἀκούει ἡμῶν
ὃ ἐὰν αἰτώμεθα,
οἴδαμεν ὅτι ἔχομεν τὰ αἰτήματα
ἃ ᾐτήκαμεν ἀπ' αὐτοῦ.

16 Ἐάν τις ἴδῃ τὸν ἀδελφὸν αὐτοῦ ἁμαρτάνοντα ἁμαρτίαν
μὴ πρὸς θάνατον,
αἰτήσει
καὶ δώσει αὐτῷ ζωήν
↑= τοῖς ἁμαρτάνουσιν μὴ πρὸς θάνατον.
ἔστιν ἁμαρτία
πρὸς θάνατον·
οὐ περὶ ἐκείνης λέγω ἵνα ἐρωτήσῃ.

17 πᾶσα ἀδικία ἁμαρτία ἐστίν,
καὶ ἔστιν ἁμαρτία
οὐ πρὸς θάνατον.

18 Οἴδαμεν ὅτι πᾶς ὁ γεγεννημένος ἐκ τοῦ θεοῦ οὐχ ἁμαρτάνει,
ἀλλ' ὁ γεννηθεὶς ἐκ τοῦ θεοῦ τηρεῖ ἑαυτὸν
καὶ ὁ πονηρὸς οὐχ ἅπτεται αὐτοῦ.

19 οἴδαμεν ὅτι ἐκ τοῦ θεοῦ ἐσμεν
καὶ [*ὅτι*] ὁ κόσμος ὅλος ἐν τῷ πονηρῷ κεῖται.

20 οἴδαμεν δὲ ὅτι ὁ υἱὸς τοῦ θεοῦ ἥκει
καὶ δέδωκεν ἡμῖν διάνοιαν,
ἵνα γινώσκωμεν τὸν ἀληθινόν,
καὶ ἐσμὲν
ἐν τῷ ἀληθινῷ
ἐν τῷ υἱῷ αὐτοῦ = Ἰησοῦ Χριστῷ.
οὗτός ἐστιν ὁ ἀληθινὸς θεὸς καὶ ζωὴ αἰώνιος.

21 Τεκνία, φυλάξατε ἑαυτὰ ἀπὸ τῶν εἰδώλων.

VERSE 13

Ταῦτα ἔγραψα ὑμῖν, ἵνα εἰδῆτε ὅτι ζωὴν ἔχετε αἰώνιον,
These things I wrote to you all so that you would know that you have eternal life,

Ταῦτα, acc. pl. neut. of the near dem. pron., serves as the dir. obj. of ἔγραψα, the 1st sg. aor. act. indic. of γράφω. The vb. is an epistolary aorist (Smalley 277; ZG 733; on this topic, see KMP 296–97; R 845–46; cf. 2:21). Ὑμῖν, dat. pl. of the 2nd pers. personal pron., functions as the indir. obj. Ἵνα introduces a purpose clause "so that" (most EVV; Culy 132; Rogers and Rogers 599). Εἰδῆτε is 2nd pl. pf. act. subjunc. from οἶδα (for the strange forms of οἶδα, see MBG 263). About two thirds of subjuncs. in the GNT are aor. tense. Roughly one-third of subjuncs. are pres. tense. Take a close look at this pf. tense subjunc. because you won't see one again for a long time (for discussion of the pf. subjunc., see Campbell 64). Ὅτι introduces the content of what is known (see

BDAG 731d; R 1034–35; Young 190). Ζωήν, the acc. sg. fem. of ζωή, serves as the direct obj. of ἔχετε, the 2nd pl. pres. act. indic. of ἔχω. Αἰώνιον, the acc. sg. fem. of the adj. αἰώνιος (see 1:2), modifies ζωήν attrib. (cf. 1:2; 2:25; 3:15; 5:11, 20). The adj. would more typically be found adjacent to the noun it modifies. Αἰώνιος is usually found behaving as a two-termination adj. (i.e., employing λόγος endings for both fem. and masc. forms), though occasionally first declension feminine endings (καρδία pattern) are found (on this topic, see BDF §59[1]; Decker 95; R 272–73; on "eternal life," see For Further Study 26 "Eternal Life"). Most commentators rightly see 1 John 5:13 as the clearest statement of the author's purpose in this short letter. John is writing to believers who are unsettled by recent defections from their community and need to be reassured of their relationship with the triune God.

τοῖς πιστεύουσιν εἰς τὸ ὄνομα τοῦ υἱοῦ τοῦ θεοῦ.
that is, to those who believe in the name of the Son of God.

The Greek text above has no equivalent to the English phrase "that is," but the words were added to clarify that this entire clause is appositional to ὑμῖν above. Most EVV translate the ptc. (placing it directly after ὑμῖν) with the sense of a rel. clause "to you who believe." Πιστεύουσιν, dat. pl. masc. pres. act. ptc. from πιστεύω, functioning subst., is in appos. to ὑμῖν. The prep. phrase εἰς τὸ ὄνομα τοῦ υἱοῦ τοῦ θεοῦ gives the object of belief (equivalent to a dat. complement with the vb. πιστεύω, see 5:10). Ὄνομα, acc. sg. neut., is the obj. of the prep. εἰς. Υἱοῦ, the gen. sg. masc. of υἱός, expresses poss. Θεοῦ, the gen. sg. masc. of θεός, is a gen. of relationship. To believe in the name of the Son of God is to believe in who he is and what he has accomplished.

VERSE 14

καὶ αὕτη ἐστὶν ἡ παρρησία ἣν ἔχομεν πρὸς αὐτόν,
And this is the confidence which we have toward him:

Greek has a plethora of conjunctions and connecting particles. Although your English teacher told you never to start a sentence with "and," it's normal and good to start Gk. sentences with καί. Αὕτη, the nom. sg. fem. of the near dem. pron. (looking forward to the following clause), serves as the subj. of ἐστίν, the 3rd sg. pres. indic. of εἰμί. Παρρησία, "boldness, confidence"(see 2:28), nom. sg. fem., serves as the pred. nom. Ἥν, acc. sg. fem. rel. pron., refers back to the antecedent παρρησία and acts as the dir. obj. of ἔχομεν, the 1st pl. pres. act. indic. of ἔχω. The prep. phrase πρὸς αὐτόν likely conveys an idea of proximity or location ("in the presence of," or "facing," see BDAG 874a; "before him," CSB, NASB; "toward him," ESV; "in approaching God," NIV). Αὐτόν, the acc. sg. masc. of the 3rd pers. personal pron., serves as obj. of the prep. πρός.

ὅτι ἐάν τι αἰτώμεθα κατὰ τὸ θέλημα αὐτοῦ ἀκούει ἡμῶν.
if we ask anything according to his will, he hears us.

Ὅτι is epex. (ZG 733; cf. Young 190), with the colon in the English translation communicating that function (so CSB, NET). Ἐάν introduces the prot. of a third class cond. sentence, holding out a situation for consideration (on third class cond., see 1:6). Τι, the acc. sg. neut. of the indef. pron., serves as the dir. obj. of αἰτώμεθα, the 1st pl. pres. mid. subjunc. of αἰτέω. "Asking" or "requesting" is an action of reciprocity (requiring two parties), so we are not surprised to find αἰτέω frequently in the middle voice (cf. R. 805; Smalley 282). The prep. phrase κατὰ τὸ θέλημα αὐτοῦ connotes correspondence or conformity (Harris 152). Θέλημα, "will, desire," acc. sg. neut., acts as the obj. of the prep. κατά. Αὐτοῦ, the gen. sg. masc. of the 3rd pers. personal pron., functions as a subj. gen. The apod. of this third class cond. sentence is: ἀκούει ἡμῶν. Ἀκούει is the 3rd sg. pres. act. indic. of ἀκούω. Ἡμῶν, gen. pl. of the 1st pers. personal pron., is the gen. obj. (or gen. complement) of the vb. ἀκούει. Ἀκούω frequently takes a gen. obj., though the vb. also appears with a dir. obj. in the acc. case. Categories of vbs. that often take objects in the gen. case include sensation, emotion, volition, sharing, ruling, and separation (KMP 107; on this topic, see also BDF §173; Moule 36–37).

VERSE 15

καὶ ἐὰν οἴδαμεν ὅτι ἀκούει ἡμῶν ὃ ἐὰν αἰτώμεθα,
And if we know that he hears us (whatever we ask),

Ἐάν introduces the prot. of a third class cond. sentence (see 1:6), though, strangely, the main vb. of the clause is in the indic. mood (cf. 1 Thess 3:8; Acts 8:31). We would have expected εἰδῶμεν (1st pl. pf. act. subj.), but the choice of the indic. probably points to the "fuzziness" of Koine Gk. patterns rather than to any special intended nuance (see Marshall 245 n. 10; BDF §372[1a]; R 1010; Z §336; contra Culy 134, who suggests the writer is possibly intending to weaken the third class cond. by using the indic. since the fact had previously been established as true in v. 14; sim., see Turner, *Syntax*, 116; cf. Burton §247; Brown 610 suggests the indic. is used here in the prot. to show its connection with the same vb. in the apod. in 15b). Οἴδαμεν is the 1st pl. pf. act. indic. of οἶδα. Ὅτι introduces the content of what is known (see BDAG 731d; R 1034–35; Young 190). Ἀκούει is the 3rd sg. pres. act. indic. of ἀκούω, with God the Father as the implied subj. Ἡμῶν, gen. pl. of the 1st pers. personal pron., is the gen. obj. (or gen. complement) of the vb. ἀκούει (see 5:14). The indef. rel. clause ὃ ἐὰν αἰτώμεθα, "whatever we ask," should likely be understood to function as an adv. acc. of reference "*with regard to* whatever we ask" (on this function, see BW 55–56; KMP 71; R 486–88; Wallace 203–4). The inclusion of the phrase is emphatic and invites the readers to petition our gracious and powerful heavenly Father. Ὃ ἐάν is the acc. sg. neut. indef. rel. pron., which functions as the dir. obj. of αἰτώμεθα, the 1st pl. pres. mid. subjunc. of αἰτέω (see 5:14 for discussion of the middle voice forms of αἰτέω). Note the relative pronoun, when combined with ἄν or ἐάν, conveys an indefinite sense, thus the above translation "whatever."

οἴδαμεν ὅτι ἔχομεν τὰ αἰτήματα ἃ ἠτήκαμεν ἀπ' αὐτοῦ.
we know that we have the requests which we have asked from him.

This clause is the apod. of the third class cond. sentence that began above. Οἴδαμεν is the 1st pl. pf. act. ind. of οἶδα. Ὅτι introduces the content of what is known. Ἔχομεν is the 1st pl. pres. act. indic. of ἔχω. Αἰτήματα is the acc. pl. neut. of αἴτημα, "request" (BDAG 30d; derivative of αἰτέω, cf. LN §33.164), and serves as the dir. obj. of ἔχομεν. Ἅ, acc. pl. neut. rel. pron., refers back to the antecedent αἰτήματα and functions as the dir. obj. of ᾐτήκαμεν, the 1st pl. pf. act. indic. of αἰτέω. The prep. phrase ἀπ' αὐτοῦ communicates the idea of origin/source (see BDAG 106a). Αὐτοῦ, gen. sg. masc. of the 3rd pers. personal pron., functions as obj. of the prep. ἀπό.

VERSE 16

Εάν τις ἴδῃ τὸν ἀδελφὸν αὐτοῦ ἁμαρτάνοντα ἁμαρτίαν μὴ πρὸς θάνατον,
If anyone sees his brother sinning a sin not to death,

Εάν introduces a third class cond. sentence (Let's consider this situation . . . what if . . . ; on third class cond., see 1:6). Τις, nom. sg. masc. of the indef. pron., serves as the subj. of ἴδῃ, the 3rd sg. aor. act. subj. of ὁράω. Ἀδελφόν, acc. sg. masc. of ἀδελφός, -οῦ, ὁ, functions as the dir. obj. of ἴδῃ. Αὐτοῦ, gen. sg. masc. of the 3rd pers. personal pron., is a gen. of relationship. The term "brother" is variously understood to refer to those who believe in the name of Jesus (e.g., Akin 207; Jobes 234; Kruse 190), to a church member (e.g., Marshall 246 n. 15), or as a broader reference to a "neighbor" or a nominal Christian (e.g., Stott 190). Ἁμαρτάνοντα, acc. sg. masc. pres. act. ptc. of ἁμαρτάνω, functions as a supplementary ptc. (see "Supplementary Participles" in the introduction; on this topic, see also BDF §416; R 480; Young 149; Wallace 181–89; cf. 4:2). Ἁμαρτίαν, acc. sg. fem. of ἁμαρτία, -ας, ἡ, is a cognate acc. (BW 50; Moule 32; ZG 733; on function, see also BDF §153[1]) and serves as the dir. obj. of ἁμαρτάνοντα. The negated prep. phrase πρὸς θάνατον qualifies ἁμαρτίαν and communicates the idea of result ("resulting in death," NET; "lead[ing] to death," CSB, ESV, NIV; see BDAG 874d; LN §89.44; cf. Harris 196). John is discussing a sin that does not result in or end in eternal spiritual death (i.e., John is *not* talking about the schismatic heretics he has been referencing throughout the letter). Θάνατον, acc. sg. masc. of θάνατος, -ου, ὁ, is the obj. of the prep. πρός.

αἰτήσει καὶ δώσει αὐτῷ ζωήν,
he should ask and he will give to him life

Αἰτήσει, 3rd sg. fut. act. indic. of αἰτέω, functions as an imperatival fut. (Porter, *Idioms*, 224; Jobes 234; Kruse 190; Marshall 246 n. 16; Yarbrough 307; contra Hiebert 258; on function, see also BDF §362; Burton §67; KMP 272–73; Young 118). The implied subj. of αἰτήσει is the one who sees his brother sinning a sin not to death. Δώσει is the 3rd sg. fut. act. indic. of δίδωμι. While it is possible to understand the subj. of δώσει also as the interceding brother (i.e., as an instr. under God; Brooke 146; Haas 150; Stott 186), it is perhaps more likely that we should understand God the Father as the implied subj. of δώσει (most EVV; Akin 207 n. 237; Jobes 234; Law 407; Marshall 246 n. 17; Smalley 287). NET Translation Notes rightly observe this option is more consistent theologically. Αὐτῷ is the dat. sg. masc. of the 3rd pers. personal pron., here functioning as a dat. of indir. obj. Ζωήν, acc. pl. fem. of ζωή, -ῆς, ἡ, serves as the dir.

obj. of δώσει (on the varied understandings of the sense of the term in this context, see discussions in Jobes 307; Kruse 191; Stott 188–89; Yarbrough 307).

τοῖς ἁμαρτάνουσιν μὴ πρὸς θάνατον.
(to those sinning not to death).

Ἁμαρτάνουσιν, dat. pl. masc. pres. act. ptc. of ἁμαρτάνω, stands in appos. to αὐτῷ. For strict grammatical concord, a singular form would have been expected, but αὐτῷ above is clearly generic, so in a *constructio ad sensum*, the apostle John shifts to the pl. The negated prep. phrase πρὸς θάνατον qualifies ἁμαρτίαν and communicates the idea of result ("those committing a sin that does not lead to death," CSB; "not resulting in death," NET). θάνατον, acc. sg. masc. of θάνατος, is the obj. of the prep. πρός.

ἔστιν ἁμαρτία πρὸς θάνατον
There is a sin to death.

Ἔστιν, the 3rd sg. pres. indic. of εἰμί, has an implied impersonal subj. ("there" in translation above; sometimes referred to as the "existential" use of εἰμί; see Decker 86). Ἁμαρτία, nom. sg. fem., serves as the pred. nom. The negated prep. phrase πρὸς θάνατον qualifies ἁμαρτία and communicates the idea of result. Θάνατον, acc. sg. masc. of θάνατος, is the obj. of the prep. πρός. The interpretation concerning the sin that leads to death has been debated throughout church history. In broad terms, the interpretations fall under three categories:

1. A specific, deadly ("mortal") sin
2. Blasphemy against the Holy Spirit

*3. Rejection of the redemptive message of Christ and his atoning work. This is a broad category encompassing nuanced positions among scholars. Yet, fundamentally the sin is one of persistent and willful rebellion against God and rejection of the saving work of Christ, with some scholars specifically viewing John as associating this sin with that of the secessionist (see Akin 210; Hiebert 263; Jobes 236; Kruse 192; Marshall 247; Smalley 285 defines the sin as "such wrong doing as is incompatible with walking in the light and living as a child of God . . . deliberately turning away from God"; sim. Yarbrough 309–11).

(For a detailed discussion on this topic, see Akin 208–10; Brown 612–19; Jobes 234–35; Kruse 193–94; Smalley 284–85.)

οὐ περὶ ἐκείνης λέγω ἵνα ἐρωτήσῃ.
Not concerning that am I saying that he should ask.

The negation particle οὐ, though modifying the vb. λέγω, is pulled forward, apparently for emphasis. The prep. phrase περὶ ἐκείνης adv. modifies λέγω (Law 407–8), communicating reference or respect. Ἐκείνης, fem. sg. acc. of the far dem. pron. and referring to the "sin to death" (most EVV; though cf. NLT), serves as the obj. of the prep. περί. Λέγω is 1st sg. pres. act. ind. Ἵνα introduces ind. discourse ("content" ἵνα, see Wallace 475; Culy 136; Jobes 236; contra Tan 2002). Ἐρωτήσῃ is the 3rd sg. aor. act. subjunc.

of ἐρωτάω. Praying for a person who is running full speed down the road to eternal death is not the kind of confident intercession that John seeks to illustrate here. In our opinion, John is not forbidding prayer for impenitent rebels, but such intercession cannot be made with the same confidence that one can pray for a straying Christian brother or sister. In this context of confident prayer, John encourages intercession for fellow believers, reflecting yet another aspect of loving one another.

VERSE 17

πᾶσα ἀδικία ἁμαρτία ἐστίν,
All unrighteousness is sin,

Πᾶσα, nom. sg. fem. of πᾶς, attrib. modifies the nom. sg. fem. ἀδικία ("unrighteousness," NASB, ESV, KJV; "wrongdoing," ESV, NIV). Note how the alpha privative (α-) on the beginning of a word is akin to the English prefix "un-." Πᾶσα ἀδικία serves as the subj. of the vb. ἐστίν, the 3rd sg. pres. indic. of εἰμί. Ἁμαρτία, nom. sg. fem., is the pred. nom. In distinguishing the "sin to death" from sin which is not to death, John feels the need to clarify that all unrighteousness is sin, even though it is valid to distinguish the category of "sin to death" in this situation.

καὶ ἔστιν ἁμαρτία οὐ πρὸς θάνατον.
and there is a sin not to death.

Ἔστιν, the 3rd sg. pres. indic. of εἰμί, has an implied impersonal subj. ("there" in translation above; see 5:16). Ἁμαρτία, nom. sg. fem., serves as the pred. nom. The negated prep. phrase πρὸς θάνατον qualifies ἁμαρτία and communicates the idea of result ("resulting in death," NET; "lead[ing] to death," CSB, ESV, NIV; see BDAG 874d; LN §89.44; cf. Harris 196). Θάνατον, the acc. sg. masc. of θάνατος, -ου, ὁ, is the obj. of the prep. πρός. Above, πρὸς θάνατον is preceded with the negation particle μή (5:16). *Variatio* (stylistic variation) seems the most likely reason for the change here.

VERSE 18

Οἴδαμεν ὅτι πᾶς ὁ γεγεννημένος ἐκ τοῦ θεοῦ οὐχ ἁμαρτάνει,
We know that everyone born from God does not continue in sin,

Οἴδαμεν is the 1st pl. pf. act. indic. of οἶδα. Ὅτι introduces the content of what is known. Πᾶς, nom. sg. masc., attrib. modifies γεγεννημένος, the nom. sg. masc. pf. pass. ptc. of γεννάω. The prep. phrase ἐκ τοῦ θεοῦ communicates the idea of source/origin (cf. 3:9). Θεοῦ, the gen. sg. masc. of θεός, functions as the obj. of the prep. ἐκ. The subst. ptc. ὁ γεγεννημένος serves as the subj. of the negated vb. ἁμαρτάνει, the 3rd sg. pres. act. indic. of ἁμαρτάνω. The vb. ἁμαρτάνει has been translated above with consideration of both the literary context and imperfective aspect of the vb. form ("continue to sin," NIV; "keep on sinning," ESV; "make a practice of sinning," NLT; see 3:6, 9). John teaches his readers that spiritual birth makes continuance in unrepentant habitual sin impossible. At the same time, John is not teaching a dispassionate class on doctrine. His statement is a strong appeal to holiness and warning against sin. Perhaps even as you, the modern reader, are considering this short verse, the Holy Spirit is bringing to your mind a sin that you must turn from. Do not delay!

ἀλλ' ὁ γεννηθεὶς ἐκ τοῦ θεοῦ τηρεῖ ἑαυτὸν
but the one begotten from God guards himself,

Ἀλλά introduces a strong adversative statement. Rather than continuing in sin, the believer assiduously guards himself. Γεννηθείς, the nom. sg. masc. aor. pass. ptc. of γεννάω, most likely refers to the Christian believer (KJV; Brown 622; Culy 137; Law 409) rather than Christ (i.e., as the "only *Begotten* Son of God," so NASB, NIV, NLT; Young 75; most commentators surveyed, e.g., Haas 151; Hiebert 265–66; Kruse 195 n. 233; Marshall 252 n. 37; Smalley 289–90; Stott 192; Yarbrough 316 n. 2). The prep. phrase ἐκ τοῦ θεοῦ communicates the idea of source/origin. Θεοῦ, gen. sg. masc. of θεός, functions as the obj. of the prep. ἐκ. The subst. ptc. γεννηθείς serves as the subj. of the vb. τηρεῖ, the 3rd sg. pres. act. indic. of τηρέω. The acc. sg. masc. reflexive pronoun ἑαυτόν acts as the dir. obj. of τηρεῖ ("keeps," CSB, NIV; "protects," ESV, NET). The decision as to whether the personal pron. αὐτόν or the reflexive pron. ἑαυτόν is original (both attested in mss.) governs to a large degree the understanding of ὁ γεννηθεὶς ἐκ τοῦ θεοῦ (though the personal pron. could convey a reflexive sense, see R 287–88; Young 75). Following the *Editio Critica Maior*, the NA[28]/UBS[5] read ἑαυτόν (supported by ℵ A Ψ 33 1735 1739 *Byz* [K L P] et al.), in contrast to αὐτόν of the NA[27]/UBS[4]. The UBS[5] committee rate their choice of ἑαυτόν with a "C" (difficult to decide; for other grammatically possible interpretations beyond the two main options of Christ keeping the believer or the believer keeping himself, see Brown 620–22; NET Translation Notes). Supporting the above translation is the fact that ὁ γεννηθεὶς ἐκ τοῦ θεοῦ is an unusual way to refer to Christ. Also, Law notes that "it does seem very improbable that, having just described the Christian as ὁ γεγεννημένος, the Apostle should immediately expect us, without a hint of any kind, to understand by ὁ γεννηθεὶς the Only-Begotten Son of God" (409). (Some scholars address the objection by suggesting John is highlighting how the Son identifies with believers, see Haas 151; Jobes 238.) Ultimately, the UBS[5] decision on the most likely original reading of the text, as well internal considerations, support the above rendering. True believers guard themselves from evil, even as God empowers and strengthens them in that task.

καὶ ὁ πονηρὸς οὐχ ἅπτεται αὐτοῦ.
and the evil one does not touch him.

Πονηρός, the subst. use of the nom. sg. masc. adj., is here employed in reference to the devil and serves as the subj. of the negated vb. ἅπτεται, the 3rd sg. pres. mid. indic. of ἅπτομαι. Ἅπτομαι is one of those unusual vbs. whose active (ἅπτω, "light on fire, kindle") and middle forms (ἅπτομαι, "touch") have quite distinct semantic ranges. The sense of ἅπτομαι here must be something like "touch so as to harm" (sim. NIV). It is an encouraging thing to remember—if you belong to Christ, the devil cannot ultimately harm you. Αὐτοῦ, the gen. masc. sg. of the 3rd pers. personal pronoun, is a gen. obj. or gen. complement of the vb.

VERSE 19

οἴδαμεν ὅτι ἐκ τοῦ θεοῦ ἐσμεν
We know that we are from God,

Οἴδαμεν is 1st pl. pf. act. ind. from οἶδα. Ὅτι introduces the content of what is known (see BDAG 731d; R 1034–35; Young 190). The prep. phrase ἐκ τοῦ θεοῦ communicates source or origin (cf. 3:9) and adv. modifies ἐσμεν, the 1st pl. pres. indic. of εἰμί.

καὶ ὁ κόσμος ὅλος ἐν τῷ πονηρῷ κεῖται.
and the whole world lies in the evil one's embrace.

Ὅλος, nom. sg. masc. attrib. adj. (though in pred. position), modifies κόσμος, nom. sg. masc., which functions as the subj. of κεῖται, the 3rd sg. pres. mid. indic. of κεῖμαι ("recline" or "lies," ESV, NASB; "is under the sway," CSB; "exist," LN §13.73; cf. use in 2 Macc 3:11; 4:31, 34). Lying down is transparently an action that one would expect to highlight subject affectedness, so it is no surprise that the vb. prefers the middle voice. The prep. phrase ἐν τῷ πονηρῷ possibly communicates a metaphorical loc./spherical idea alongside the idea of dominance over (see Harris 118). BDAG notes that "esp[ecially] in Paul[ine] or Joh[annine] usage, [the preposition ἐν is used] to designate a close personal relation in which the referent of the ἐν-term is viewed as the controlling influence: *under the control of, under the influence of, in close association with*" (327d). A more literal translation of the Greek reads in English as: "And the whole world lies/reclines in the evil one." Some liberties have been taken in the translation above to render it in a more easily understood English expression. The sense must be not only the control exercised by the evil one, but the culpable passivity of his victim. Πονηρῷ, the dat. sg. masc. subst. adj. from πονηρός, -ά, -όν, functions as the obj. of the prep. ἐν.

VERSE 20

οἴδαμεν δὲ ὅτι ὁ υἱὸς τοῦ θεοῦ ἥκει καὶ δέδωκεν ἡμῖν διάνοιαν,
And we know that the Son of God has come and has given to us understanding,

Οἴδαμεν is 1st pl. pf. act. ind. from οἶδα. Although John prefers καί as a connecting particle in this letter, he does employ postpositive δέ ten times, one of them here. Ὅτι introduces the content of what is known. Υἱός, nom. sg. masc., serves as the subj. of ἥκει, the 3rd sg. pres. act. indic. of ἥκω, "have come, be present" (BDAG 435b–c), a pres. form with a stative nuance, and δέδωκεν, the 3rd sg. pf. act. indic. of δίδωμι. Θεοῦ, gen. sg. masc. of θεός, is a gen. of relationship. Ἡμῖν, dat. pl. of the 1st pers. personal pron., functions as the indir. obj. of the vb. δέδωκεν. Διάνοιαν, acc. sg. fem. of διάνοια, -ας, ἡ, ("understanding," most EVV; "insights," BDAG 234b; "the process of reasoning that leads to perception," Smalley 292; see also M. Lattke, *EDNT* 1:309b–10a), is the dir. obj. of δέδωκεν.

ἵνα γινώσκωμεν τὸν ἀληθινόν,
so that we may know the true one,

Ἵνα introduces a purpose clause (Rogers and Rogers 599; most EVV). Γινώσκωμεν is the 1st pl. pres. act. subjunc. of γινώσκω. The subst. adj. ἀληθινόν, acc. sg. masc. from ἀληθινός, -ή, -όν, "true, genuine" (see 2:8), functions as the dir. obj. of γινώσκωμεν, with God the Father as the referent.

καὶ ἐσμὲν ἐν τῷ ἀληθινῷ,
and we are in the true one,

Ἐσμέν is 1st pl. pres. ind. from εἰμί. The prep. phrase ἐν τῷ ἀληθινῷ communicates a metaphorical loc./spatial idea (on prep., see BDAG 326c; R 585–86; Moule 75–76). The subst. adj. ἀληθινῷ, dat. sg. masc., refers to God the Father and is the obj. of the prep. ἐν.

ἐν τῷ υἱῷ αὐτοῦ Ἰησοῦ Χριστῷ.
in his Son, Jesus Christ.

In this clause, there is an ellipsis of ἐσμέν, the 1st pl. pres. indic. from εἰμί. The prep. phrase ἐν τῷ υἱῷ αὐτοῦ communicates a metaphorical loc./spatial idea. Υἱῷ, dat. sg. masc. from υἱός, -οῦ, ὁ, is the obj. of the prep. ἐν. Αὐτοῦ, gen. sg. masc. of the 3rd pers. personal pron., is a gen. of relationship. Ἰησοῦ Χριστῷ is in appos. to υἱῷ (on dative in simple appos., see KMP 138).

οὗτός ἐστιν ὁ ἀληθινὸς θεὸς καὶ ζωὴ αἰώνιος.
This one is the true God and eternal life.

Οὗτός, nom. sg. masc. of the near dem. pron., is most naturally understood as referring to the closest antecedent, Ἰησοῦ Χριστῷ (Akin 214–15; Brown 625–26; Culy 139–40; Haas 153; Hiebert 272; Jobes 241; Marshall 254 n. 47; Yarbrough 320; scholars who view the dem. pron. as referring to the Father include Brooke 152–53; Smalley 294; Stott 195; for discussion on views, see Wallace 326–27; Hiebert 271; Brown 625–26). John begins and ends his letter with a strong statement of Jesus's divine status; it is right and good to speak of the Messiah Jesus as "eternal life" who has existed eternally with God the Father and even to call Jesus, "the true God," *not* in a modalistic sense, but in the sense that he is, in essence, true deity (as well as truly human). Οὗτός serves as the subj. of ἐστιν, the 3rd sg. pres. indic. of εἰμί. The attrib. adj. ἀληθινός, "true, genuine," nom. sg. masc., modifies the first item of the compound predicate nom. θεός, nom. sg. masc. The second member of the compound predicate nom. is ζωή, nom. sg. fem., modified by the attrib. adj. αἰώνιος, "eternal, never-ending," also nom. sg. fem. (see BDF §59[1]; Decker 95; R 272–73 for a discussion of the forms for this [normally] two-termination adj.)

VERSE 21

Τεκνία, φυλάξατε ἑαυτὰ ἀπὸ τῶν εἰδώλων.
Dear children, guard yourselves from idols.

Τεκνία, voc. pl. neut. of the diminutive form of τέκνον, reminds John's readers of his affection for them and their familial dependence upon him. Φυλάξατε, 2nd pl. aor. act. impv. from φυλάσσω, "guard, protect" (BDAG 1068c), is likely in the aor. tense because the procedural nature of the activity described is envisioned from a wholistic perspective (i.e., "to guard oneself from idols" is viewed as a whole, including any beginning or ending). Ἑαυτά, acc. pl. neut. of the reflexive pron., acts as the dir. obj. of φυλάξατε. The neut. form is chosen to match the gender of the voc. τεκνία. The prep. phrase ἀπὸ τῶν εἰδώλων communicates the idea of separation/disassociation. Εἰδώλων, -ου, τό, gen. pl. neut. of εἴδωλον ("idol, image of false god"; "views of God that are divorced from the truth of God's self-revelation in Christ," BDAG 281b; see also LN §12.23) functions as the obj. of the prep. ἀπό. The mng. of John's final exhortation of the letter is debated (Brown 641 lists ten possible views). Marshall understands the reference of idolatry is likely "referring to false conceptions of God" (255). Other commentators surveyed have a similar view and associate the warning with the teachings of those who have withdrawn from the church (see Akin 215–16; Brown 627–29; Jobes 245; Kruse 202; Smalley 296–97; Stott 196). Ben Merkle has an excellent article on how 1 John 5:21 is actually a very fitting final injunction (see For Further Study 41 "Keep Yourself from Idols").

FOR FURTHER STUDY

39. Prayer (5:14–16)

Bonhoeffer, Dietrich. *Life Together: The Classic Exploration of Christian Community*. Translated by John W. Doberstein. New York: HarperOne, 1954 (see 81–89).

Brown, C. *NIDNTT* 2:882–86.

Coggan, F. Donald. *The Prayers of the New Testament*. New York: Harper and Row, 1967 (see 87–167).

Grudem 376–96.

Osborne, Grant R. "Moving Forward on Our Knees: Corporate Prayer in the New Testament." *JETS* 53, no. 2 (2010): 243–67.

Mullins, Terence Y. "Petition as Literary Form." *NovT* 5 (1962): 46–54.

Peterson, D. G. "Prayer in the General Epistles." Pages 102–18 in *Teach Us to Pray: Prayer in the Bible and the World*. Edited. by D. A. Carson. Grand Rapids: Baker, 1990.

Tan, Randall K. J. "Should We Pray for Straying Brethren?: John's Confidence in 1 John 5:16–17." *JETS* 45, no. 4 (2002): 599–609.

Thompson, Marianne Meye. "Intercession in the Johannine Community: 1 John 5:16 in the Context of the Gospel and Epistles of John." Pages 225–45 in *Worship, Theology and Ministry in the Early Church: Essays in Honor of Ralph P. Martin*. Edited by Michael J. Wilkins and Terence Paige. JSNTSup 87. Sheffield, UK: Sheffield Academic Press, 1992.

Wilkins, M. J. *DLNT*, 941–48.

40. Christology/Deity of Christ (5:21)

Bauckham, Richard. *Jesus and the God of Israel: God Crucified and Other Studies on the New Testament's Christology of Divine Identity*. Grand Rapids: Eerdmans, 2008.

Bavinck 3:233–319.

*Bowman, Robert M., J. Ed Komoszewski, and Darrell L. Bock. *Putting Jesus in His Place: The Case for the Deity of Christ*. Illustrated ed. Grand Rapids: Kregel, 2007.

Capes, D. B. *DLNT*, 955–61.

Dunn, J. D. G. *ABD* 1:979–91.

Grudem 529–53.

Hamerton-Kelly, R. G. *Pre-Existence, Wisdom, and The Son of Man: A Study of the Idea of Pre-Existence in the New Testament*. Cambridge: Cambridge University Press, 1973.

Harris, Murray J. *Jesus as God: The New Testament Use of Theos in Reference to Jesus*. Eugene, OR: Wipf & Stock, 2008.

Hurtado, L. W. *DLNT*, 170–84 (see esp. 175–76).

———. *Lord Jesus Christ: Devotion to Jesus in Earliest Christianity*. Grand Rapids: Eerdmans, 2003.

———. *One God, One Lord: Early Christian Devotion and Ancient Jewish Monotheism*. Philadelphia: Fortress, 1988.

Longenecker, Richard N., ed. *Contours of Christology in the New Testament*. Grand Rapids: Eerdmans, 2005.

Marshall, I. H. *Jesus the Savior: Studies in New Testament Theology*. Downers Grove, IL: InterVarsity, 1990.

Pollard, T. E. *Johannine Christology and the Early Church*. Cambridge: Cambridge University Press, 2005.

Rowdon, Harold H., ed. *Christ the Lord: Studies in Christology Presented to Donald Guthrie*. Downers Grove, IL: InterVarsity, 1982.

41. "Keep Yourself from Idols" (5:21)

Hills, Julian. "'Little Children, Keep Yourselves from Idols': 1 John 5:21 Reconsidered." *CBQ* 51, no. 2 (1989): 285–310.

Merkle, Benjamin L. "What Is the Meaning of 'Idols' in 1 John 5:21?" *BSac* 169 (2012): 328–40.

HOMILETICAL SUGGESTIONS

Things Known: Final Words of Assurance (5:13–21)

1. Purpose of the letter: knowing you have eternal life (v. 13)
2. Confidence in prayer: knowing we are heard (vv. 14–17)
3. Three things known (vv. 18–20)
    a. Children of God do not practice (continue to) sin (v. 18)
    b. Believers are of God; the world is in the grips of the evil one (v. 19)
    c. The Son of God has given us understanding (v. 20)
4. A pastor's final words: guard yourself from the world's false teachings that are counter to your knowledge of Jesus Christ (v. 21)

2 JOHN

I. Opening Greeting (1–3)

This initial section reflects the expected structure of a Greco-Roman letter with sender, recipient, and greeting. The themes of truth and love are introduced in the opening (ἀλήθεια, 4× in vv. 1–4 and ἀγάπη or ἀγαπάω, 4× in vv. 1–6). Those in the church are loved by John and all who know the truth (v. 1), and this love is because of the truth (v. 2a). Verse 3 provides a wish or, more accurately, an affirmation (Kruse 206) that grace, mercy, and peace will be with them, which come from God the Father and Jesus Christ in love and truth.

1 Ὁ πρεσβύτερος
ἐκλεκτῇ κυρίᾳ
καὶ τοῖς τέκνοις αὐτῆς,
οὓς ἐγὼ ἀγαπῶ ἐν ἀληθείᾳ,
καὶ οὐκ ἐγὼ μόνος [ἀγαπῶ],
ἀλλὰ καὶ πάντες οἱ ἐγνωκότες τὴν ἀλήθειαν
[ἀγαπῶσιν],

2 διὰ τὴν ἀλήθειαν τὴν μένουσαν ἐν ἡμῖν
καὶ μεθ' ἡμῶν ἔσται εἰς τὸν αἰῶνα.

3 ἔσται μεθ' ἡμῶν χάρις ἔλεος εἰρήνη
παρὰ θεοῦ πατρὸς
καὶ παρὰ Ἰησοῦ Χριστοῦ = τοῦ υἱοῦ τοῦ πατρὸς
ἐν ἀληθείᾳ
καὶ ἀγάπῃ.

VERSE 1

Ὁ πρεσβύτερος ἐκλεκτῇ κυρίᾳ καὶ τοῖς τέκνοις αὐτῆς,
The elder. To the elect lady and to her children,

Πρεσβύτερος, nom. sg. masc., functions as a nom. abs. (on use, see BW 5–6; KMP 60–61; Wallace 49–51), identifying the sender of the letter. Alternately, one could hypothesize the ellipsis of γράφει, the 3rd sg. pres. act. indic. of γράφω. Ἐκλεκτῇ, dat. sg. fem. attrib. adj. from ἐκλεκτός, -ή, -όν, "elect, chosen, selected" (see BDAG 306b–c), modifies κυρίᾳ, the dat. sg. fem. of κυρία, -ας, ἡ, "a woman of special status, lady, mistress" (BDAG 576b; on term, see also MM 364b–c; J. A. Fitzmyer, *EDNT* 2:328b). Κυρίᾳ is in the dat. to signify whom is being addressed in the letter (as also τέκνοις, dat. pl. neut. of τέκνον; see Wallace 148–49 on dat. of recipient). Alternately, one could say that κυρίᾳ and τέκνοις are the compound indir. obj. of the implied vb. γράφει. Αὐτῆς, gen. sg. fem. of the 3rd pers. personal pron., is a gen. of relationship. The author of this letter is either *(1) the apostle John, as favored by early church history and early titular evidence (see introductory matters above); or (2) some other prominent Christian leader in the early church who wrote with apostolic authority. The recipients of this letter are either *(1) an early church metaphorically referred to as "an elect lady and her children" (most commentators surveyed, e.g., Brown 654–55; Jobes 255; Kruse 204; Marshall 60; Smalley 305–6; Stott 202–3; Yarbrough 334); or (2) an actual early prominent Christian lady (perhaps named Κυρία) and her dependents or the Christian assembly which meets in her home (Hiebert 281–83; Marshall 60 n. 5 notes various older scholars who held to this view including Morris, A. Plummer, Smith, and Ross). For discussion on views, see Smalley 305–6.

οὓς ἐγὼ ἀγαπῶ ἐν ἀληθείᾳ,
whom I love in truth,

Οὕς, acc. pl. masc. of the rel. pron., refers back to τοῖς τέκνοις αὐτῆς and functions as the dir. obj. of ἀγαπῶ, 1st sg. pres. act. ind. Though grammatically unnecessary, the explicit pron. subj. of ἀγαπῶ is present (i.e., ἐγώ, nom. sg. of the 1st pers. personal pron.). John perhaps further reinforces his personal care and affection for this congregation by including the pronoun ἐγώ. The prep. phrase ἐν ἀληθείᾳ adv. modifies ἀγαπῶ. Ἀληθείᾳ, dat. sg. fem. of ἀλήθεια, -ας, ἡ, functions as the obj. of the prep. ἐν. The prep. phrase may (1) communicate manner; (2) indicate the metaphorical realm/sphere of the truth; or *(3) be intentionally ambiguous to overlap the ideas of manner and realm (cf. Jobes 256; Marshall 61–62; see also Smalley 307, who emphasizes the deep significance of "truth" for John).

καὶ οὐκ ἐγὼ μόνος ἀλλὰ καὶ πάντες οἱ ἐγνωκότες τὴν ἀλήθειαν,
and not only I, but also all who know the truth,

There are two ellipses of the vb. ἀγαπῶ in this clause (i.e., "and not only I *love* [ἀγαπῶ, 1st sg. pres. ind.], but also all who know the truth *love* [ἀγαπῶσιν, 3rd pl. pres. ind.]"). Οὐκ negates the implied vb. ἀγαπῶ. Ἐγώ, nom. sg. of the 1st pers. personal pron., is the subj. of the implied vb. ἀγαπῶ. Μόνος, nom. sg. masc., functions as an attrib. adj. modifying ἐγώ. Πάντες, nom. pl. masc. of πᾶς, attrib. modifies the art. ptc. οἱ ἐγνωκότες, the nom. pl. masc. pf. act. ptc. of γινώσκω, which is functioning subst. The English translation above reflects the stative aspect of the pf. ptc. Ἀλήθειαν, acc. sg. fem. of ἀλήθεια, functions as the dir. obj. of the ptc. ἐγνωκότες.

VERSE 2

διὰ τὴν ἀλήθειαν τὴν μένουσαν ἐν ἡμῖν καὶ μεθ' ἡμῶν ἔσται εἰς τὸν αἰῶνα.
because of the truth which remains in us all and will be with us forever.

The large prep. phrase beginning with διά above expresses causality and adv. modifies the two implied forms of ἀγαπῶ in the previous verse (see 2 John 1). Ἀλήθειαν, acc. sg. fem. of ἀλήθεια, -ας, ἡ, is the obj. of the prep. διά. Ἀλήθειαν is modified attrib. by the ptc. μένουσαν, acc. sg. fem. of pres. act. ptc. of μένω. The prep. phrase ἐν ἡμῖν expresses a metaphorical loc./spherical idea. Ἡμῖν, dat. pl. of the 1st pers. personal pron., is the obj. of the prep. ἐν. The truth that abides in John and his recipients is further described with this phrase: μεθ' ἡμῶν ἔσται εἰς τὸν αἰῶνα. Ἡμῶν, gen. pl. of the 1st pers. personal pron., serves as the obj. of the prep. μετά. The prep. phrase μεθ' ἡμῶν expresses the idea of accompaniment (see BDAG 636c) and adv. modifies ἔσται, the 3rd sg. fut. mid. indic. of εἰμί. The prep. phrase εἰς τὸν αἰῶνα expresses extent of time and adv. modifies ἔσται. Αἰῶνα, acc. sg. masc. of αἰών, -ῶνος, ὁ, is the obj. of the prep. εἰς. The prep. phrase literally means "into the age," but it is usually viewed as an idiom meaning "forever" (on the phrase, see Harris 94; *NIDNTTE* 1:196; see also discussion on 1 John 2:17). Perhaps the phrase also implies an idea of continuing into the eternal and never-ending eschatological age of divine fulfillment.

VERSE 3

ἔσται μεθ' ἡμῶν χάρις ἔλεος εἰρήνη
Grace, mercy, and peace will be with us,

Ἔσται, 3rd sg. fut. mid. ind. from εἰμί, is a sg. vb. with a compound subj: χάρις ἔλεος εἰρήνη (a Pindaric constr.; see KMP 46; R 404–5; see 1 John 2:17). Ἔλεος, -ους, τό, means "mercy" (see BDAG 316b; *NIDNTTE* 2:167–72). We might have expected two occurrences of καί inserted between the elements of the formulaic blessing, but John's staccato style conforms to early ecclesiastical formulae (1 Tim 1:2; 2 Tim 1:2). Stott notes, "peace indicates the character of salvation, mercy our need of it and grace God's free provision of it in Christ" (206). The prep. phrase μεθ' ἡμῶν expresses accompaniment and adv. modifies ἔσται. Ἡμῶν, gen. pl. of the 1st pers. personal pron., functions as the obj. of the prep. μετά. Students, don't forget that μετά followed by a vowel with a smooth breathing mark becomes μετ', while μετά followed by a vowel with rough breathing mark becomes μεθ'.

παρὰ θεοῦ πατρὸς καὶ παρὰ Ἰησοῦ Χριστοῦ τοῦ υἱοῦ τοῦ πατρὸς ἐν ἀληθείᾳ καὶ ἀγάπῃ.
from God the Father and from Jesus Christ, the Son of the Father, in truth and love.

The prep. phrases παρὰ θεοῦ πατρὸς καὶ παρὰ Ἰησοῦ Χριστοῦ τοῦ υἱοῦ τοῦ πατρός adv. modify ἔσται (see clause above) and express source/origin (on sense of παρά, see BDAG 756b). Θεοῦ, gen. sg. masc. of θεός, functions as the obj. of the prep. παρά. Πατρός, gen. sg. masc. of πατήρ, ὁ, is in appos. to θεοῦ. Ἰησοῦ Χριστοῦ, gen. sg. masc. of Ἰησοῦς and Χριστός, serves as the obj. of the second prep. παρά. Τοῦ υἱοῦ is in appos. to Ἰησοῦ Χριστοῦ. The second instance of πατρός (gen. sg. masc. of πατήρ) in the clause above is a gen. of relationship. The prep. phrase ἐν ἀληθείᾳ καὶ ἀγάπῃ modifies ἔσται and expresses manner, or perhaps metaphorical loc./sphere. Both ἀληθείᾳ and ἀγάπῃ are dat. sg. fem., respectively from ἀλήθεια, -ας, ἡ, and ἀγάπη, -ης, ἡ, and function as a compound obj. of the prep. ἐν. Culy notes, "The function of the preposition is difficult to label. It appears to point to the context or circumstances in which grace, mercy and peace will be experienced: clinging to the truth and loving one another (143).

FOR FURTHER STUDY

42. Ancient Letters/Letter Writing

Doty, W. G. *Letters in Primitive Christianity*. Philadelphia: Fortress, 1973.

Klauck, H. J., and D. P. Bailey. *Ancient Letters and the New Testament: A Guide to Context and Exegesis*. Waco: Baylor University Press, 2006.

Morello, R., and A. D. Morrison. *Ancient Letters: Classical and Late Antique Epistolography*. Oxford: Oxford University Press, 2007.

*Stowers, S. K. *Letter Writing in Greco-Roman Antiquity*. Philadelphia: Westminster, 1986.

Watson, D. F. *DLNT*, 649–55.

Weima, J. A. D. *DNTB*, 640–44.

White, J. L. *Light from Ancient Letters*. Philadelphia: Fortress, 1986.

HOMILETICAL SUGGESTIONS

Opening Greeting: In Truth and Love (vv. 1–3)

1. The writer: the elder (v. 1)
2. The recipient: a local church and its members (v. 1)
   a. Loved by the elder
   b. Loved by all believers who know the truth
   c. Loved because of the abiding, eternal truth (v. 2)
3. The affirmation: grace, mercy, and peace will be with us from God the Father and from Jesus Christ. (v. 3)
   a. In truth
   b. In love

Love and Truth (vv. 1–3)

1. A church that is loved (vv. 1–2)
   a. Loved by John
   b. Loved by all who know the truth
   c. Loved because of the truth
2. A church that is affirmed (v. 3)
   a. Grace, mercy, and peace will be with them
      (1) From God the Father and the Son
      (2) In truth and in love
3. Love and truth in our local church body:
   a. Dedication to studying and growing in the truth revealed in God's word
   b. Commitment to walking in the truth
   c. Loving one another

II. A New Command: Love One Another (4–6)

The ὅτι clause of v. 4 provides the reason the author has rejoiced greatly, because he has found some of the members are walking in the truth (the vb. περιπατέω occurs twice more in v. 6 of the section). The ἵνα clause of v. 5 indicates the purpose of the writing and provides the exhortation to love one another. The two epex. ἵνα clauses of v. 6 characterize this love as walking according to God's commandments.

4 Ἐχάρην λίαν
ὅτι εὕρηκα ἐκ τῶν τέκνων σου περιπατοῦντας
ἐν ἀληθείᾳ,
καθὼς ἐντολὴν ἐλάβομεν
παρὰ τοῦ πατρός.

5 καὶ νῦν ἐρωτῶ σε, κυρία,
οὐχ ὡς ἐντολὴν γράφων σοι καινὴν
ἀλλʼ [*ὡς ἐντολὴν γράφων*]
ἣν εἴχομεν ἀπʼ ἀρχῆς
ἵνα ἀγαπῶμεν ἀλλήλους

6 καὶ αὕτη ἐστὶν ἡ ἀγάπη,
ἵνα περιπατῶμεν
κατὰ τὰς ἐντολὰς αὐτοῦ·
αὕτη ἡ ἐντολή ἐστιν
καθὼς ἠκούσατε
ἀπʼ ἀρχῆς,
ἵνα ἐν αὐτῇ περιπατῆτε.

VERSE 4

Ἐχάρην λίαν ὅτι εὕρηκα ἐκ τῶν τέκνων σου περιπατοῦντας ἐν ἀληθείᾳ,
I rejoiced exceedingly because I have found some of your children walking in the truth,

Ἐχάρην, 1st sg. aor. pass. ind. from χαίρω, might also be parsed as a "medial-passive," as the vb. is a passive form conveying a middle idea (see R 817). Verbs of emotion (subj.-affected actions) often appear in the middle voice. Λίαν, "exceedingly" (see BDAG 594b), is an adv. expressing degree. Ὅτι introduces a causal clause. Εὕρηκα is the 1st sg. pf. act. indic. of εὑρίσκω. The prep. phrase ἐκ τῶν τέκνων expresses a partitive idea (BDAG 297d; cf. BDF §164.2; i.e., it is as if there were an ellipsis of the word τινάς [acc. pl. masc. of τις, "some"] before the prep. phrase). Τέκνων, gen. pl. neut. of τέκνον, -ου, τό, is the obj. of the prep. ἐκ. Σου, gen. sg. of the 2nd pers. personal pron., is a gen. of relationship. Περιπατοῦντας, acc. pl. masc. pres. act. ptc. of περιπατέω (see 1 John 1:6–7; 2:6, 11; 3 John 3), functions as a supplementary ptc. (see "Supplementary Participles" in the introduction). The prep. phrase ἐν ἀληθείᾳ adv. modifies the ptc. περιπατοῦντας and communicates the metaphorical idea of realm/sphere (Harris 134). Harris notes the phrase "describes a way of life, embracing both thought and action, that is informed, molded, and regulated by Christian truth" (134). Ἀληθείᾳ, dat. sg. fem. of ἀλήθεια, -ας, ἡ, is the obj. of the prep. ἐν.

Καθὼς ἐντολὴν ἐλάβομεν παρὰ τοῦ πατρός.
just as we received a commandment from the Father.

Καθώς introduces a comparison. Ἐντολήν, acc. sg. fem. of ἐντολή, -ῆς, ἡ, serves as the dir. obj. of ἐλάβομεν, the 1st pl. aor. act. indic. of λαμβάνω. The prep. phrase παρὰ τοῦ πατρός expresses origin/source. Πατρός, gen. masc. sg. of πατήρ, ὁ, is the obj. of the prep. παρά.

VERSE 5

καὶ νῦν ἐρωτῶ σε, κυρία, οὐχ ὡς ἐντολὴν γράφων σοι καινὴν
And now, I ask you, dear lady (not that I am writing to you a new commandment,

The NET Translation Notes observe: "The introductory καὶ νῦν (*kai nun*) has some adversative (contrastive) force: The addressees are already 'living according to the truth' (v. 4) but in the face of the threat posed by the opponents, the author has to stress obedience all the more." Νῦν expresses current time and adv. modifies ἐρωτῶ, the 1st sg. pres. act. ind. from ἐρωτάω. Σε, acc. sg. of the 2nd pers. personal pron., functions as the dir. obj. of ἐρωτῶ. Κυρία, see v. 1. Ὡς introduces a ptc. expressing indir. discourse (see Goodwin §1593; Smyth §2120–22). Σοι, dat. sg. of the 2nd pers. personal pron., serves as the indir. obj. of γράφων. Ἐντολήν, acc. sg. fem. of ἐντολή, -ῆς, ἡ, functions as the dir. obj. of γράφων and is modified by καινήν, the acc. sg. fem. of καινός, -ή, -όν. An attrib. adj. is commonly found next to the noun it modifies. Perhaps John separates the two words (ἐντολὴν . . . καινήν) to help set apart the clause for his original hearers (i.e.,

John may employ hyperbaton). In this verse, John continues addressing the church metaphorically as a "lady" (cf. 2 John 1). The adj. "dear" has been added in the translation above to comport with the emotional tenor of the context (see CSB, ESV).

ἀλλ' ἣν εἴχομεν ἀπ' ἀρχῆς, ἵνα ἀγαπῶμεν ἀλλήλους.
but that I am writing to you a commandment which we've had from the beginning) that we love one another.

Adversative ἀλλά introduces a contrast in John's statement of indir. discourse. The apostle is, in fact, only reminding this church of a divine injunction that it has had since its founding. There is an ellipsis of ὡς ἐντολὴν γράφων, "that I am writing a commandment" (see above and Goodwin §1593). Ἥν, acc. sg. fem. rel. pron., refers back to the elided noun ἐντολήν and functions as the dir. obj. of εἴχομεν, the 1st pl. impf. act. indic. of ἔχω. The spelling of the impf. (εἴχομεν, not ἤχομεν) is because of its root σεχ. Adding an *epsilon* augment (a syllabic vowel), causes the σ (now intervocalic) to drop out, leaving the two vowels (εε) which contract to ει (see MBG 206 n. 10). The imperfective aspect of εἴχομεν communicates well the community's ongoing possession of the love commandment. The prep. phrase ἀπ' ἀρχῆς communicates an extension of time and is an intriguing, repeated phrase in John's Letters (1 John 1:1; 2:7, 13, 14, 24; 3:8, 11; 2 John 6; for developed study on the topic, see Hong). Ἀρχῆς, gen. sg. fem. of ἀρχή, ἡ, acts as the obj. of the prep. ἀπό. Ἵνα introduces the content of what is requested by the apostle (Rogers and Rogers 600). Ἀγαπῶμεν is the 1st pl. pres. act. subjunc. of ἀγαπάω and ἀλλήλους is the acc. pl. masc. of the reciprocal pron., here serving as the dir. obj. of ἀγαπῶμεν. The exhortation to "love one another" also occurs at 1 John 3:11, 23; 4:7, 11, 12.

VERSE 6

καὶ αὕτη ἐστὶν ἡ ἀγάπη, ἵνα περιπατῶμεν κατὰ τὰς ἐντολὰς αὐτοῦ·
And this is love: that we walk in accord with his commandments.

Αὕτη, nom. sg. fem. of the near dem. pron., functions as the subj. of ἐστίν, the 3rd sg. pres. indic. of εἰμί. Ἀγάπη, nom. sg. fem. from ἀγάπη, -ης, ἡ, serves as the pred. nom. Abstract nouns are often art. (BW 74; R 758), as here (ἡ ἀγάπη). Ἵνα introduces an epex. clause (Culy 146; cf. Wallace 475–76). Περιπατῶμεν is the 1st pl. pres. act. subjunc. of περιπατέω. Many biblical authors use walking as a metaphor for a consistent pattern of life (e.g., Prov 8:20; Eph 4:1; Col 1:10; in John's Letters, see 1 John 1:6, 7; 2:6, 11; 2 John 4; 3 John 3, 4). The prep. phrase κατὰ τὰς ἐντολὰς αὐτοῦ communicates a standard (see BDAG 512c) and adv. modifies περιπατῶμεν. Ἐντολάς, acc. sg. fem. of ἐντολή, -ῆς, ἡ, is the obj. of the prep. κατά. Αὐτοῦ, gen. sg. masc. of the 3rd pers. personal pron., is a subj. gen.

αὕτη ἡ ἐντολή ἐστιν, καθὼς ἠκούσατε ἀπ' ἀρχῆς, ἵνα ἐν αὐτῇ περιπατῆτε.
This commandment is—just as you all heard from the beginning—that we walk in it.

Αὕτη, nom. sg. fem. of the near dem. pron., attrib. modifies ἡ ἐντολή, nom. sg. fem. (dem. prons. occur in the pred. position when modifying nouns). Ἐντολή functions as subj. of ἐστιν, 3rd sg. pres. indic. of εἰμί. Note the shift from a pl. form earlier in v. 6 (ἐντολάς) to a sg. in the opening clause above (ἐντολή). Marshall writes that "'*the* command' is that we should love one another, while 'the commands' are the detailed requirements which unfold the structure of this central command" (67). The sg. "commandment" is used in 1 John 2:7, 8; 3:23; 4:21; 2 John 4, 5, 6; the pl. "commandments" is used in 1 John 2:3, 4; 3:22, 24; 2 John 6. Love is the preeminent and summary commandment (cf. Matt 22:36–40). Καθώς introduces a comparison. Ἠκούσατε is the 2nd pl. aor. act. indic. of ἀκούω. The prep. phrase ἀπ' ἀρχῆς communicates an extension of time and is an intriguing, repeated phrase in John's Letters (1 John 1:1; 2:7, 13, 14, 24; 3:8, 11; 2 John 5; see Hong). Ἀρχῆς, gen. sg. fem. of ἀρχή, ἡ, acts as the obj. of the prep. ἀπό. Ἵνα introduces a clause epex. (see above) to αὕτη ἡ ἐντολή. Περιπατῆτε is the 2nd pl. pres. act. subjunc. of περιπατέω. The prep. phrase ἐν αὐτῇ adv. modifies περιπατῆτε and perhaps communicates a metaphorical loc./spherical sense in accord with the metaphor of ambulation. This metaphorical sense is similar to the idea of reference/respect. The believer's pattern of life (walking) is to be shaped consistently with reference to God's command of love. Αὐτῇ, dat. sg. fem. of the 3rd pers. personal pron., is the obj. of the prep. ἐν. The referent of the pron. could potentially be: (1) ἀγάπη (Haas 166; Hiebert 300–301; Kruse 208–9; Marshall 68 n. 11; Smalley 314; Stott 210; "in love," CSB, NIV); (2) ἐντολή (Brooke 174); or (3) ἀληθεία from v. 4 (Jobes 262). Though pleonastic, normal syntactical patterns favor αὕτη ἡ ἐντολή as the referent for αὐτῇ and John's wording is frequently pleonastic, it is also possible (and perhaps more easily understood by the reader) if the referent for αὐτῇ is ἀγάπη (so CSB, NIV).

FOR FURTHER STUDY

See For Further Study 16 "Love/Ἀγαπάω/Ἀγάπη Word Study" and 19 "Loving One Another."

HOMILETICAL SUGGESTIONS

Loving and Obeying (vv. 4–6)

1. A faithful flock: walking in the truth as commanded by God (v. 4) (Are we walking in truth?)
2. A new command: love one another (v. 5) (Are we loving one another?)
3. Obedience as an expression of this love (v. 6) (Do our words and actions reflect someone who "walks in love"?)

III. Beware of False Teachers (7–11)

The ὅτι clause that begins the sections indicates the reason for the emphasis of v. 6, on walking according to God's command of love (v. 6): many deceivers have come into the world. The phrase *οἱ μὴ ὁμολογοῦντες Ἰησοῦν Χριστὸν ἐρχόμενον ἐν σαρκί* stands in appos. to *πλάνοι*. The impv. of v. 8 provides the exhortation for the believers to guard themselves against such deceivers who have not remained in the teaching of Christ (v. 9). Verses 10–11 build on the impv. of v. 8 with two further impvs., exhorting the readers to not receive or welcome those who bring a teaching other than that of Christ.

7 Ὅτι πολλοὶ πλάνοι ἐξῆλθον εἰς τὸν κόσμον = οἱ μὴ ὁμολογοῦντες Ἰησοῦν Χριστὸν
ἐρχόμενον ἐν σαρκί·
οὗτός ἐστιν ὁ πλάνος καὶ ὁ ἀντίχριστος.

8 βλέπετε ἑαυτούς,
ἵνα μὴ ἀπολέσητε ἃ εἰργασάμεθα
ἀλλὰ μισθὸν πλήρη ἀπολάβητε.

9 Πᾶς ὁ προάγων καὶ μὴ μένων ἐν τῇ διδαχῇ τοῦ Χριστοῦ θεὸν οὐκ ἔχει·
ὁ μένων ἐν τῇ διδαχῇ,
οὗτος καὶ τὸν πατέρα καὶ τὸν υἱὸν ἔχει.

10 εἴ τις ἔρχεται πρὸς ὑμᾶς
καὶ ταύτην τὴν διδαχὴν οὐ φέρει,
μὴ λαμβάνετε αὐτὸν εἰς οἰκίαν
καὶ χαίρειν αὐτῷ μὴ λέγετε·

11 ὁ λέγων γὰρ αὐτῷ χαίρειν κοινωνεῖ
τοῖς ἔργοις αὐτοῦ τοῖς πονηροῖς.

VERSE 7

Ὅτι πολλοὶ πλάνοι ἐξῆλθον εἰς τὸν κόσμον,
For many deceivers have gone forth into the world,

Ὅτι begins a causal clause, "introducing the grounds for the previous exhortation" (Culy 147). Πολλοί, nom. pl. masc. of πολύς, attrib. modifies πλάνοι, the nom. pl. masc. of πλάνος, -ον, "deceiver, imposter" (BDAG 822d; see also LN §31.9). Πλάνοι serves as the subj. of ἐξῆλθον, the 3rd pl. aor. act. indic. of ἐξέρχομαι. The prep. phrase εἰς τὸν κόσμον communicates loc./sphere (see BDAG 289a). Κόσμον, acc. masc. sg. of κόσμος, -ου, ὁ, is the obj. of the prep. εἰς.

οἱ μὴ ὁμολογοῦντες Ἰησοῦν Χριστὸν ἐρχόμενον ἐν σαρκί
those who do not confess Jesus Christ as coming in the flesh.

Οἱ μὴ ὁμολογοῦντες is in appos. to πολλοὶ πλάνοι above. The negated subst. ptc. ὁμολογοῦντες is a nom. pl. masc. pres. act. ptc. from ὁμολογέω. Ἰησοῦν Χριστόν, both forms acc. sg. masc., respectively from Ἰησοῦς and Χριστός, serves as the dir. obj. of ὁμολογοῦντες. Ἐρχόμενον, acc. sg. masc. pres. mid. ptc. of ἔρχομαι, is a supplementary ptc. indicating indir. discourse after a vb. of communication (see "Supplementary Participles" in the introduction; Wallace 645–46, followed by Jobes 264; Young 149 notes concerning the cstr. that "the participle and its subject will be in the accusative case, since the noun phrase of which they are a part is actually the object of a verb of speaking"; R 1123 addresses the topic of this ptc. cstr., noting "in principle it is the double accusative . . . only the second acc. is a predicate adj., not a substantive"; Culy 147 suggests the ptc. is functioning as the complement in an object-complement double acc. cstr.; see also R 480, 1040–42; BDF §416; Burton §460; KMP 343). The phrasing of the above clause is sim. to 1 John 4:2 (see discussion there), though here we have the pres. tense ptc. ἐρχόμενον rather than pf. ἐληλυθλότα of 1 John 4:2. While the pres. tense ptc. could possibly be viewed as pointing toward Christ's second coming, a reference to Christ's incarnation is more likely (Hiebert 302; Jobes 265; Kruse 209; NET Translation Notes). Marshall suggests the shift contributes to affirming not only that Jesus had come, but that he "*still existed* 'in flesh'" (70; so also Stott 212; cf. Aiken 229; Brooke 175; Yarbrough 343–44). Moule notes the pres. ptc. here is functioning as the equivalent to ἐληλυθλότα in 1 John 4:2. Culy (following Porter) suggests the tenses emphasize "different focal semantic elements," the pf. focusing attention on the subject and the pres. on the action (147). The prep. phrase ἐν σαρκί adv. modifies ἐρχόμενον and communicates manner (i.e., Jesus came in a fully human body, Culy 148). Σαρκί, dat. sg. fem. of σάρξ, σαρκός, ἡ, is the obj. of the prep. ἐν.

οὗτός ἐστιν ὁ πλάνος καὶ ὁ ἀντίχριστος.
This is the deceiver and the antichrist.

Οὗτός is the nom. sg. masc. of the near dem. pron. and functions as the subj. of ἐστιν, the 3rd sg. pres. indic. of εἰμί. Οὗτός here functions as a generic sg., "such a person" (Wallace 332), referring to any deceiver or false confessor from the categories discussed immediately above. The compound pred. nom. is πλάνος (nom. sg. masc., "deceiver, imposter") and ἀντίχριστος (nom. sg. masc., "antichrist"; cf. 1 John 2:18, 22; 4:3). Here ἀντίχριστος is used "to characterize people who are radically opposed to the true doctrine about Christ and are thus supremely his opponents" (Marshall 71).

VERSE 8

βλέπετε ἑαυτούς,
Watch yourselves,

βλέπετε is 2nd pl. pres. act. impv. of βλέπω. The pres. impv. calls on John's recipients to adopt a spiritually watchful stance in life. Ἑαυτούς, acc. pl. masc. of the reflexive pron., is the dir. obj. of βλέπετε. Humans have a tendency to watch (and judge!) one another. John reminds these believers to watch *themselves*.

ἵνα μὴ ἀπολέσητε ἃ εἰργασάμεθα
so that you all do not lose what we worked for,

Ἵνα introduces a purpose statement (first with a neg. component, then a positive; "so that," CSB; cf. Moule 145). Why should believers watch themselves? So that they do not lose what they worked for! Ἀπολέσητε is the 2nd pl. aor. act. subjunc. of ἀπόλλυμι, neg. with μή, as expected for nonindicative mood vbs. Ἅ, acc. pl. neut. rel. pron., introduces a headless rel. clause and functions as the dir. obj. of εἰργασάμεθα, the 1st pl. aor. mid. indic. of ἐργάζομαι. The 1st pl. of the vb. has strong ms. support (including B 1175 *Byz* [K L P]). The 2nd pl. form has significant ms. support as well (including ℵ A Ψ and significant minuscules). The UBS^5 committee gives the 1st pl. choice a "B" rating (almost certain). The entire headless rel. clause (ἃ εἰργασάμεθα) serves as the dir. obj. of ἀπολέσητε.

ἀλλὰ μισθὸν πλήρη ἀπολάβητε.
but so that you receive a full reward.

This clause continues the purpose statement introduced by ἵνα above. Μισθόν, acc. sg. masc. of μισθός, -οῦ, ὁ, "reward, pay" (on this term, see BDAG 653b–d; LN §38.14), is modified by πλήρη, acc. sg. masc. of πλήρης, -ες, "complete, full, in full" (BDAG 827b; ZG 734), and serves as the dir. obj. of ἀπολάβητε, the 2nd pl. aor. act. subjunc. of ἀπολαμβάνω, "receive" (LN §34.53; see also BDAG 115b). Although salvation is completely by grace, eschatological rewards and punishments are frequently appealed to by biblical authors as an impetus for faithfulness.

VERSE 9

Πᾶς ὁ προάγων καὶ μὴ μένων ἐν τῇ διδαχῇ τοῦ Χριστοῦ θεὸν οὐκ ἔχει·
Everyone who goes on ahead and does not remain in the teaching of Christ does not have God.

Πᾶς, nom. sg. masc., attrib. modifies προάγων and μένων, both nom. sg. masc. pres. act. ptc., respectively from προάγω ("go in advance of, lead forward" or "to go beyond bounds, to fail to obey," LN §36.25; "goes beyond," CSB; "runs ahead," NIV) and μένω. Note how the sg. art. (ὁ) governs multiple sg. substs. connected by καί, with the subs. having the same referent (as expected by the Granville Sharp rule, see Wallace 275; also, KMP 161–63). Note also how the nonindicative μένων is negated by μή, as expected. The prep. phrase ἐν τῇ διδαχῇ communicates a metaphorical spatial idea. Διδαχῇ, dat. sg. fem. of διδαχή, -ῆς, ἡ, "the content of training, teaching" (BDAG 241c; on the term, see also H. F. Weiss, *EDNT* 1:320b; Rengstorf, *TDNT* 2:163–65), is the obj. of the prep. ἐν. Χριστοῦ, gen. sg. masc. of Χριστός, -οῦ, is a subj. gen. (Brooke 177; Brown 675; Stott 214; for the position that supports viewing the gen. as obj., see Culy 150; Marshall 72–73 n. 13; Smalley 319). The subject (including all modifiers) of the vb. ἔχει is: Πᾶς ὁ προάγων καὶ μὴ μένων ἐν τῇ διδαχῇ τοῦ Χριστοῦ. The neg. vb. ἔχει is the 3rd sg. pres. act. indic. of ἔχω. Θεόν, acc. sg. masc. of θεός, is the dir. obj. of ἔχει.

ὁ μένων ἐν τῇ διδαχῇ, οὗτος καὶ τὸν πατέρα καὶ τὸν υἱὸν ἔχει.
The one who remains in the teaching—this person has both the Father and the Son.

Μένων, nom. sg. masc. pres. act. ptc. of μένω, is a subst. use of the ptc. The prep. phrase ἐν τῇ διδαχῇ communicates a metaphorical spatial idea. Διδαχῇ, dat. sg. fem. of διδαχή, -ῆς, ἡ, is the obj. of the prep. ἐν. Culy helpfully observes the structure of this clause: "The whole substantival construction [i.e., ὁ μένων ἐν τῇ διδαχῇ] serves as the topic of what follows and will be picked up with the resumptive dem. pron. οὗτος" (150). Οὗτος, nom. sg. masc. of the near dem. pron., serves as the subj. of the vb. ἔχει, the 3rd sg. pres. act. indic. of ἔχω. The cstr. "καί [noun] καί [noun]" is often best translated "both [noun] and [noun]," as here. The compound dir. obj. of ἔχει is καὶ τὸν πατέρα καὶ τὸν υἱόν. Πατέρα is the acc. sg. masc. of πατήρ, πατρός, ὁ, and υἱόν is the acc. sg. masc. of υἱός, -οῦ, ὁ.

VERSE 10

εἴ τις ἔρχεται πρὸς ὑμᾶς καὶ ταύτην τὴν διδαχὴν οὐ φέρει,
If anyone comes to you all and does not bring this teaching,

Εἴ introduces a first class cond. clause, with the prot. assumed true (if only for the sake of argument; cf. Moule 149; on this topic, see BW 182; Wallace 690–94). Τις, nom. sg. masc. of the indef. pron., functions as the subj. of ἔρχεται, the 3rd sg. pres. mid. indic. of ἔρχομαι. The prep. phrase πρὸς ὑμᾶς adv. modifies ἔρχεται and communicates a spatial or loc. nuance. Ὑμᾶς, acc. pl. of the 2nd pers. personal pron., is the obj. of the prep. πρός. Ταύτην, acc. sg. fem. of the near dem. pron., attrib. modifies διδαχήν, acc. sg. fem. of διδαχή, -ῆς, ἡ. Τις also functions as the subj. of φέρει (in addition to ἔρχεται), with ταύτην τὴν διδαχὴν as the dir. obj. of φέρει, the 3rd sg. pres. act. indic. of φέρω (negated with οὐ, as expected of indic. vbs.).

μὴ λαμβάνετε αὐτὸν εἰς οἰκίαν καὶ χαίρειν αὐτῷ μὴ λέγετε
do not receive him into your house and do not say a greeting to him.

The neg. particle μή alerts us to anticipate a nonindicative mood vb., which we find in λαμβάνετε, 2nd pl. pres. act. impv. of λαμβάνω. Αὐτόν, acc. sg. masc. of the 3rd pers. personal pron., functions as the dir. obj. of λαμβάνετε. The prep. phrase εἰς οἰκίαν adv. modifies λαμβάνετε and communicates a spatial/loc. idea. Οἰκίαν, acc. sg. fem. of οἰκία, -ας, ἡ, is the obj. of the prep. εἰς (the object of a prep. is often considered def. without the art., see R 791–92; the pron. "your" is inserted for clarity in most EVV). Χαίρειν, pres. act. inf. of χαίρω, is an idiomatic greeting (BDAG 1075b; cf. Acts 15:23; 23:26; Jas 1:1). Here the inf. χαίρειν acts as the dir. obj. of the negated vb. λέγετε, 2nd pl. pres. act. impv. of λέγω (rendered as such by most EVV). One could also describe χαίρειν as direct discourse (i.e., "Do not say, 'Greetings' to him"). Αὐτῷ, dat. sg. masc. of the 3rd pers. personal pron., functions here as an indir. obj. in relation to the vb. λέγετε. As Robertson notes, "It is not a case of mere hospitality to strangers" (Robertson, *Pictures* 6:255). Smalley writes, "Jesus himself welcomed those with whom he disagreed and ate with them (Matt 9:10–12). . . . The presbyter is warning the members of his community against the dangers of entertaining heretics and their views in such a way as to strengthen and develop their erroneous position, and so compromise the truth" (321).

VERSE 11

ὁ λέγων γὰρ αὐτῷ χαίρειν κοινωνεῖ τοῖς ἔργοις αὐτοῦ τοῖς πονηροῖς.
For the person who speaks a greeting to him shares in his evil works.

Postpositive γάρ introduces an explanatory statement. Λέγων, nom. sg. masc. of pres. act. ptc. from λέγω, is functioning subst., serves as the subj. of κοινωνεῖ, 3rd sg. pres. act. ind. from κοινωνέω ("share, participate," BDAG 553c; "participates in," NASB; "shares in," CSB, NET). Χαίρειν, pres. act. inf. of χαίρω, is an idiomatic greeting (cf. Acts 15:23; 23:26; Jas 1:1). Here the inf. χαίρειν acts as the dir. obj. of λέγων. One could also describe χαίρειν as dir. discourse (i.e., "the person who says "Greetings" to him). Αὐτῷ, dat. sg. masc. of the 3rd pers. personal pron., functions here as an indir. obj. in relation to the ptc. λέγων. Ἔργοις, dat. pl. neut. of ἔργον, -ου, τό, is the dat. obj. or dat. complement of κοινωνεῖ. Αὐτοῦ, gen. sg. masc. of the 3rd pers. personal pron., is a subj. gen. Πονηροῖς, dat. pl. neut. of πονηρός, -ά, -όν, functions as an attrib. adj. modifying ἔργοις.

FOR FURTHER STUDY

See For Further Study 18 "Abiding/Remaining/Μένω" and 27 "Assurance."

HOMILETICAL SUGGESTIONS

Beware of False Teachers! (vv. 7–11)

1. Do not be deceived! Deceivers have come into the world (v. 7)
   a. They deny that Jesus Christ has come in the flesh
   b. They are mouthpieces of the Antichrist
2. Beware! The danger and implications of being influenced by false teaching (v. 8)
3. Abide! To remain in relation with the Father and Son one must continue in the apostolic teaching of Christ (v. 9)
4. Discern! Do not give validity or support to such false teachers (vv. 10–11)
   a. We are called to show the love of Christ to others
   b. Yet, we are warned here to not support or contribute to false teachers' destructive works

IV. Final Greetings (12–13)

This section reflects the expected closing structure for a typical Hellenistic letter. The ἵνα of v. 12 indicates the purpose of the author's desire to see the readers in person, "that our joy may be fulfilled." Both the references to "joy" and "your elect sister" offer an inclusio to the beginning of the letter (Jobes 276–77).

12 Πολλὰ ἔχων ὑμῖν γράφειν
οὐκ ἐβουλήθην διὰ χάρτου καὶ μέλανος,
ἀλλ' ἐλπίζω γενέσθαι πρὸς ὑμᾶς
καὶ στόμα πρὸς στόμα λαλῆσαι,
ἵνα ἡ χαρὰ ἡμῶν ᾖ πεπληρωμένη.

13 Ἀσπάζεταί σε τὰ τέκνα τῆς ἀδελφῆς σου τῆς ἐκλεκτῆς.

VERSE 12

Πολλὰ ἔχων ὑμῖν γράφειν οὐκ ἐβουλήθην διὰ χάρτου καὶ μέλανος,
Although I have many things to write to you all, I do not want to communicate through a piece of papyrus and ink,

Πολλά, acc. pl. neut. of πολύς, functioning here as a subst. adj., serves as the dir. obj. of ἔχων, the nom. sg. masc. pres. act. ptc. of ἔχω. Ἔχων is an adv. ptc. conveying a concessive nuance (i.e., translated with "although" above, so Rogers and Rogers 601; Yarbrough 358; ZG 734; on this function of ptc., see KMP 335). Ὑμῖν, dat. pl. of the 2nd pers. personal pron., is an indir. obj. in relation to γράφειν, pres. act. inf. of γράφω, here functioning as an epex. inf. (an inf. that "clarifies, explains, or qualifies a noun or adjective," Wallace 607) qualifying πολλά (on epex. inf., see also BDF §394; KMP 376–77; Young 175). The negated vb. ἐβουλήθην is the 1st sg. aor. pass. indic. of βούλομαι. Although pass. in form, ἐβουλήθην here is perhaps more accurately parsed as a "medial passive," because the pass. form conveys a middle idea (not uncommon in Koine Gk.). Verbs of volition (e.g., βούλομαι) frequently prefer the middle voice, and one can transparently see the "subject affected" nature of volitional activities. The aor. tense of ἐβουλήθην should likely be understood as an epistolary aor. (thus the pres.

tense translation in English above). The prep. phrase διὰ χάρτου καὶ μέλανος modifies an implied inf. in complementary relationship to ἐβουλήθην (e.g., λαλῆσαι or some other vb. of communication). Χάρτου is the gen. sg. masc. of χάρτης, -ου, ὁ, "piece of papyrus." Μέλανος is the gen. sg. masc. of μέλας, -ους, τό, "black, black ink." Χάρτου and μέλανος serve as a compound object of the prep. διά.

ἀλλ' ἐλπίζω γενέσθαι πρὸς ὑμᾶς καὶ στόμα πρὸς στόμα λαλῆσαι,
but I hope to be with you all and to speak face to face,

Ἀλλά introduces a contrast to communication by letter from a distance, as mentioned above. Ἐλπίζω ("hope, to look forward to someth. in view of the measures one takes to ensure fulfillment," BDAG 319c) is 1st sg. pres. act. ind. Γενέσθαι, aor. mid. inf. of γίνομαι, functions here as the first of two complementary infs. (on function, see BDF §392; KMP 365–66). The prep. phrase πρὸς ὑμᾶς adv. modifies γενέσθαι and expresses an idea of accompaniment. Πρός plus acc. can convey the sense of "in the presence of" or "with" (cf. John 1:1; on use of πρός, see BDAG 875b–c). The second of the complementary infinitives is λαλῆσαι, the aor. act. inf. of λαλέω. The phrase στόμα πρὸς στόμα (lit. "mouth to mouth") is a Gk. idiom meaning essentially the same thing as the modern English idiom "face to face" (most EVV; see LN §83.39). The phrase στόμα πρὸς στόμα adv. modifies λαλῆσαι, expressing manner.

ἵνα ἡ χαρὰ ἡμῶν ᾖ πεπληρωμένη.
so that our joy may be fulfilled.

Ἵνα introduces a purpose clause followed by the 3rd sg. pres. subjunc. of εἰμί (ᾖ). Πεπληρωμένη is the nom. sg. fem. pf. pass. ptc. of πληρόω (gender agrees with the fem. noun χαρά). The ptc. is employed in a periph. cstr. (εἰμί + ptc.; see Turner, *Syntax*, 88–89; KMP 345–46). The pf. ptc. conveys the idea that the action (i.e., to complete or perfect) is finished and an ongoing state continues. We might *overtranslate* this clause, "that our joy may reach a state of lasting completion." The subj. of this purpose clause is χαρά, nom. sg. fem. Ἡμῶν, pl. gen. of the 1st pers. personal pron., is a subj. gen. Ἡμῶν "our," is well supported by ms. evidence (including ℵ Ψ *Byz* [K L P] syr$^{ph, h}$ et al., followed by most EVV). The variant ὑμῶν "your," is well attested, including the uncials A and B (followed by NASB). Yet, as Smalley notes, the variant probably "results from scribal assimilation to the second persons (ὑμίν, "to you," ὑμᾶς, "you,") earlier in the sentence" (302). The UBS[5] identifies the variant with a black diamond (the highest level of uncertainty, mng. it could equally be adopted).

VERSE 13

Ἀσπάζεταί σε τὰ τέκνα τῆς ἀδελφῆς σου τῆς ἐκλεκτῆς.
The children of your elect sister greet you.

Ἀσπάζεταί, 3rd sg. pres. act. indic. of ἀσπάζομαι, "greet, welcome," is followed by its dir. obj. σε, the acc. sg. of the 2nd pers. personal pron., which metaphorically refers to the church to whom the letter is addressed with a sg. pron. Τέκνα, nom. pl. neut.

of τέκνον, -ου, τό, is the subj. of ἀσπάζεταί (neut. pl. subjects frequently take sg. vbs.; see BDF §133; R 403–4; Wallace 399–400). Ἀδελφῆς, gen. sg. fem. of ἀδελφή, ῆς, ἡ, "sister," is a gen. of relationship. Σου, gen. sg. of the 2nd pers. personal pron. is also a gen. of relationship. The attrib. adj. ἐκλεκτῆς, gen. sg. fem. of ἐκλεκτός, -ή, -όν, modifies ἀδελφῆς. The "elect sister" is almost certainly another congregation referred to metaphorically. It is instructive to note how many greetings, often steeped in affection or encouragement, appear in the New Testament.

FOR FURTHER STUDY

See For Further Study 42 "Ancient Letters/Letter Writing"

HOMILETICAL SUGGESTIONS

Final Words for the Community of Faith (vv. 12–13)

1. The elder's desire to visit face to face (v. 12)
    a. The authority of a letter
    b. The joy of personal relations and firsthand fellowship and growth
2. Greetings from the church from which the elder is writing (v. 13)
    a. Fellowship of believers
    b. Unity of the family of God

The Love and Hope of a Pastor (vv. 12–13)

1. The love of a pastor (v. 12)
    a. A desire to guide church members to live faithfully in this world ("I have much to write to you")
    b. A desire to be invested in the lives of church members (Desire to be face to face)
2. The hope of a pastor: "that our joy may be complete (v. 12)
    a. 1 John 1:4
    b. 3 John 4
    c. Joy from fellowship with one another
    d. Joy with one another is based on fellowship with God made available through the atoning sacrifice of Christ

3 JOHN

I. Opening Greeting (1–4)

The section reflects the standard opening for a Greco-Roman letter, providing both the sender and recipient within the introductory greeting as well as a wish for good health (v. 3). The voc. ἀγαπητέ (v. 2), reflecting the warm relation between the elder and Gaius, is encountered again in vv. 5 and 11. Verses 3–4 convey the author's joy at Gaius's walking in the truth (ἀλήθεια, 4× in vv. 1–4), a theme found also in 1 John 1:4 and 2 John 4 (Kruse 221).

1 Ὁ πρεσβύτερος
Γαΐῳ τῷ ἀγαπητῷ,
ὃν ἐγὼ ἀγαπῶ ἐν ἀληθείᾳ.

2 Ἀγαπητέ,
περὶ πάντων
εὔχομαί σε εὐοδοῦσθαι
καὶ ὑγιαίνειν,
καθὼς εὐοδοῦταί σου ἡ ψυχή.

3 ἐχάρην γὰρ λίαν
ἐρχομένων ἀδελφῶν καὶ μαρτυρούντων
σου τῇ ἀληθείᾳ,
καθὼς σὺ ἐν ἀληθείᾳ περιπατεῖς.

4 μειζοτέραν τούτων οὐκ ἔχω χαράν,
ἵνα ἀκούω τὰ ἐμὰ τέκνα ἐν ἀληθείᾳ περιπατοῦντα.

VERSE 1

Ὁ πρεσβύτερος Γαΐῳ τῷ ἀγαπητῷ, ὃν ἐγὼ ἀγαπῶ ἐν ἀληθείᾳ.
The elder, to Gaius the beloved, whom I love in truth.

Πρεσβύτερος, nom. sg. masc., functions as a nom. abs., identifying the sender of the letter. Alternately, one could hypothesize the ellipsis of γράφει, the 3rd sg. pres. act.

indic. of γράφω. Γαΐῳ, dat. sg. masc. of Γάϊος, "Gaius," signifies the recipient of the letter. Ἀγαπητῷ, dat. sg. masc. of ἀγαπητός, -ή, -όν, is in appos. to Γαΐῳ. Ὅν, acc. sg. masc. of the rel. pron., refers back to ἀγαπητῷ and functions as the dir. obj. of ἀγαπῶ, 1st sg. pres. act. ind. Though grammatically unnecessary, the explicit pron. subj. of ἀγαπῶ is present (i.e., ἐγώ, nom. sg. of the 1st pers. personal pron.). John perhaps further reinforces his personal care and affection for this Gaius by including the pronoun ἐγώ. The prep. phrase ἐν ἀληθείᾳ adv. modifies ἀγαπῶ. Ἀληθείᾳ, dat. sg. fem. of ἀλήθεια, -ας, ἡ, functions as obj. of the prep. ἐν. The prep. phrase may (1) communicate manner (cf. Marshall 82: "the kind of love shown by God himself"); (2) indicate the metaphorical realm/sphere of the truth (e.g., Stott 226: "the sphere in which their mutual love existed and flourished"; see also Hiebert 323); or *(3) be intentionally ambiguous to overlap the ideas of manner and realm. Note the almost identical beginning to 2 John.

VERSE 2

Ἀγαπητέ, περὶ πάντων εὔχομαί σε εὐοδοῦσθαι καὶ ὑγιαίνειν,
Beloved, I hope that in every way you may be getting along well and may be in good health,

Ἀγαπητέ is voc. sg. masc. of ἀγαπητός. The prep. phrase περὶ πάντων likely communicates reference/respect (i.e., "with reference to all" = "in every way," CSB). Blass and Debrunner observe that "περὶ πάντων εὔχομαί σε εὐοδοῦσθαι καὶ ὑγιαίνειν corresponds to the frequent salutation in letters in the papyri πρὸ μὲν πάντων ('above all') εὔχομαι σε ὑγιαίνειν, although περί with the gen. in this sense does not appear to be attested otherwise" (BDF §229[2], cited by Culy 155). Πάντων, gen. pl. neut., is the obj. of the prep. περί. Εὔχομαί ("hope, wish," see LN §25.6; BDAG 417b; "pray," see BDAG 417a; LN §33.178) is 1st sg. pres. mid. ind., and although the word can mean "pray" (cf. Jas 5:16; most EVV; cf. "wish," KJV), it is frequently used at the beginning of letters in this time period to express a wish, hope, or desire on the part of the writer for his recipient (Culy 156; see also Brown 703; Haas 176). Note also the main vb. has two accents because σε is an enclitic (see Carson, *Greek Accents*, 47–51). Εὔχομαί is followed by two infs. functioning as compound complementary infs. (on function, see BDF §392; KMP 365–66). Culy rightly observes that the infs. will be labeled as either complementary or "indirect discourse" depending on whether the main vb. means "wish" or "pray" (157). The first of the two infs. is εὐοδοῦσθαι, the pres. mid. inf. of εὐοδόω ("have things turn out well, prosper, succeed" or "to experience and enjoy favorable circumstances," LN §22.47; "prosper," CSB, NASB, KJV; "may go well," ESV, NET). Σε, acc. sg. of the second pers. personal pron., serves as the subj. of the inf. εὐοδοῦσθαι. The second complementary inf. in the compound cstr. is ὑγιαίνειν, the pres. act. inf. of ὑγιαίνω, "to be in good physical health, be healthy" (see BDAG 1023a). In our right reaction against the so-called health and wealth gospel, let us not forget there is scriptural warrant to desire and rejoice in the health and general prosperity of others.

καθὼς εὐοδοῦταί σου ἡ ψυχή.
just as your soul is getting along well.

Καθώς introduces a comparison. The apostle John is confident of Gaius's spiritual state. Can others say the same of you? Εὐοδοῦταί is the 3rd sg. pres. mid. indic. of εὐοδόω, "have things turn out well, prosper, succeed." Ψυχή, nom. sg. fem., is the subj. of εὐοδοῦταί. Σου, gen. sg. of the 2nd pers. personal pron., is perhaps best labeled a poss. gen.

VERSE 3

ἐχάρην γὰρ λίαν ἐρχομένων ἀδελφῶν καὶ μαρτυρούντων σου τῇ ἀληθείᾳ,
For I rejoiced exceedingly when brothers came and testified to your truth,

Postpositive γάρ introduces an explanation of how John knew that Gaius's soul was getting along well (v. 1). Ἐχάρην, 1st sg. aor. pass. indic. of χαίρω, should more accurately be labeled as "medial-passive" because the passive form clearly conveys a middle sense (see R 817). The middle voice is common for vbs. of emotion. Λίαν, "exceedingly, very" (LN §78.1), is an adv. that modifies ἐχάρην. The latter half of the sentence above is a gen. abs. cstr. with a gen. noun (ἀδελφῶν) as the subj. and two gen. ptcs. (ἐρχομένων, μαρτυρούντων) as the vbs. As is the case in most gen. abs. cstr., a temp. adv. relationship fits the literary context. Ἀδελφῶν is the gen. pl. masc. of ἀδελφός, -οῦ, ὁ. Ἐρχομένων is the gen. pl. masc. pres. mid. ptc. of ἔρχομαι. Μαρτυρούντων is the gen. pl. masc. pres. act. ptc. of μαρτυρέω. The final phrase σου τῇ ἀληθείᾳ (translated literally above) is intriguing. Perhaps the cstr. means something like "your fidelity" (CSB) or "your faithfulness to the truth" (NIV). Ἀληθείᾳ, dat. sg. fem. of ἀλήθεια, -ας, ἡ, is a dat. obj. or complement for μαρτυρούντων. Σου, gen. sg. of the 2nd pers. personal pron., is probably best understood as a subj. gen.

καθὼς σὺ ἐν ἀληθείᾳ περιπατεῖς
just as you are walking in truth.

Καθώς introduces a pleonastic comparative clause ("as indeed," ESV; see BDAG 493c). Note the subord. conj. could also be viewed as introducing indir. discourse (NASB; BDF §453[2]; see BDAG 494a). Σύ, nom. sg. of the 2nd pers. personal pron., serves as the subj. of περιπατεῖς, the 2nd sg. pres. act. indic. of περιπατέω. Walking is often employed in the Bible as a metaphor for a pattern of living (e.g., Prov 8:20; Eph 4:1; Col 1:10; in John's Letters, see 1 John 1:6, 7; 2:6, 11; 2 John 4; 3 John 3, 4). The explicit inclusion of the subj. pron. (σύ) perhaps highlights Gaius's exemplary faithfulness (i.e., *he* stands out). The prep. phrase ἐν ἀληθείᾳ adv. modifies περιπατεῖς and conveys a metaphorical nuance of realm/sphere (see BDAG 326c; R 585–86, 589; Moule 75–76). Ἀληθείᾳ, dat. sg. fem. of ἀλήθεια, is the obj. of the prep. ἐν. Note what brings the apostle John exceeding joy: to hear of the faithfulness of another Christian.

VERSE 4

μειζοτέραν τούτων οὐκ ἔχω χαράν,
I do not have greater joy than these things:

Μειζοτέραν, acc. sg. fem. of the comparative adj. μέγας, attrib. modifies χαράν, acc. sg. fem. (on use of the comparative, see KMP 173–74; R 276–78, 662–64). Perhaps μειζοτέραν is spatially (and thus audibly) distanced from χαράν to help segment the text into discourse units for the reader/listener (i.e., hyperbaton is employed by John). Τούτων, gen. pl. neut. of the near dem. pron. functioning subst. as a gen. of comparison. Note that most EVV use a sg. dem. pron. in translation (i.e., "this"), but retaining the pl. "these things," although awkward in English, reminds us that John likely heard multiple and varied accounts of how Gaius and other early believers under his tutelage were living in faithfulness. The negated vb. ἔχω is 1st sg. pres. act. ind., with χαράν as the dir. obj.

ἵνα ἀκούω τὰ ἐμὰ τέκνα ἐν ἀληθείᾳ περιπατοῦντα.
to hear that my children are walking in the truth.

Ἵνα introduces an epex. clause (Robertson, *Pictures* 6:260; Culy 159; cf. "appos.," Jobes 293; Yarbrough 368 n. 7), explaining what τούτων is. Ἀκούω is a 1st sg. pres. act. subjunc., followed by a dir. obj. (τὰ ἐμὰ τέκνα) and a supplementary ptc. (περιπατοῦντα), communicating indir. discourse (see "Supplementary Participles" in the introduction). Τέκνα, acc. pl. neut. of τέκνον, -ου, τό, is modified by grammatically matching pronominal adj. ἐμά (from ἐμός). Περιπατοῦντα is the acc. pl. neut. pres. act. ptc. of περιπατέω (describing the activity of the acc. neut. pl. τέκνα). The prep. phrase ἐν ἀληθείᾳ adv. modifies περιπατοῦντα and conveys a nuance of metaphorical realm. Ἀληθείᾳ, dat. sg. fem. of ἀλήθεια, -ας, ἡ, is the obj. of the prep. ἐν. Does hearing of other Christians' faithfulness bring to you incomparable joy?

FOR FURTHER STUDY

See For Further Study 42 "Ancient Letters/Letter Writing"

HOMILETICAL SUGGESTIONS

Opening Greeting (vv. 1–4)

1. The writer: the elder (v. 1)
2. The recipient: the beloved Gaius (v. 1)
    a. Loved by the elder
    b. Loved in the truth
3. A prayer for Gaius's physical well-being during his spiritual prospering (v. 2)
4. A pastor's joy at a believer's faithfulness to the truth and demonstration of it (vv. 3–4)

II. Affirmation and Exhortation (5–8)

Verses 5–8 convey both affirmation and exhortation. The section begins with the repetition of the voc. (v. 5) that begins the main body of the letter. Gaius is commended for his actions for the brothers (ἀδελφοὺς), the pl. noun functioning as the antecedent of the two rel. prons. that follow in v. 6. The second rel. clause reflects an exhortation or request that Gaius continue to act faithfully toward these traveling Christian workers. The conjunction of v. 7 develops the second rel. clause, providing two reasons to send out such ones in a manner worthy of God. The ἵνα clause of v. 8 offers a final reason for supporting such travelers: "that we may be fellow workers in the truth."

5 Ἀγαπητέ,
πιστὸν ποιεῖς
ὃ ἐὰν ἐργάσῃ
εἰς τοὺς ἀδελφοὺς
καὶ τοῦτο ξένους,

6 οἳ ἐμαρτύρησάν σου τῇ ἀγάπῃ
ἐνώπιον ἐκκλησίας,

οὓς καλῶς ποιήσεις προπέμψας ἀξίως τοῦ θεοῦ·

7 ὑπὲρ γὰρ τοῦ ὀνόματος ἐξῆλθον
μηδὲν λαμβάνοντες
ἀπὸ τῶν ἐθνικῶν.

8 ἡμεῖς οὖν ὀφείλομεν ὑπολαμβάνειν τοὺς τοιούτους,
ἵνα συνεργοὶ γινώμεθα
τῇ ἀληθείᾳ.

VERSE 5

Ἀγαπητέ, πιστὸν ποιεῖς ὃ ἐὰν ἐργάσῃ εἰς τοὺς ἀδελφοὺς καὶ τοῦτο ξένους,
Beloved, you are acting faithfully regarding whatever you do for the brothers (and this for strangers!).

Ἀγαπητέ is the voc. sg. masc. of ἀγαπητός, -ή, -όν. Πιστόν, acc. sg. neut. of πιστός -ή, -όν, functions as an adv. to modify ποιεῖς, the 2nd sg. pres. act. indic. of ποιέω. "The neuter singular form of an adjective is frequently used to form an adverb" (Culy 160). The indef. rel. pron. ὃ ἐὰν (neut. sg. acc.) functions as an adv. acc. of reference, "regarding whatever," or perhaps simply as a dir. obj. of ἐργάσῃ, 2nd sg. aor. mid. subjunc. of ἐργάζομαι. The prep. phrase εἰς τοὺς ἀδελφούς communicates advantage (see BDAG 290d; "*for* the brothers," most EVV). Ἀδελφούς, acc. pl. masc. of ἀδελφός, -οῦ, ὁ, is the obj. of the prep. εἰς. There is an ellipsis of the repeated ἐργάσῃ in the final phrase of the clause above (i.e., and *you are doing* this for strangers!). Τοῦτο, acc. sg. neut. of the near dem. pron., then, is the dir. obj. of the implied vb. ἐργάσῃ. There also appears to be an ellipsis of εἰς before ξένους (Culy 160). ξένους, acc. pl. masc. of ξένος, -η, -ον ("strangers," most EVV; see BDAG 684b), communicates the nuance of advantage as the obj. of the implied prep. εἰς.

VERSE 6

οἳ ἐμαρτύρησάν σου τῇ ἀγάπῃ ἐνώπιον ἐκκλησίας,
They testified to your love before the church.

Οἵ, nom. pl. masc. of the rel. pron., has been rendered above as a personal pron. in English, "they," for greater readability (as most EVV). The antecedent of οἵ is τοὺς ἀδελφούς (v. 5), and οἵ functions as the subj. of ἐμαρτύρησάν, 3rd pl. aor. act. indic. of μαρτυρέω. Ἀγάπῃ, dat. sg. fem. of ἀγάπη, -ης, ἡ, is the dat. obj. or dat. complement to ἐμαρτύρησάν. Σου, gen. sg. of the 2nd pers. personal pron., functions as a subj. gen. The prep. phr. ἐνώπιον ἐκκλησίας expresses location. Ἐκκλησίας, gen. sg. fem. of ἐκκλησία, -ας, ἡ, is the obj. of the prep. ἐνώπιον. Ἐνώπιον is the second most common improper prep., occurring ninety-four times in the GNT (Ἕως is the most common at 146× in the GNT). Improper preps. began their semantic life as adverbs and only later "improperly" began to be used as preps. — thus the unfortunate moniker they bear (see Harris 239–65).

οὓς καλῶς ποιήσεις προπέμψας ἀξίως τοῦ θεοῦ·
You will do well by sending out such ones in a manner worthy of God.

The text more literalistically reads, "whom you will do well sending out worthily of God." Οὕς, acc. pl. masc. of the rel. pron., refers back to the antecedent τοὺς ἀδελφούς (v. 5) and acts as the dir. obj. of ποιήσεις, the 2nd sg. fut. act. indic. of ποιέω. Καλῶς adv. modifies ποιήσεις, expressing manner: "You will do well" (most EVV). Καλῶς is often noted as "a common, polite phrase in letters (papyri) like our 'please'" (Robertson, *Pictures* 6:261; see also Moulton 228; Jobes 302; Marshall 85; cf. NIV). Προπέμψας is the nom. sg. masc. aor. act. ptc. of προπέμπω ("to assist someone in making a journey, send on one's way," BDAG 873c; "implying provision for the journey," ZG 736; on the term, see also LN §15.72; MM 544a). The ptc. adv. communicates means/instr. in relation to καλῶς ποιήσεις. Ἀξίως, "worthily, in a worthy manner," adv. modifies προπέμψας. Θεοῦ, gen. sg. masc. of θεός, -οῦ, is a complement of ἀξίως (Culy 161). John is exhorting Gaius to treat the human representatives of God with the honor and deference appropriate to messengers representing the Almighty.

VERSE 7

ὑπὲρ γὰρ τοῦ ὀνόματος ἐξῆλθον μηδὲν λαμβάνοντες ἀπὸ τῶν ἐθνικῶν.
For on behalf of the Name, they went forth, receiving nothing from the pagans.

Postpositive γάρ introduces a reason why Gaius should support the itinerant Christian workers (i.e., they are not being supported by the fallen world). The prep. phrase ὑπὲρ . . . τοῦ ὀνόματος (cf. Rom 1:5) adv. modifies ἐξῆλθον and communicates the nuance of representation ("for the sake of the Name," most EVV; Harris 210). Ὀνόματος, gen. sg. neut. of ὄνομα, τό, is the obj. of the prep. ὑπέρ. "The Name," while alluding to many OT statements about "the name of the Lord," likely points more specifically to the person and work of Jesus as God the Son (most commentators surveyed, e.g., Akin 244; Hiebert 332; Jobes 303; Kruse 223–24; Marshall 86; Smalley 337, Stott 230; cf. Brown 711–12 and Yarbrough 372, who see possible reference to both Jesus and God the Father). Ἐξῆλθον is the 3rd pl. aor. act. indic. of ἐξέρχομαι, with the implied subj. of οἱ ἀδελφοί from v. 5. Μηδέν, acc. sg. neut. of μηδείς, is the dir. obj. of λαμβάνοντες, the nom. pl. masc. pres. act. ptc. of λαμβάνω. The ptc. λαμβάνοντες functions adv., modifying ἐξῆλθον, communicating the manner in which "the brothers" went out on their mission. The prep. phrase ἀπὸ τῶν ἐθνικῶν communicates source. Ἐθνικῶν, gen. pl. masc. of ἐθνικός, -ή, -όν ("Gentile, pagan" or "those who are not Christians," Jobes 303; on the term, see also BDAG 276c; K. L. Schmidt, *TDNT* 2:364–72), is the obj. of the prep. ἀπό. The NET Translation Notes observe, "The word ἐθνικός (*ethnikos*) occurs only 4 times in the NT (the other three are in Matt 5:47; 6:7; and 18:17). It is virtually synonymous here with the far more common ἔθνος (*ethnos*, used some 162 times in the NT). Both refer to the Gentiles (that is, pagans)."

VERSE 8

ἡμεῖς οὖν ὀφείλομεν ὑπολαμβάνειν τοὺς τοιούτους,
So, we ought to support such ones,

Postpositive particle οὖν introduces an inference drawn from the preceding discussion. Ἡμεῖς, nom. pl. of the 1st per. personal pron. is the subj. of ὀφείλομεν, 1st pl. pres. act. indic. of ὀφείλω, "ought, should." In the GNT, ὀφείλω is followed by a complementary inf. twenty-five times. Of those twenty-five infs., nineteen are present tense, as here (ὑπολαμβάνειν, pres. act. inf. of ὑπολαμβάνω, "receive as a guest, support," BDAG 1038c; "to support," CSB, ESV, NASB; "to show hospitality," NIV; see Baugh, *Tense*

Form Choice, 74). Τοιούτους, acc. pl. masc. of τοιοῦτος, -αύτη, -οῦτον, "such one, such a kind as," is the subst. use of the correlative adj. as the dir. obj. of ὑπολαμβάνειν.

ἵνα συνεργοὶ γινώμεθα τῇ ἀληθείᾳ.
so that we become colaborers in the truth.

Ἵνα introduces a purpose clause. Γινώμεθα is the 1st pl. pres. mid. subj. of γίνομαι. Συνεργοί, nom. pl. masc. of συνεργός, -όν ("fellow worker," LN §42.44; on term, see also BDAG 969c; M. Seifrid, *DLNT*, 267–86), functions as the pred. nom. Ἀληθείᾳ, dat. sg. fem. of ἀλήθεια, -ας, ἡ, is variously rendered as "*with* the truth" (CSB, NET) reflecting an associative idea (i.e., believers cooperation with the truth itself, see Brooke 187; Brown 714; Haas 181; Hiebert 335) or as "*for* the truth" (Lenski 584; NIV, ESV), which could be understood as a dat. of advantage (aligning with the rendering "*for* the truth," see Akin 245; Jobes 304; Kruse 224; Marshall 87 n. 16). Likely τῇ ἀληθείᾳ should be classified as a dat. of reference/respect (cf. Culy 162; on use, see BW 36; KMP 127–28; Young 46–47).

FOR FURTHER STUDY

43. Hospitality (vv. 5–6)

*Barton, S. C. *DLNT*, 501–7.
Bietenhard, H. *NIDNTT* 1:686–90.
Carroll, M. "A Biblical Approach to Hospitality." *RevExp* 108 (2011): 519–26.
Fitzgerald, J. T. *DNTB*, 522–25.
Jipp, Joshua W. *Saved by Faith and Hospitality*. Grand Rapids: Eerdmans, 2017.
Koenig, J. *ABD* 3:299–301.
———. *New Testament Hospitality: Partnership with Strangers as Promise and Mission*. Eugene, OR: Wipf & Stock, 2001.
Pohl, C. D. *NDBT*, 561–63.
Kruse 215–16 (see "A Note on Hospitality").
Malina, Bruce J. "The Received View and What It Cannot Do: III John and Hospitality." *Semeia* 35 (1986): 171–94.
Stählin, G. *TDNT* 5:17–25.

HOMILETICAL SUGGESTIONS

Working Together for the Truth (vv. 5–8)

1. The right way to support Christian workers: in a manner that honors God (v. 6).
2. The right motivation of true Christian workers: they go out for the sake of the Name (v. 7).
3. The responsibility for support for Christian ministry is on fellow Christians (v. 7).
4. Showing hospitality to (or supporting) Christian ministry allows us the privilege of working together for the truth (v. 8).

III. Conflict with Diotrephes (9–10)

Verses 9–10 address a conflict with a certain Diotrephes. Verse 9 introduces the issue and the character of Diotrephes (the name standing in appos. to ὁ φιλοπρωτεύων αὐτῶν). Verse 10 indicates the elder will call attention to his works on account of this (διὰ τοῦτο). The subsection of v. 10 highlights the behavior of Diotrephes.

9 Ἔγραψά τι
τῇ ἐκκλησίᾳ·
ἀλλ' ὁ φιλοπρωτεύων αὐτῶν = Διοτρέφης οὐκ ἐπιδέχεται ἡμᾶς.

10 διὰ τοῦτο,
↓ἐὰν ἔλθω,
ὑπομνήσω αὐτοῦ τὰ ἔργα
ἃ ποιεῖ
λόγοις πονηροῖς φλυαρῶν ἡμᾶς,
καὶ ↓μὴ ἀρκούμενος ἐπὶ τούτοις
οὔτε αὐτὸς ἐπιδέχεται τοὺς ἀδελφοὺς
καὶ τοὺς βουλομένους κωλύει
καὶ ἐκ τῆς ἐκκλησίας ἐκβάλλει.

VERSE 9

Ἔγραψά τι τῇ ἐκκλησίᾳ·
I wrote something to the church,

Ἔγραψά, 1st pl. aor. act. indic. of γράφω, is not an epistolary aor. (i.e., referring to John's current letter) but instead references an earlier letter. Τι is acc. sg. neut. of the indef. pron. and the dir. obj. of ἔγραψα. Concerning variant readings here, Metzger notes ἔγραψα ἄν, "I would have written," was introduced into various manuscripts ($\aleph^2$ 33 81 307 436 vg et al.) in order to avoid the conclusion that an apostolic letter had been lost (656). He adds that the reading ἔγραψα without τι (attested in C Ψ *Byz* [K L P] most minuscules, followed by TR) was introduced "to avoid undue deprecation of apostolic authority" (Metzger 655). The reading ἔγραψάς τι has little external support and is an obvious transcriptional error. Ἔγραψά τι is well supported (א* A [B] 048 1241 1739 [cop^sa bo]) and best explains the origin of other readings. The UBS⁵ gives ἔγραψά τι a "B" rating (indicating that the text is almost certain). Ἐκκλησίᾳ, dat. sg. fem. of ἐκκλησία, serves as an indir. obj.

ἀλλ' ὁ φιλοπρωτεύων αὐτῶν Διοτρέφης οὐκ ἐπιδέχεται ἡμᾶς.
but the one who loves to be first over them, Diotrephes, does not welcome us.

Φιλοπρωτεύων, nom. sg. masc. pres. act. ptc. of φιλοπρωτεύω (a *hapax legomenon*, "wish to be first, like to be a leader," BDAG 1058d; see also LN §25.110), is a subst. ptc. acting as subj. of the negated vb. ἐπιδέχεται, 3rd sg. pres. mid. indic. of ἐπιδέχομαι ("receive," CSB; "welcome," NIV; "acknowledge," NET; see BDAG 371c; LN §§34.53, 36.14). The term (occurring only in 3 John 9–10 in the NT) can, as noted, convey the sense of "welcoming." Yet, it can also convey the sense of "acknowledging" or "accepting the authority of." Contextually, it seems both mngs. fit in v. 9 (Brown 718; Smalley 343; see also Kruse 227; Marshall 88 n. 2). Αὐτῶν, gen. pl. masc. of the 3rd pers. personal pron., is a gen. of subordination (on topic, see Wallace 103–4) or a gen. complement in relationship to φιλοπρωτεύων. Διοτρέφης, "Diotrephes," nom. sg. masc., is in appos. to ὁ φιλοπρωτεύων αὐτῶν. Ἡμᾶς, acc. pl. of the 1st pers. personal pron., is the dir. obj. of ἐπιδέχεται.

VERSE 10

διὰ τοῦτο, ἐὰν ἔλθω, ὑπομνήσω αὐτοῦ τὰ ἔργα ἃ ποιεῖ λόγοις πονηροῖς φλυαρῶν ἡμᾶς,
On account of this, when I come, I will call attention to his works which he is doing, slandering us with evil words.

Τοῦτο, acc. sg. neut. of the near dem. pron., refers to the previous descriptions of Diotrephes's schismatic behavior. Τοῦτο functions as the obj. of the prep. διά. Ἐάν introduces a third class cond. clause, which usually considers a future possibility ("think about this . . . what if . . . "; cf. 1 John 1:6), but can also be used to refer to expected future events of undetermined timing (cf. 1 John 2:29; 3:2; on third class cond., see BW 183; Porter, *Idioms*, 262; Young 228; Moule 148–52; Z §320; Wallace 696–99; KMP 447–48). It is difficult to determine here whether ἐάν should be translated as "if" (see CSB, ESV, NET; Brown 718–19; Culy 164; Jobes 314; Kruse 227) or "when," (see NIV, NLT; Akin 248; Smalley 343), but considering the specificity of John's description of his coming rebuke, we have opted for "when." Ἔλθω is the 1st sg. aor. act. subjunc. of ἔρχομαι. Ὑπομνήσω is the 1st sg. fut. act. indic. of ὑπομιμνῄσκω ("bring up," ESV; "call attention to," NASB, NET, NIV; "remind," CSB; see BDAG 1060c; LN §29.10). Ἔργα, acc. pl. neut. of ἔργον, -ου, τό, serves as the dir. obj. of ὑπομνήσω. Αὐτοῦ, gen. sg. masc. of the 3rd pers. personal pron., is a subj. gen. Ἅ, acc. pl. neut. of the rel. pron., refers back to the antecedent ἔργα and serves as the dir. obj. of ποιεῖ, the 3rd sg. pres. act. indic. of ποιέω. Φλυαρῶν, nom. sg. masc. pres. act. ptc. of φλυαρέω (a *hapax legomenon*, "talk nonsense [about], disparage," BDAG 1060c;

on the term, see also LN §33.374; MM 673a; H. Balz, *EDNT* 3:429a), is an adv. ptc. expressing epex. what "the bad works" are. Culy labels φλυαρῶν as an adv. ptc. of means (164). Ἡμᾶς, acc. pl. of the 1st pers. personal pron., is the dir. obj. of φλυαρῶν. Λόγοις, dat. pl. masc. of λόγος, -ου, ὁ, expresses means/instr. in relation to the ptc. The adj. πονηροῖς, dat. pl. masc. of πονηρός, -ά, -όν, attrib. modifies λόγοις.

καὶ μὴ ἀρκούμενος ἐπὶ τούτοις οὔτε αὐτὸς ἐπιδέχεται τοὺς ἀδελφοὺς
And not being content with these things, neither does he welcome the brothers,

The negated ptc. ἀρκούμενος, nom. sg. masc. pres. mid. ptc. of ἀρκέω, "be satisfied/ content w. someth." (BDAG 132a), functions as an adv. causal ptc. in relation to the vb. ἐπιδέχεται, the 3rd sg. pres. mid. indic. of ἐπιδέχομαι, "receive, welcome, acknowledge." The prep. phrase ἐπὶ τούτοις perhaps is best labeled as conveying cause or basis (i.e., Diotrephes is not content on the basis of these things alone; on this use of prep. ἐπί, see BDAG 364d). Normally, ἀρκέω would be followed by a dat. obj. or dat. complement. Τούτοις, dat. pl. neut. of the near dem. pron., serves as the obj. of the prep. ἐπί. Αὐτός, nom. sg. masc. of the 3rd pers. personal pron., serves as the subj. of ἐπιδέχεται. Ἀδελφούς, acc. sg. masc. of ἀδελφός, -οῦ, ὁ, is the dir. obj. of ἐπιδέχεται.

καὶ τοὺς βουλομένους κωλύει καὶ ἐκ τῆς ἐκκλησίας ἐκβάλλει.
and those who do wish to welcome them, he forbids and throws out of the church.

Βουλομένους, acc. pl. masc. pres. mid. ptc. of βούλομαι, is a subst. ptc. functioning as the dir. obj. of κωλύει, 3rd sg. pres. act. indic. of κωλύω, "hinder, prevent, forbid" (BDAG 580a). After βουλομένους, a complementary inf. from ἐπιδέχομαι and the object τοὺς ἀδελφοὺς, "to welcome the brothers," is implied from the previous clause. The prep. phrase ἐκ τῆς ἐκκλησίας expresses disassociation or separation. Ἐκκλησίας, gen. sg. fem. of ἐκκλησία, -ας, ἡ, is the obj. of the prep. ἐκ. Ἐκ τῆς ἐκκλησίας adv. modifies ἐκβάλλει, the 3rd sg. pres. act. indic. of ἐκβάλλω.

FOR FURTHER STUDY

44. Church Discipline

Leeman, Jonathan. *Church Discipline: How the Church Protects the Name of Jesus.* Wheaton, IL: Crossway, 2012.

See also For Further Study 7 "Obedience/ Christian Growth" and 8 "Christian Ethics"

HOMILETICAL SUGGESTIONS

Conflict and Discipline within the Church (vv. 9–10)

1. The example of Diotrephes who "loves to be first" (vv. 9–10)
    a. His behavior
        (1) Talks maliciously about them
        (2) Refuses to welcome believers

(3) Stops others who want to welcome believers and puts them out of the church

b. Issues of behavior in the local church today

2. The behavior will be addressed (v. 10)
   a. The elder will call attention to what Diotrephes is doing (v. 10)
   b. The need for biblical, gracious, and faithful discipline in the church

A Teachable Moment (vv. 9–10)

1. The deeds of Diotrephes who "likes to put himself first" (vv. 9–10)
   a. Rebels against the Elder's authority
   b. Disparages the Elder and those with him
   c. Refuses to welcome the brothers
   d. Stops others who seek to welcome the brothers and puts others out of the church
2. Lessons from Diotrephes (vv. 9–10)
   a. Immediate context
      (1) Diotrephes offers a contrast to Demetrius who "has received a good testimony from everyone" (v. 12).
      (2) The actions of Diotrephes provides background to the Elder's command to "not imitate evil but imitate good" (v. 11)
   b. Broader context
      (1) Diotrephes highlights the importance of unity in the church, a common theme in the New Testament
         (a) 1 Peter 3:8
         (b) 1 Corinthians 1:10
         (c) 2 Corinthians 13:11
         (d) Romans 15:5
         (e) Philippians 2:1–2; 4:2
      (2) Diotrephes highlights the importance of church discipline in the church
         (a) Matthew 18:15–20
         (b) Example: 1 Corinthians 5
         (c) To be practiced prayerfully and graciously
            (i) For the good of the individual
            (ii) For the good of the church body
            (iii) For the name of Christ

IV. Commendation of Demetrius (11–12)

This section offers a contrasting character to that of Diotrephes in the person of Demetrius. Verse 11 begins, once again, with the voc. ἀγαπητέ followed by the only impv. in the body of the letter (the closing has one other). "Do not imitate what is evil (μὴ μιμοῦ), but good." Verse 12 offers a commendation to Gaius of Demetrius, emphasizing the testimony concerning him (μαρτυρία; μαρτυρέω 2x).

11 Ἀγαπητέ,
μὴ μιμοῦ τὸ κακὸν
ἀλλὰ [*μιμοῦ*] τὸ ἀγαθόν.
ὁ ἀγαθοποιῶν ἐκ τοῦ θεοῦ ἐστιν·
ὁ κακοποιῶν οὐχ ἑώρακεν τὸν θεόν.

12 Δημητρίῳ μεμαρτύρηται
ὑπὸ πάντων
καὶ ὑπὸ αὐτῆς τῆς ἀληθείας·
καὶ ἡμεῖς δέ μαρτυροῦμεν,
καὶ οἶδας ὅτι ἡ μαρτυρία ἡμῶν ἀληθής ἐστιν.

VERSE 11

Ἀγαπητέ, μὴ μιμοῦ τὸ κακὸν ἀλλὰ τὸ ἀγαθόν.
Beloved, do not imitate what is evil but what is good.

Ἀγαπητέ is the voc. sg. masc. of ἀγαπητός, -ή, -όν (cf. 3 John 1, 2, 5; also 1 John 2:7; 3:2, 21; 4:1, 7). Μή negates the impv. μιμοῦ, 2nd sg. pres. mid. impv. from μιμέομαι, "to use as a model, imitate" (see BDAG 651c; LN §41.44). Κακόν, acc. sg. neut. of κακός, -ή, -όν, is the subst. use of the adj. as the dir. obj. of μιμοῦ. There is an ellipsis of μιμοῦ at the end of v. 11 (i.e., Gaius is being commanded to *imitate* what is good). Ἀγαθόν, acc. sg. neut. of ἀγαθός, -ή, -όν, is the subst. use of the adj. as the dir. obj. of the elided μιμοῦ.

ὁ ἀγαθοποιῶν ἐκ τοῦ θεοῦ ἐστιν
The person doing good is from God.

Ἀγαθοποιῶν, nom. sg. masc. pres. act. ptc. of ἀγαθοποιέω, "do good," is a subst. use of the ptc. and the subj. of ἐστιν, 3rd sg. pres. indic. of εἰμί. The prep. phrase ἐκ τοῦ θεοῦ expresses source/origin (on the prep., see BDAG 296c; cf. 1 John 2:16; 3:9, 10; 4:2–7; 5:19). Θεοῦ, gen. sg. masc. of θεός, -οῦ, ὁ, is the obj. of the prep. ἐκ.

ὁ κακοποιῶν οὐχ ἑώρακεν τὸν θεόν.
The person doing evil has not seen God.

Κακοποιῶν, nom. sg. masc. pres. act. ptc., of κακοποιέω, "do evil," is a subst. use of the ptc. and the subj. of the negated vb. ἑώρακεν, the 3rd sg. pf. act. indic. of ὁράω. Θεόν, acc. sg. masc. of θεός, serves as the dir. obj. of ἑώρακεν.

VERSE 12

Δημητρίῳ μεμαρτύρηται ὑπὸ πάντων καὶ ὑπὸ αὐτῆς τῆς ἀληθείας·
For Demetrius, it has been testified to by all and by the truth itself,

At the risk of poor readability, a very literal translation has been provided above. Δημητρίῳ, dat. sg. masc. of Δημήτριος, -ου, ὁ, "Demetrius," is probably a dat. of advantage (i.e., for Demetrius's benefit/advantage, it has been testified to by all; see Culy 166–67). Μεμαρτύρηται, "testify favorably, speak well (of), approve" (BDAG 618c; see also LN §33.262), the 3rd sg. pf. pass. indic. of μαρτυρέω, has an implied impersonal subj. (on use, see BDAG 618c). The prep. phrase ὑπὸ πάντων adv. modifies μεμαρτύρηται and expresses agency. Πάντων, gen. pl. masc. of πᾶς, is the obj. of ὑπό. The prep. phrase ὑπὸ αὐτῆς τῆς ἀληθείας also expresses agency, personifying the truth. Ἀληθείας, gen. sg. fem. of ἀλήθεια, -ας, ἡ, is intensified by αὐτῆς in the pred. position. Αὐτῆς is the gen. sg. fem. of the 3rd pers. personal pron.

καὶ ἡμεῖς δὲ μαρτυροῦμεν,
and we now testify,

Ἡμεῖς, nom. pl. of the 1st pers. personal pron., serves as the subj. of μαρτυροῦμεν, the 1st pl. pres. act. indic. of μαρτυρέω. Δέ in this context is translated as "now" (BDAG 213b); cf. "also" (CSB, ESV, NET).

καὶ οἶδας ὅτι ἡ μαρτυρία ἡμῶν ἀληθής ἐστιν.
and you know that our testimony is true.

Οἶδας is the 2nd sg. pf. act. indic. of οἶδα (John uses οἶδα and γινώσκω synonymously). Ὅτι introduces the content of what is known (see BDAG 731d; R 1034–35; Young 190). Μαρτυρία, nom. sg. fem., is the subj. of ἐστιν, the 3rd sg. pres. indic. of εἰμί. Ἡμῶν, gen. pl. of the 1st pers. personal pron., is a subj. gen. (Young 30). Ἀληθής, "true," nom. sg. fem., is a pred. adj.

FOR FURTHER STUDY

See For Further Study 7 "Obedience/Christian Growth," 15 "Knowing God/Knowledge of the Believer," and 18 "Abiding/Remaining/Μένω."

HOMILETICAL SUGGESTIONS

The Example of Demetrius (vv. 11–12)

1. The elder's command to Gaius (v. 11)
   a. Imitate what is good
   b. The one who does good is from God
2. The elder's commendation of Demetrius (v. 12)
   a. Spoken well of by the elder and by all
   b. The contrast of Diotrephes and Demetrius

What Is Testified about You? (vv. 11–12)

1. John's command (v. 11)
   a. Do not imitate what is evil but what is good
   b. Functions as a connector between the bad example (Diotrephes, vv. 9–10) and the good example (Demetrius, v. 12)
   c. Who are you imitating, consciously or unconsciously?
2. Demetrius's testimony from others (v. 12)
   a. A good testimony from "everyone"
   b. A good testimony from the truth itself
      (1) Truth referring to the truth of the gospel (or possibly the Christian message broadly)
      (2) The truth testifying simply means Demetrius's manner of conduct measured against the truth of the gospel is a witness to his commitment and faithfulness
      (3) What standard do you look to as a reference for your own deeds and words?
   c. A good testimony from the elder and his church
   d. Note the people and standard that testify to Demetrius
      (1) The views of the worldly are not our guide
      (2) The testimonies that offer guidance to our walk
         1. The testimony of our own actions in light of the gospel
         2. The testimony of our pastors/elders about us
         3. The testimony of our fellow brothers and sisters in Christ about us

V. Final Greeting (13–15)

The section closes the letter with a structure typical of a Hellenistic letter. Verses 13–14 reflect very similar language as that in 2 John 12. Verse 15 closes the letter with a greeting.

13 Πολλὰ εἶχον γράψαι σοι
ἀλλ' οὐ θέλω ↓διὰ μέλανος καὶ καλάμου σοι
γράφειν·

14 ἐλπίζω δὲ εὐθέως σε ἰδεῖν,
καὶ στόμα πρὸς στόμα λαλήσομεν.

15 Εἰρήνη σοι.
ἀσπάζονταί σε οἱ φίλοι.
ἀσπάζου τοὺς φίλους
κατ' ὄνομα.

VERSE 13

Πολλὰ εἶχον γράψαι σοι ἀλλ' οὐ θέλω διὰ μέλανος καὶ καλάμου σοι γράφειν·
I had many things to write to you, but I am not wanting to write to you via ink and reed pen.

Πολλά, acc. pl. neut. of πολύς, πολλή, πολύ, serves as the dir. obj. of εἶχον, the 1st sg. impf. act. indic. of ἔχω. Γράψαι, aor. act. inf. of γράφω, is an epex. inf. (on this use of inf., see BW 141; KMP 376; Wallace 607–8; Young 175). Σοι, dat. sg. of the 2nd pers. personal pron., is an indir. obj. Θέλω is 1st sg. pres. act. ind. Διὰ μέλανος καὶ καλάμου is a prep. phrase communicating means. Μέλανος, gen. sg. neut. of μέλαν, -ανος, τό, "black ink" (cf. 2 John 12), and καλάμου, gen. sg. masc. of κάλαμος, -ου, ὁ, "reed pen" (BDAG 502c; see also LN §6.56), serve as a compound obj. of the prep. διά. Σοι is the dat. sg. of the 2nd pers. personal pron., functioning here as an indir. obj. Γράφειν, pres.

act. inf. of γράφω, is a complementary inf. completing the verbal idea of the vb. θέλω (on this topic, see KMP 365–66).

VERSE 14

ἐλπίζω δὲ εὐθέως σε ἰδεῖν, καὶ στόμα πρὸς στόμα λαλήσομεν.
Now I hope to see you straightaway, and face to face we will speak.

Postpositive δέ carries the conversation forward. Ἐλπίζω, "hope" (cf. 2 John 12), is 1st sg. pres. act. ind. Εὐθέως, "immediately, straightaway," is an adv. modifying the complementary inf. ἰδεῖν, the aor. act. inf. of ὁράω (the inf. completing the verbal idea of ἐλπίζω). Σε, acc. sg. of the 2nd pers. personal pron., is the dir. obj. of the inf. ἰδεῖν. The phrase στόμα πρὸς στόμα (lit. "mouth to mouth") is a Greek idiom mng. essentially the same thing as the modern English idiom "face to face" (cf. 2 John 12). The phrase στόμα πρὸς στόμα adv. modifies λαλήσομεν, expressing manner. Λαλήσομεν is the 1st pl. fut. act. indic. of λαλέω.

VERSE 15

Εἰρήνη σοι. ἀσπάζονταί σε οἱ φίλοι. ἀσπάζου τοὺς φίλους κατ' ὄνομα.
Peace to you. The friends greet you. Greet the friends there each by name.

Εἰρήνη, -ης, ἡ, nom. sg. fem., is used in a formulaic blessing with an implied form of εἰμί, "peace *be* to you." As Marshall writes, "Here the elder takes over the well-known Jewish greeting which had already been filled with deeper significance for Christians by its use by Jesus (John 20:19, 21, 26)" (94). Σοι is the dat. sg. of the 2nd pers. personal pron. Ἀσπάζονταί is the 3rd pl. pres. mid. indic. of ἀσπάζομαι. Σε, acc. sg. of the 2nd pers. personal pron., is the dir. obj. of ἀσπάζονταί. Φίλοι, nom. pl. masc. of φίλος, ὁ, "friend," is subj. of ἀσπάζονταί. Ἀσπάζου is the 2nd sg. pres. mid. impv. of ἀσπάζομαι. Φίλους, acc. pl. masc. of φίλος, is the dir. obj. of ἀσπάζου. Possibly, "friends" in this context has the mng. "brothers" (Kruse 234, who notes "it may have derived from Jesus's description of his disciples as his 'friends' in John 15:13–15"; so also Stott 240; Yarbrough 386; cf. Jobes 335). The prep. phrase κατ' ὄνομα conveys a distributive sense (Culy 168; ZG 737; see BDAG 512b, 712a). Ὄνομα is acc. sg. neut. and the obj. of the prep. κατά. John 10:3 is the only other occurrence of κατ' ὄνομα in the GNT, though Robertson notes the idiom occurs often in the papyri letters (Robertson, *Pictures* 6:266).

FOR FURTHER STUDY

See For Further Study 42 "Ancient Letters/Letter Writing."

HOMILETICAL SUGGESTIONS

Closing Words to the Community of Faith (vv. 13–14)

1. The elder's desire to visit face to face (vv. 13–14a)
   a. The authority of a letter
   b. The need for pastoral care
2. Greetings from the church from which the elder is writing (v. 15)
   a. "Peace to you"
   b. The church from which the elder writes sends greetings
   c. The strength of fellowship and unity among the community of faith

Grammar Index

S

V

Scripture Index

2 John

3 John

Revelation